# Seriously Good
# Mug Cakes

# Seriously Good
# Mug Cakes

### Over 70 Recipes for Mug Cakes in Minutes

Kate Calder, Christelle Huet-Gomez,
Lene Knudsen and Sandra Mahut

photography by Richard Boutin, Sandra Mahut,
David Japy and Clare Winfield

**Quadrille**

Quadrille, Penguin Random House UK, One Embassy Gardens, 8 Viaduct Gardens, London SW11 7BW

Quadrille Publishing Limited is part of the Penguin Random House group of companies whose addresses can be found at global.penguinrandomhouse.com

Penguin Random House UK

Text copyright © Kate Calder, Christelle Huet-Gomez, Lene Knudsen and Sandra Mahut 2025

Recipes on pages 14, 17, 19, 20, 23, 24, 45, 54, 57, 68, 70, 73, 74, 93, 103, 108, 130 and 157 © Lene Knudsen
Recipes on pages 27, 111, 113, 114, 117, 118, 120, 123, 125 and 126 © Christelle Huet-Gomez
Recipes on pages 29, 30, 33, 42, 48, 51, 52, 59, 60, 77, 78, 95, 96, 100, 132, 135, 136, 138, 141, 143, 144, 146 and 150 © Sandra Mahut
Recipes on pages 34, 37, 39, 46, 62, 65, 81, 82, 85, 86, 90, 98, 104, 152, 154, 158, 161, 162, 165, 166 and 168 © Kate Calder

Photography credits on page 176

Kate Calder, Christelle Huet-Gomez, Lene Knudsen and Sandra Mahut have asserted their right to be identified as the authors of this Work in accordance with the Copyright, Designs and Patents Act 1988

No part of this book may be used or reproduced in any manner for the purpose of training artificial intelligence technologies or systems. In accordance with Article 4(3) of the DSM Directive 2019/790, Penguin Random House expressly reserves this work from the text and data mining exception.

Published by Quadrille in 2025

Text is taken from:
*Mug Cakes* by Lene Knudsen, published by Hardie Grant Books in 2014 (originally published by Hachette Marabout in 2013)
*Mug Cakes Chocolate* by Sandra Mahut, published by Hardie Grant Books in 2015 (originally published by Hachette Marabout in 2014)
*Mug Crumbles* by Christelle Huet-Gomez, published by Hardie Grant Books in 2015 (originally published by Hachette Marabout in 2015)
*Happiness in a Mug Cake* by Kate Calder, published by Hardie Grant Books in 2023

www.penguin.co.uk

A CIP catalogue record for this book is available from the British Library

ISBN 9781837834877
10 9 8 7 6 5 4 3 2 1

Managing Director: Sarah Lavelle
Commissioning Editor: Isabel Gonzalez-Prendergast
Project Editor: Ellie Spence
Series Designer: Katy Everett
Designer: Alicia House
Photographers: Richard Boutin, Sandra Mahut, David Japy and Clare Winfield
Head of Production: Stephen Lang
Production Controller: Sumayyah Waheed

Colour reproduction by F1

Printed in China by C&C Offset Printing Co., Ltd.

The authorized representative in the EEA is Penguin Random House Ireland, Morrison Chambers, 32 Nassau Street, Dublin D02 YH68.

Penguin Random House is committed to a sustainable future for our business, our readers and our planet. This book is made from Forest Stewardship Council® certified paper.

FSC MIX Paper | Supporting responsible forestry FSC® C018179

# Contents

6
Introduction

9
Useful Equipment

11
Tips for Better Bakes

12
Totally Fruity

40
Chocolate Heaven

66
Utterly Nutty

88
Caramel & Coffee

106
Mug Crumbles

128
Melt-in-the-Middle

148
Celebrations & Holidays

170
Index

176
Picture Credits

# Introduction

Let's face it, there are few things greater in life than cake. But baking time and clean-up can be enough to put off all but the keenest of bakers. Have you ever had a cake craving but not felt bothered to line a tin, weigh out ingredients, then to sit and wait for what seems like forever? Mug cakes are here to change all that. These delicious, single-serve miracles of science are ready to eat in minutes, and most of them are mixed, baked and eaten in a single mug. Less time making, more time eating.

Choose the recipe to suit your mood and treat your taste buds; these cakes are perfect for the whole family (minus the ones with alcohol!) but also a great quick fix just for yourself. The speed and simplicity mean you no longer need to wait for a birthday as an excuse. As well as being a great dessert, a mug cake makes a perfect mid-afternoon snack – and they're also great to make with the kids after school. In fact, they're so easy to whip up that kids can even take charge with minimal adult supervision. The speed makes kids feel included and engaged as they watch their creations come to life before their eyes.

If you fancy getting creative, you can top your cakes with your favourite icing or serve them with ice cream, custard or simply a dusting of sugar. Whether you're craving a classic vanilla sponge with sprinkles or a sophisticated amaretto and chocolate bake, there's a seriously good mug cake for everyone in this book.

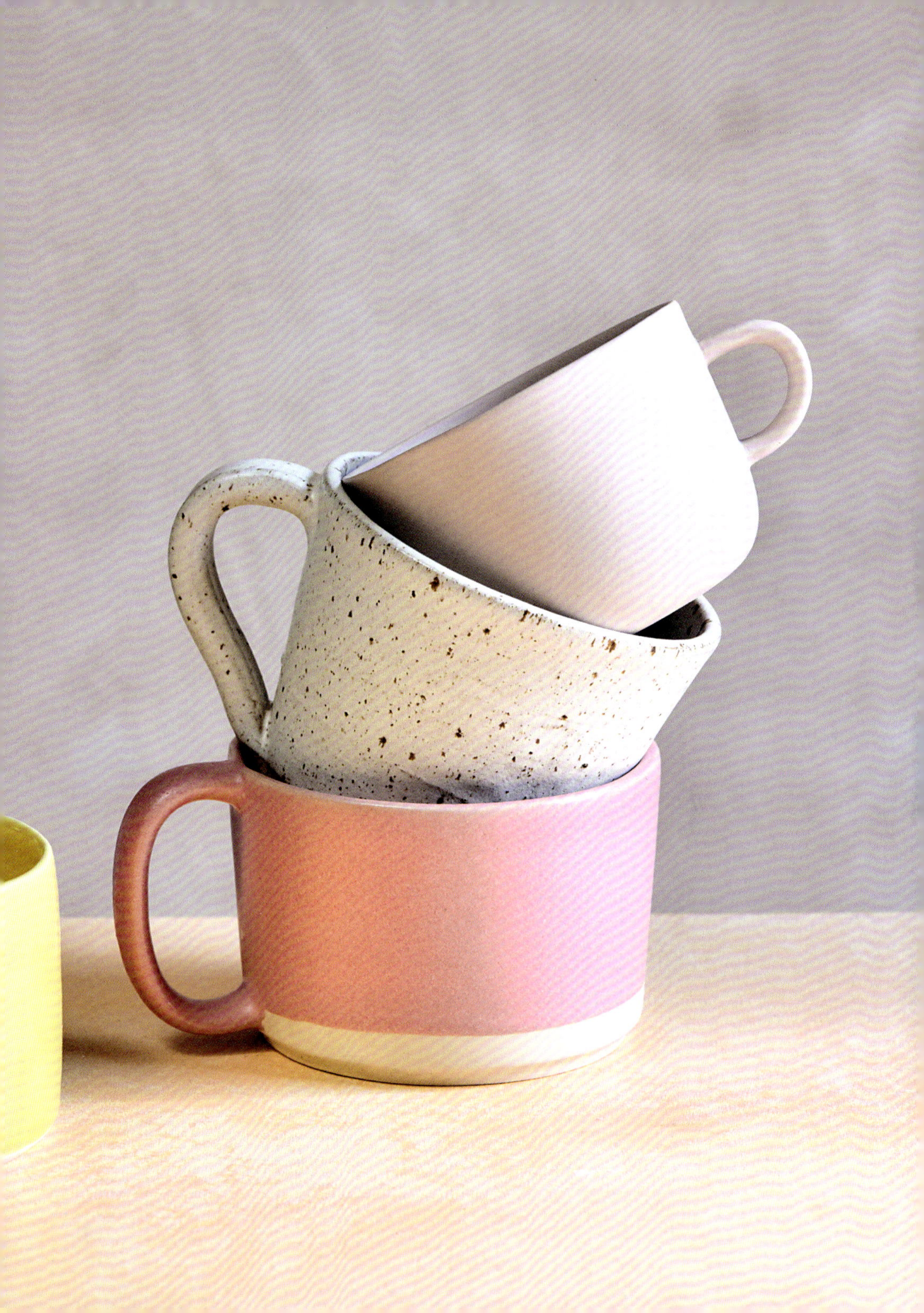

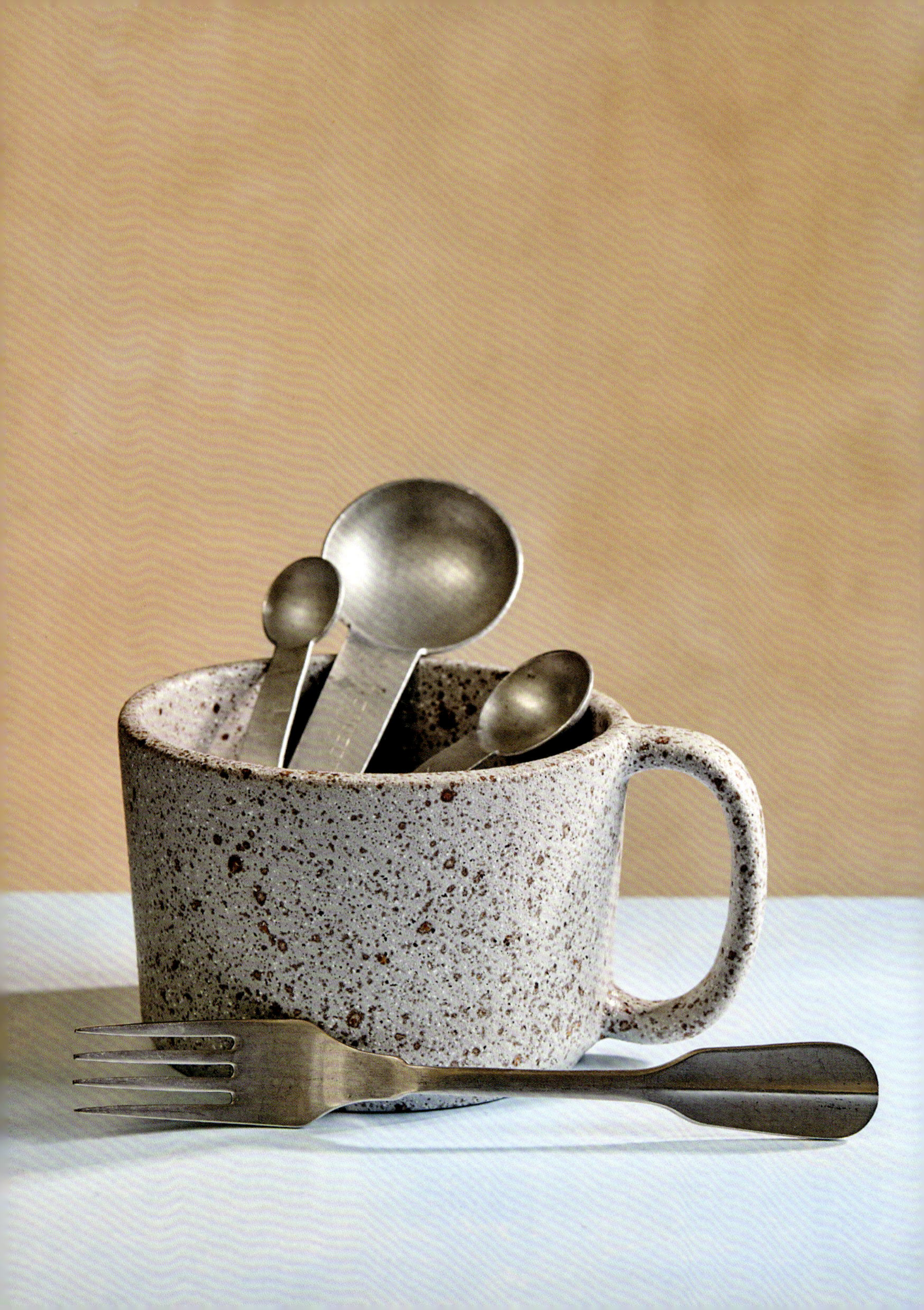

# Useful Equipment

Minimal equipment is required for these bakes, and you'll probably have everything in your kitchen already. You just need:

- a microwave-safe mug

- a fork

- measuring spoons

- a microwave

**And that's it!**

The rise of each cake will vary. Watching through the glass of the microwave door, you may be alarmed at the heights they can reach! They will have a big rise while cooking, but then collapse like a soufflé once out of the microwave. Depending on the ingredients, some will shrink further, while others will stay risen just above the rim of the mug. Because of this variation, I make mine in a standard straight-edged 300ml (10fl oz/1¼ cup) mug, which accommodates all manner of bakes. But as you begin your mug cake journey, you will soon discover your own favourite mug: the one that suits the occasion and pairs best with your microwave.

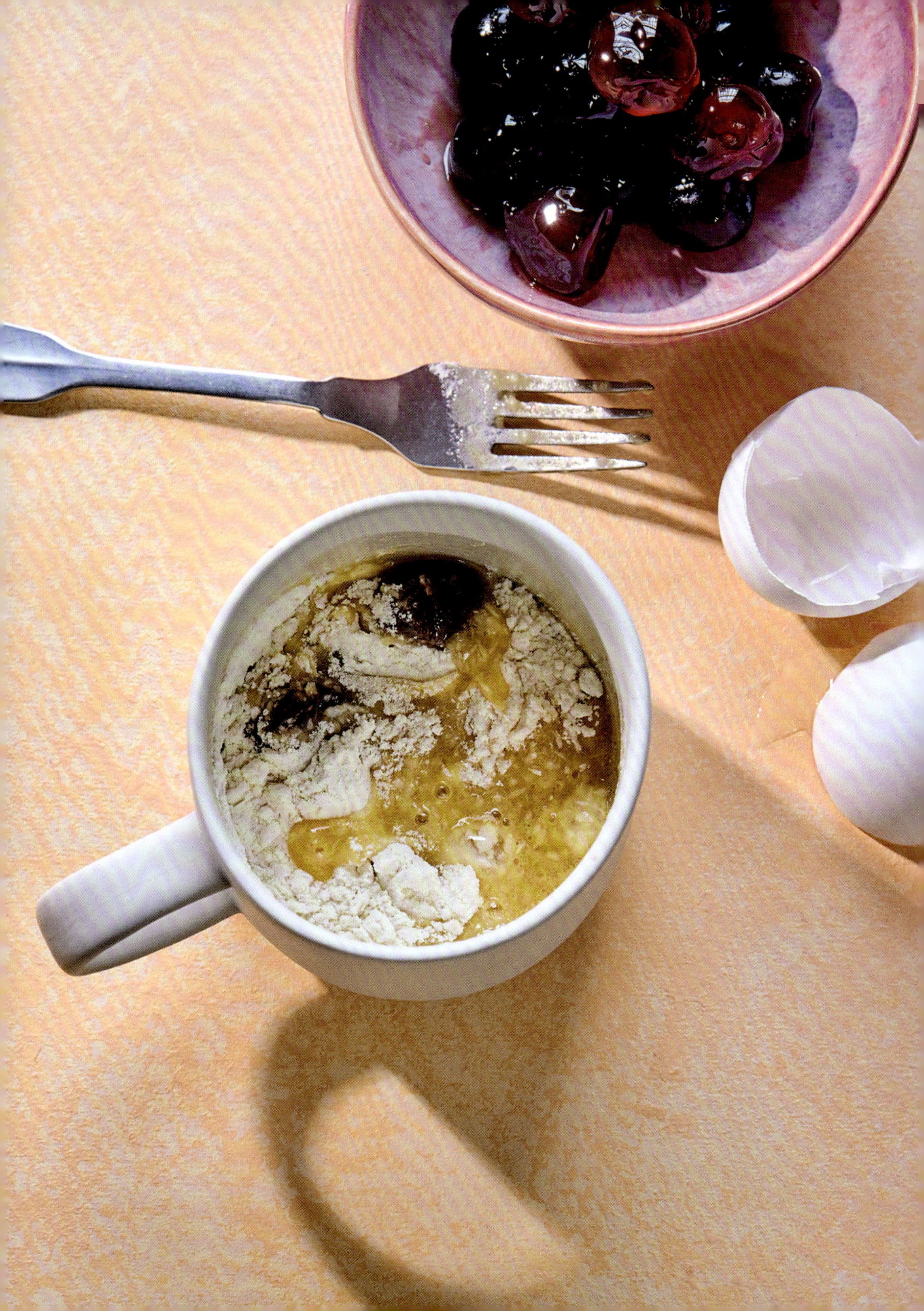

# Tips for
# **Better Bakes**

- The recipes are written for an 800-watt microwave. It may take a little trial and error, varying things by a few seconds here and there, until you find your microwave's sweet spot for timings.

- All the mixing for these cakes takes place in the mug itself. Use a fork to mix the batter. Like a mini whisk, it allows all the ingredients to come together quicker, avoiding any lumps.

- Once the flour has been added, mix just until you get a smooth batter. Overmixing can result in a rubbery cake.

- Accuracy of measurements is key. When the recipes refer to 1 tablespoon, that means 1 level tablespoon (15ml). They will say 'heaped' otherwise.

- To avoid overflowing spills, your mug should only ever be about half full of batter.

- Once baked, the top of your cake may look like it needs more time, but rest assured it will cook from the inside out. Overcook it and the cake will taste dry.

- The cakes are extremely hot when they come out of the microwave, so leave them to cool for a few minutes before eating! Especially if you're adding icing – you don't want it to slide off immediately!

- They do dry out quite quickly, however, so don't wait too long – these treats are best enjoyed soon after baking and should not be kept for later.

- If you are making multiple cakes, you must cook them in individual mugs one at a time in the microwave.

- All eggs are medium (UK) or large (US).

- We recommend using slightly salted butter in all the recipes.

- Use the milk of your choice for the recipe. If you avoid dairy, simply swap in a plant-based alternative.

Totally
# Fruity
───────

## Zesty
# Lemon Cake

*This sunny yellow mug cake is perfect for fans of a classic lemon drizzle. If you can find lemon-coloured sugar strands, great, or just use multi-coloured sprinkles or a little extra lemon zest grated over the top.*

**SERVES 1**

**TAKES 5 minutes**

1 slice of butter 1cm (½in) thick (30g/1oz)
4 tablespoons caster (superfine) sugar
2 teaspoons lemon zest
1 egg
½ teaspoon vanilla sugar
4 teaspoons single (light) cream
6 tablespoons plain (all-purpose) flour
½ teaspoon baking powder

**Icing & Decoration**
4 tablespoons icing (confectioners') sugar
yellow food colouring
1 teaspoon lemon yellow sugar strands (optional)

In a mug, melt the butter in a bowl in the microwave for 20 seconds.

Beat in one by one the sugar, lemon zest, egg, vanilla sugar, cream, flour, and baking powder.

Cook in the microwave for 1 minute 40 seconds, or until risen and springy to the touch.

To make the yellow icing, combine the icing sugar, 1 teaspoon of water and a few drops of food colouring in a small bowl. Pour it over the mug cake and top with the lemon yellow sugar strands, if using.

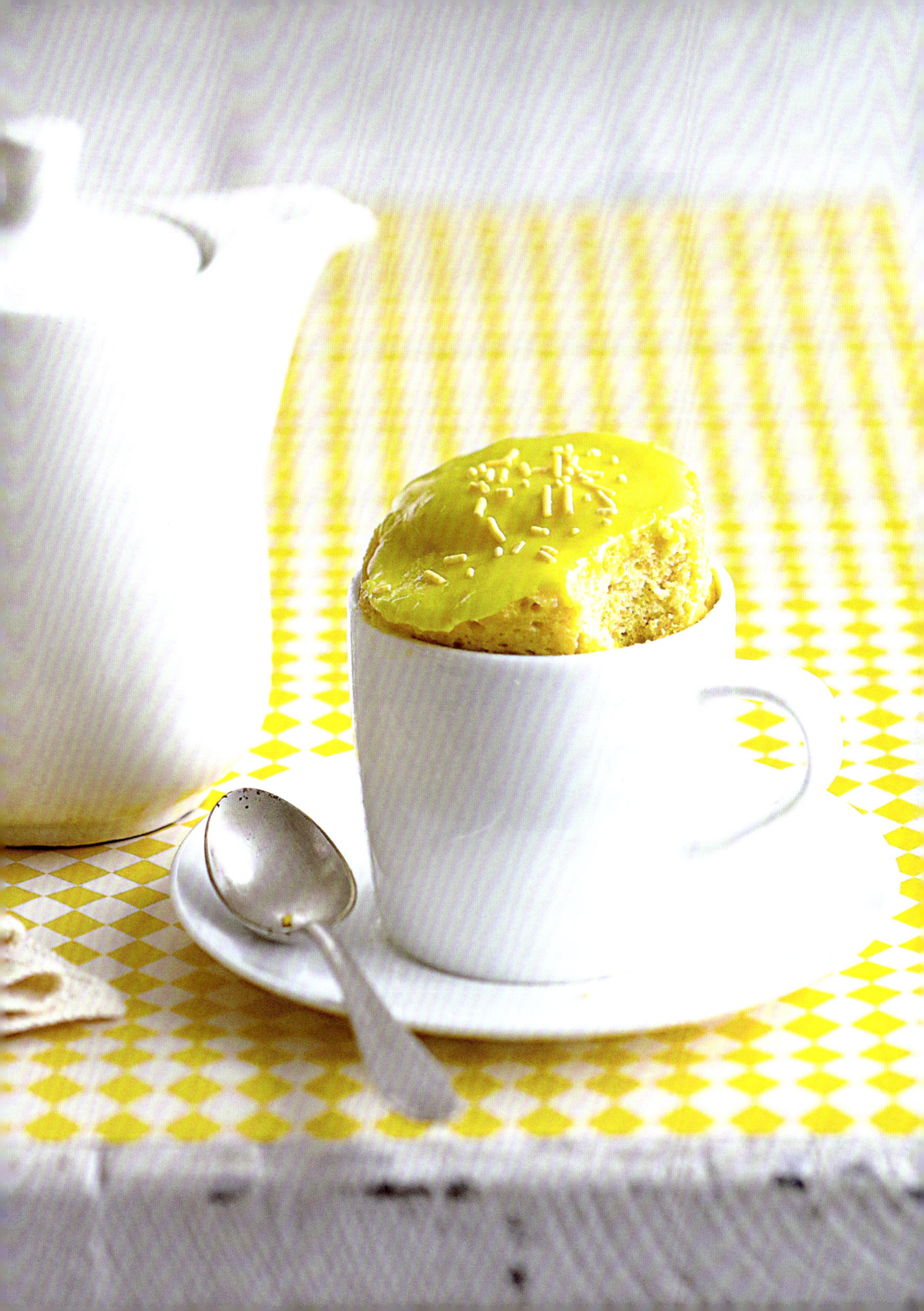

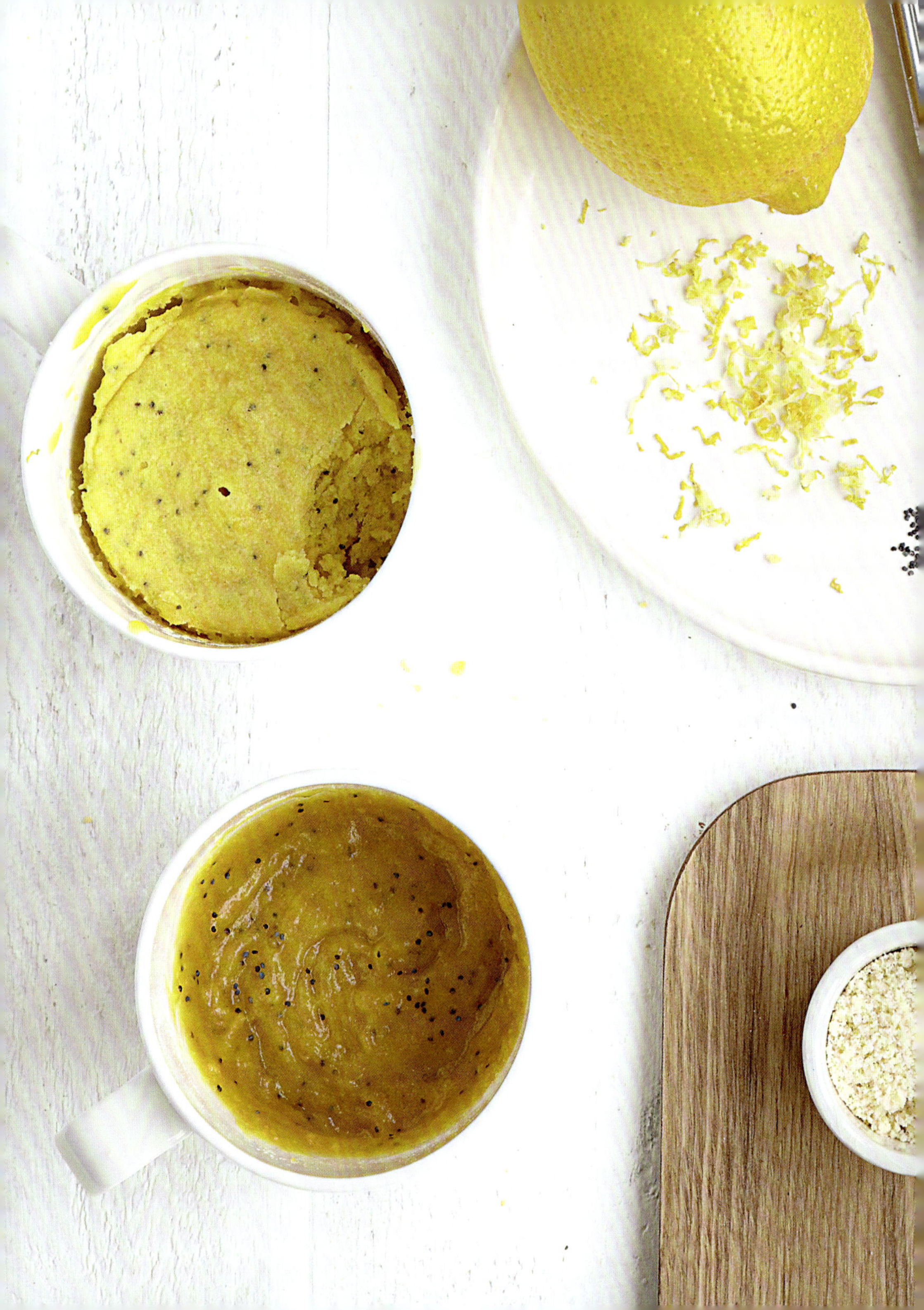

## Mug Cookie with
# Lemon & Poppy Seeds

*Poppy seeds add a great nutty flavour to this zesty little cookie, and added ground almonds in place of some flour will make sure it's moist and delicious.*

**SERVES 1**

**TAKES 4 minutes**

1 slice of butter 5mm (¼in) thick (15g/½oz)
1 tablespoon caster (superfine) sugar
½ teaspoon lemon zest
1 egg yolk
2 tablespoons plain (all-purpose) flour
2 tablespoons ground almonds
½ teaspoon poppy seeds

In a mug, melt the butter in the microwave for 20 seconds.

Beat in one by one the sugar, lemon zest, egg yolk, flour, ground almonds and poppy seeds.

Cook in the microwave for 1 minute, or until risen and springy to the touch.

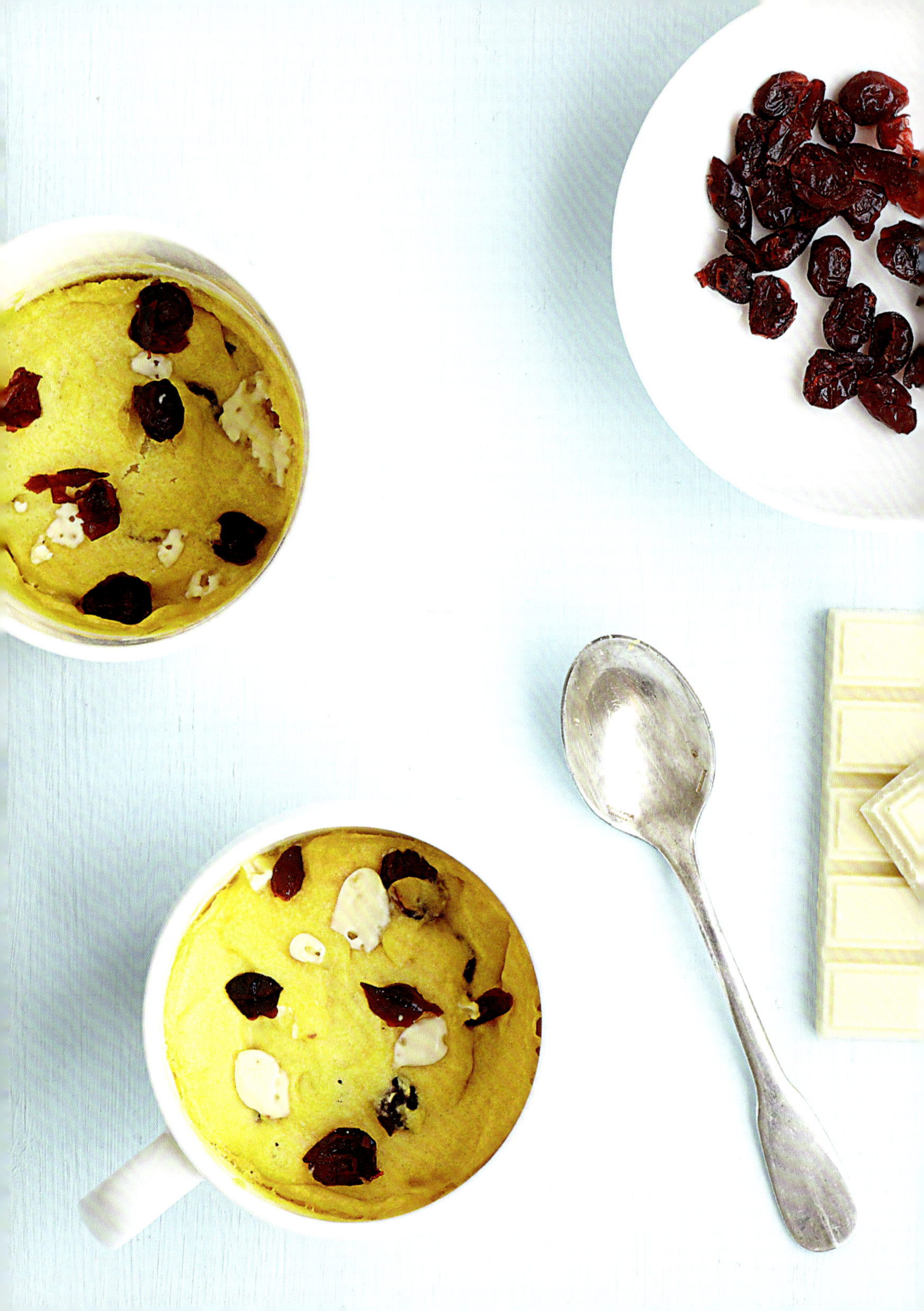

# White Chocolate & Cranberry
# Mug Cookie

*The slight sharpness of cranberries and the caramelized sweetness of white chocolate make these two a flavour match made in heaven. Combine them in this super quick mug cookie that can be ready in less than five minutes!*

**SERVES 1**

**TAKES 4 minutes**

1 slice of butter 5mm (¼in) thick (15g/½oz)
1½ tablespoons soft brown sugar
½ teaspoon vanilla sugar
1 egg yolk
4 tablespoons plain (all-purpose) flour
1 tablespoon dried cranberries
2 squares of white chocolate (10g/⅓oz), roughly chopped

In a mug, melt the butter for 20 seconds.

Beat in one by one the brown sugar, vanilla sugar, egg yolk, flour, half of the cranberries and half the white chocolate.

Add the remaining cranberries and white chocolate to the top of the mixture.

Cook in the microwave for 1 minute, or until risen and springy to the touch.

# White Chocolate, Almond & Pear Cake

*This is a mug cake with a hint of sophistication. Dig in and feel your spoon move through soft sponge to find fragrant juicy pear hidden in the centre, all topped with a sweet white chocolate drizzle.*

**SERVES 1**

**TAKES 6 minutes**

½ pear, peeled and core removed
1 slice of butter 1cm (½in) thick (30g/1oz)
1 egg
2 tablespoons caster (superfine) sugar
1 teaspoon vanilla sugar
1 tablespoon single (light) cream
6 tablespoons plain (all-purpose) flour
½ teaspoon baking powder
2 tablespoons flaked (slivered) almonds

**White Chocolate Sauce & Decoration**
6 squares of white chocolate (30g/1oz)
2 tablespoons single (light) cream
½ teaspoon icing (confectioners') sugar

Place the pear half in a bowl with 1 tablespoon of water and cook in the microwave for 1 minute 10 seconds, then drain.

In a mug, melt the butter for 20 seconds, then beat in one by one the egg, sugar, vanilla sugar, cream, flour, baking powder and 1 tablespoon of the flaked almonds. Push in the pear half and sprinkle with the remaining flaked almonds.

Cook in the microwave for 1 minute 40 seconds, or until risen and springy to the touch.

To make the white chocolate sauce, place the white chocolate and single cream in a mug and melt in the microwave for about 30 seconds, then stir until it is an even consistency. If it's too thick, return to the microwave for a further 10 seconds.

Top the mug cake with white chocolate sauce and dust with icing sugar.

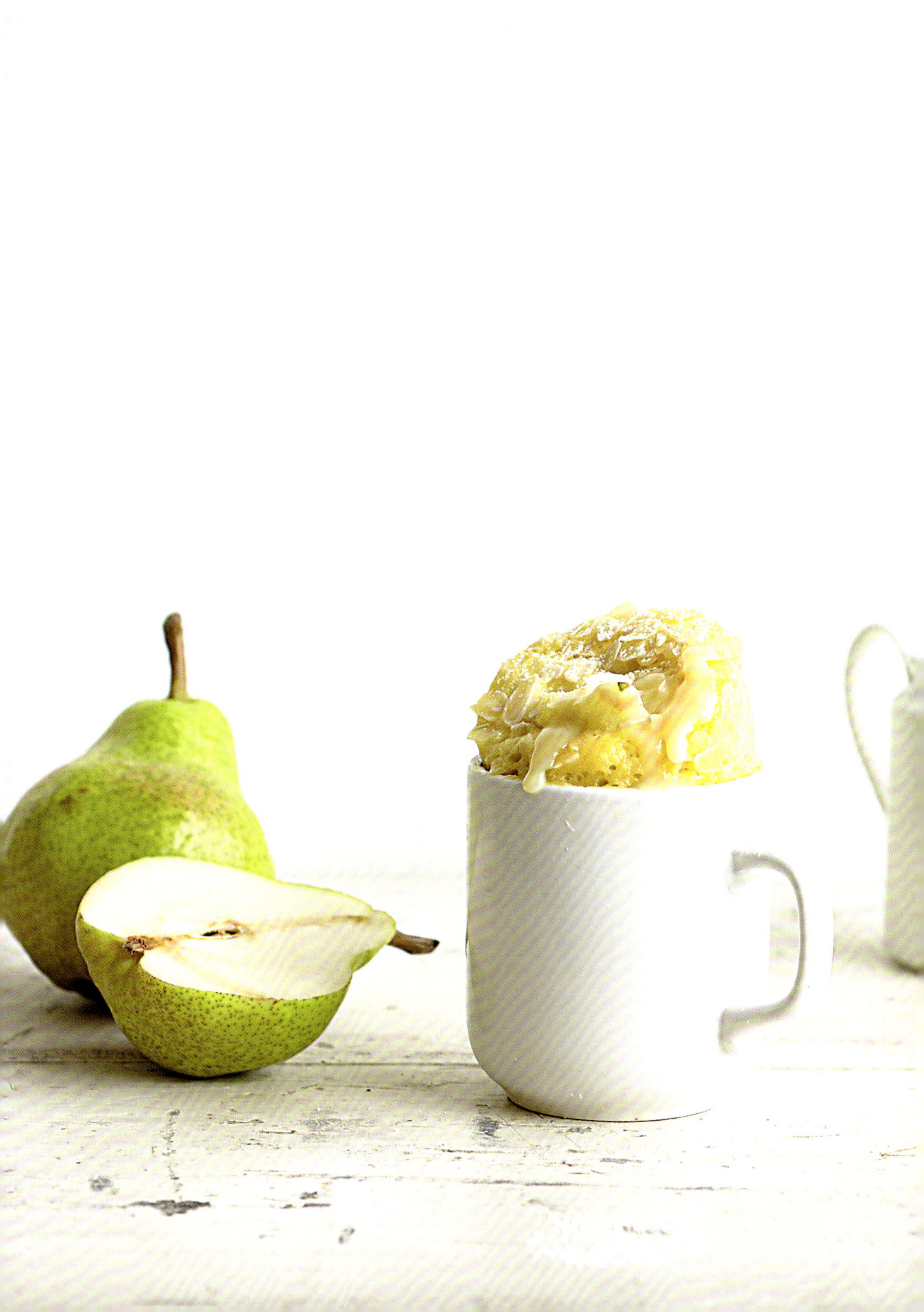

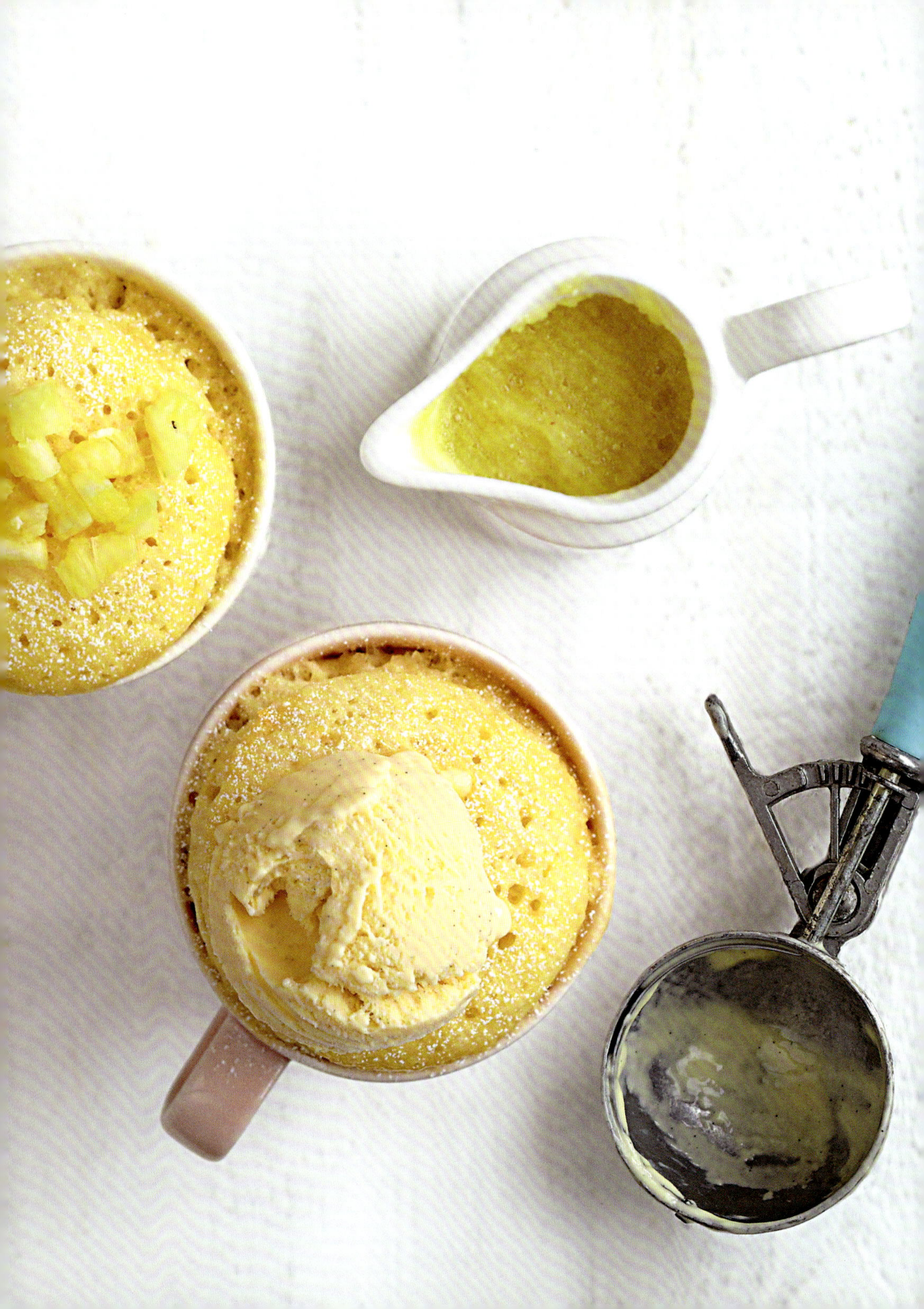

## Rum & Pineapple
# Tropical Cake

*Whip up the tropical taste of the Caribbean on a cold and dreary day! If pineapple is out of season, you can drain and use a canned variety, but try to find the premium 'gold' pineapple, as this tends to be the sweetest and deepest in colour.*

**SERVES 1**

**TAKES 5 minutes**

1 slice of butter 1cm (½in) thick (30g/1oz)
1 egg
2 tablespoons caster (superfine) sugar
1 teaspoon vanilla sugar
1 tablespoon single (light) cream
5 tablespoons plain (all-purpose) flour
2 tablespoons desiccated (dried shredded) coconut
½ teaspoon baking powder
1 tablespoon finely chopped pineapple
1 tablespoon rum
½ teaspoon icing (confectioners') sugar
vanilla ice cream, to serve

In a mug, melt the butter in the microwave for 20 seconds.

Beat in one by one the egg, sugar, vanilla sugar, cream, flour, coconut, baking powder, half of the pineapple and the rum.

Cook in the microwave for 1 minute 40 seconds, or until risen and springy to the touch.

Decorate with the remaining pieces of pineapple and dust with the icing sugar. Serve with a scoop of ice cream.

# Blueberry-Ricotta
# Swirl Cake

*Creamy ricotta, sweet bursting blueberries and a hint of lemon make this such a comforting treat. Frozen blueberries tend to break down and become more juicy when cooked, so use these if you want to make sure you get a great swirl.*

**SERVES 1**

**TAKES 5 minutes**

1 slice of butter 1cm (½in) thick (30g/1oz)
1 egg
2 tablespoons caster (superfine) sugar
1 teaspoon vanilla sugar
1½ tablespoons ricotta
2 or 3 pinches of finely grated lemon zest
5 tablespoons plain (all-purpose) flour
½ teaspoon baking powder
2 tablespoons fresh blueberries (or 1 tablespoon frozen blueberries)

In a mug, melt the butter in a bowl in the microwave for 20 seconds.

Beat in one by one the egg, sugar, vanilla sugar, ricotta, lemon zest, flour and baking powder.

Stir in the blueberries.

Cook in the microwave for 1 minute 40 seconds, or until risen and springy to the touch.

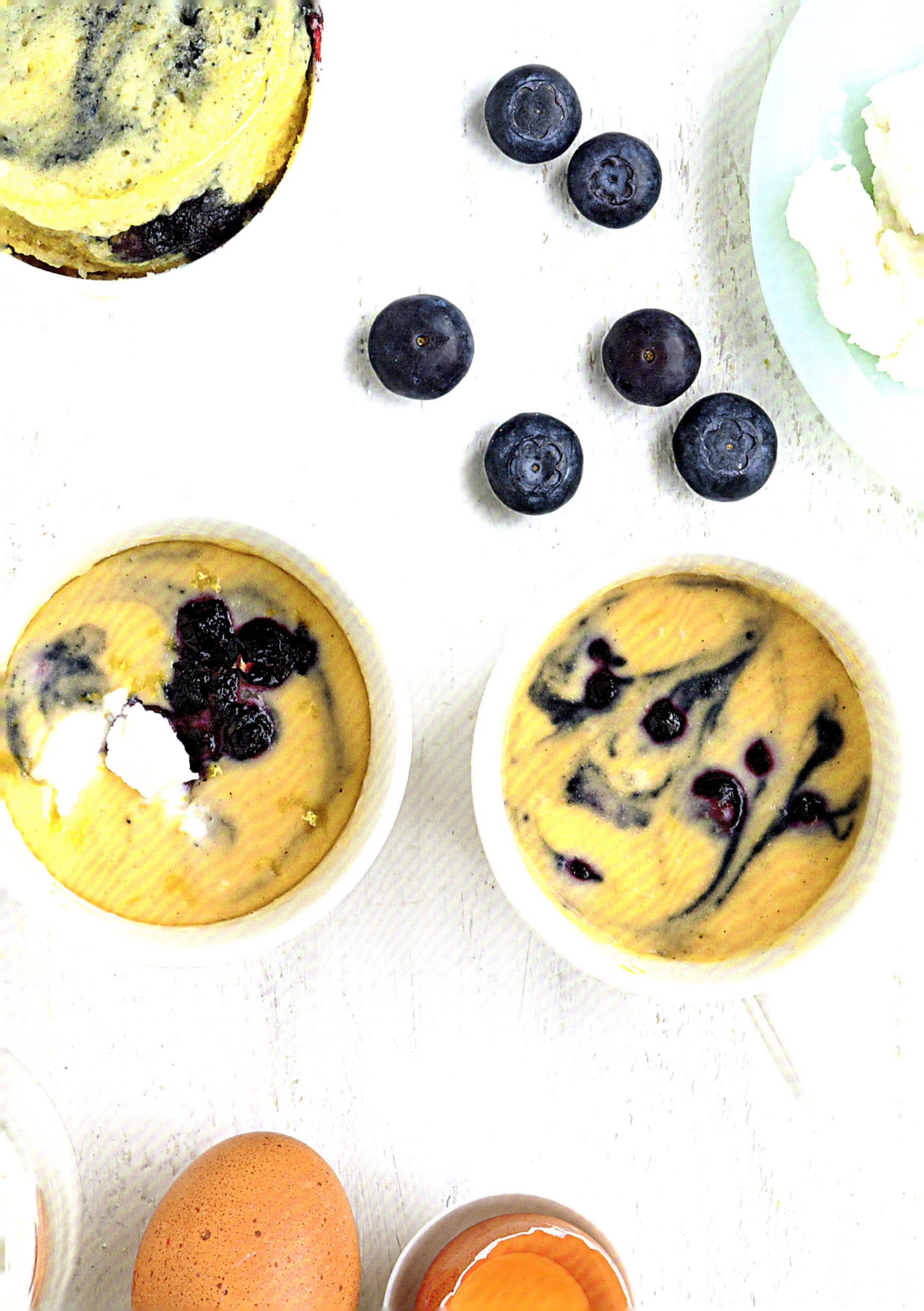

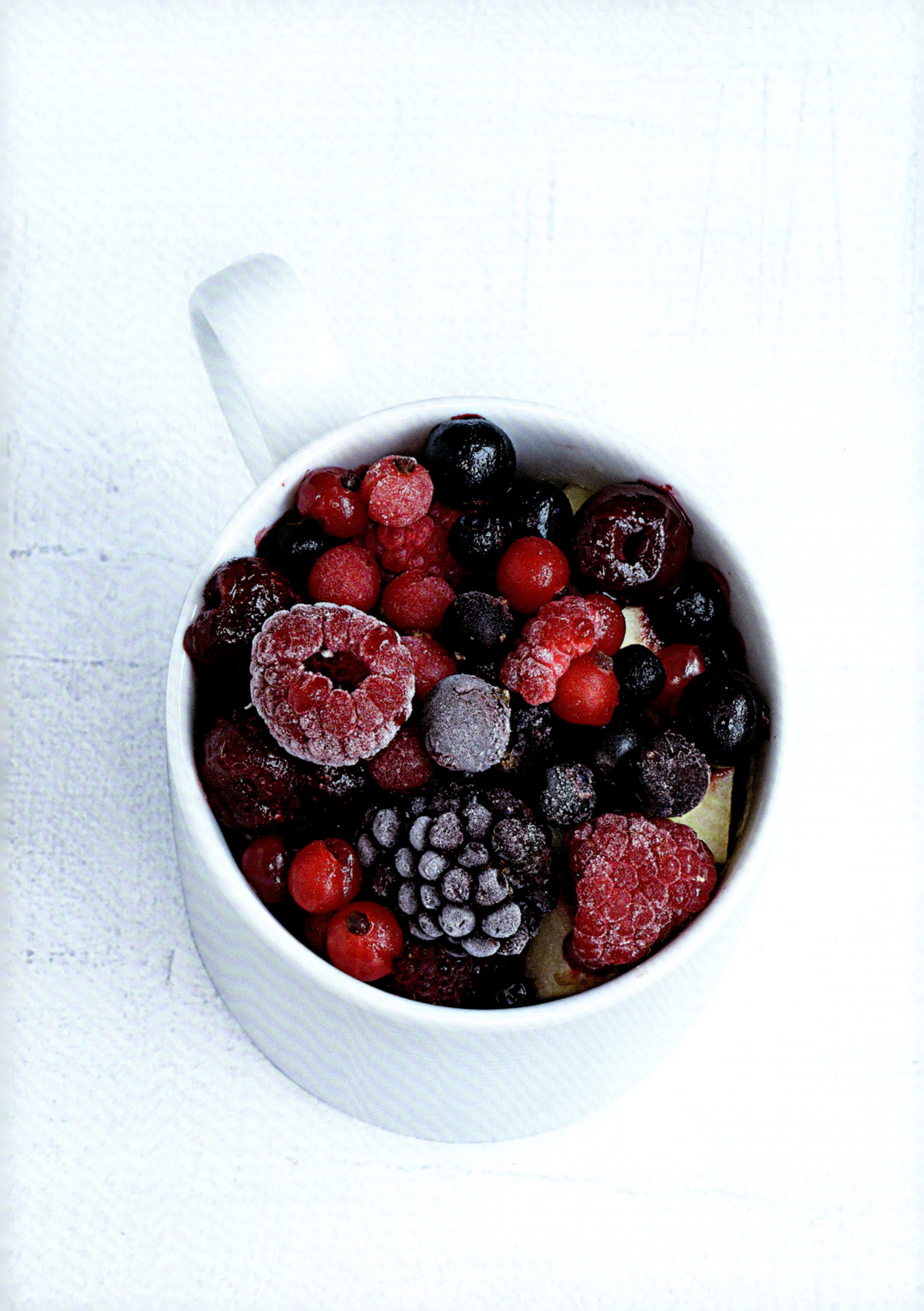

## Red Berry, Apple & Shortbread
# Mug Crumble

*Apple and berry crumble is classic comfort food, and by using ready-made shortbread biscuits to quickly make a crumble topping, this one can be ready in no time at all.*

**SERVES 1**

**TAKES 5 minutes**

1 apple, peeled, cored and diced
2 tablespoons frozen mixed red berries
1 tablespoon caster (superfine) sugar
a knob of butter

**Crumble**
1 slice of butter 5mm (¼in) thick (15g/½oz)
1 tablespoon soft brown sugar
2 crumbled petits-beurre or shortbread biscuits
1 heaped tablespoon plain (all-purpose) flour
a pinch of salt

In a mug, mix the apple with the red berries, sugar and butter. Cover the mug with cling film (plastic wrap) pierced several times.

Cook in the microwave for 1 minute, then pour off any excess liquid and stir again.

In a bowl, mix the butter, soft brown sugar, petits-beurre biscuits, flour and salt with your fingertips to form a dough.

Crumble it into the mug and cook in the microwave for 1 minute. Let it cool a little before eating.

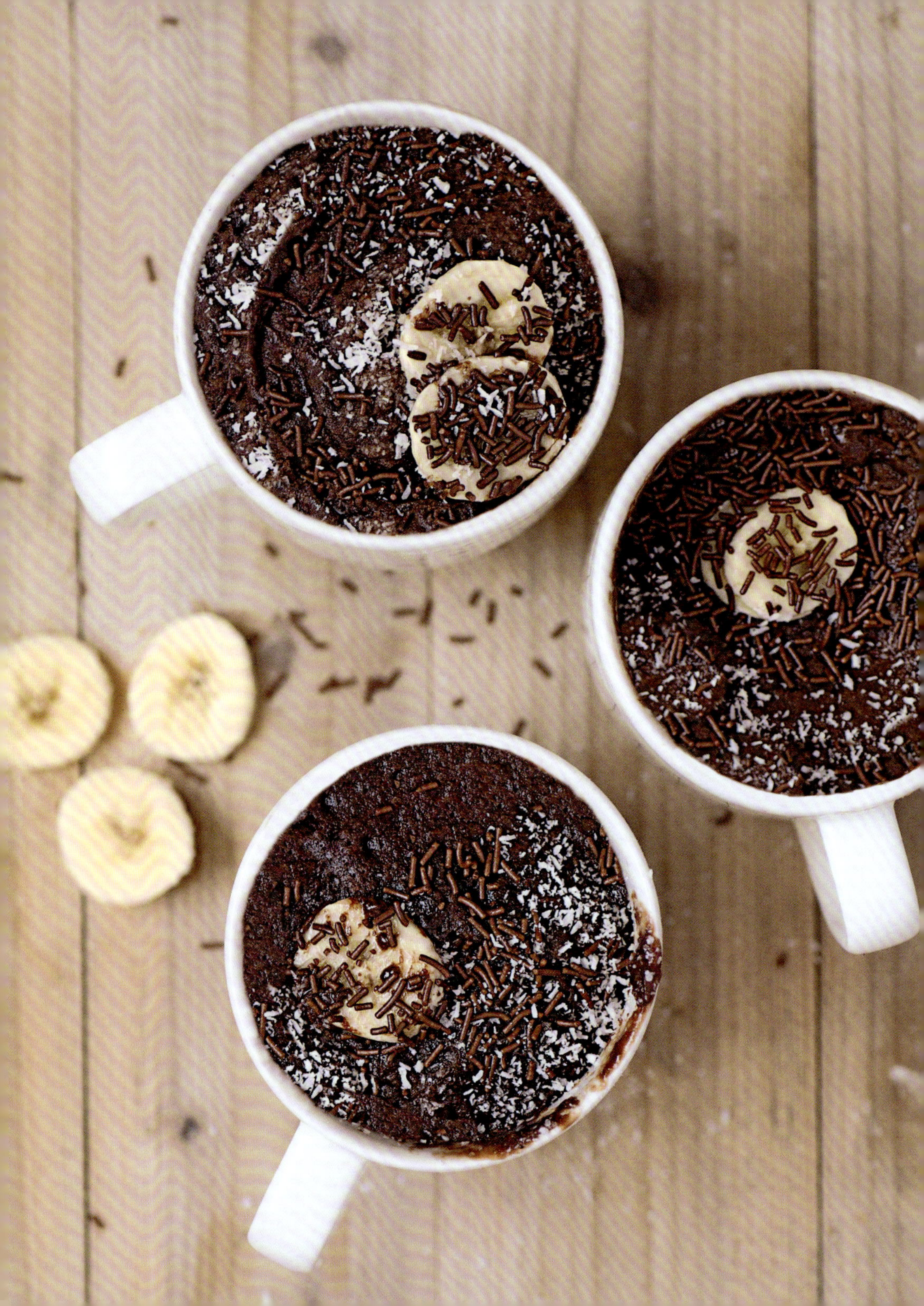

# Chocolate Mug Cake with
# **Banana & Coconut**

*The nostalgia is strong in this one, so it's sure to be a hit with adults and kids alike. The coconut adds an extra flavour dimension to the classic choc-banana combo.*

**SERVES 1**

**TAKES 5 minutes**

1 slice of butter 5mm (¼in) thick (15g/½oz)
6 squares of milk chocolate (30g/1oz)
½ mashed banana (50g/2oz)
1 egg
2 tablespoons soft brown sugar
1 tablespoon desiccated (dried shredded) coconut
4½ tablespoons plain (all-purpose) flour
½ teaspoon baking powder

**Decoration**
a few slices of banana
a pinch of chocolate sprinkles
1 teaspoon desiccated (dried shredded) coconut

In a mug, melt the butter with the chocolate in the microwave for 30–40 seconds. Beat the mixture until smooth, then allow it to cool slightly.

One by one, whisk in the mashed banana, egg, sugar, coconut, flour and baking powder. Cook in the microwave for 1 minute 30 seconds, or until risen and springy to the touch.

Place a few slices of banana on top, then decorate with chocolate sprinkles and desiccated coconut.

Allow to cool for 1 minute before eating.

# White Chocolate & Raspberry
# Matcha Mug Cake

*A wonderful twist on your daily cuppa, make a mug of green tea cake filled with plump and juicy raspberries. The fresh, slightly bitter flavour of the tea is great with sweet white chocolate – it's the perfect matcha!*

**SERVES 1**

**TAKES 5 minutes**

1 slice of butter 1cm (½in) thick (30g/1oz)
6 squares of white chocolate (30g/1oz)
1 egg
2 tablespoons caster (superfine) sugar
5 tablespoons plain (all-purpose) flour
½ teaspoon baking powder
½ teaspoon matcha green tea
5 fresh raspberries

In a mug, melt the butter with the chocolate in the microwave for 30 seconds.

Beat the mixture until smooth, then allow it to cool slightly. One by one, whisk in the egg, sugar, flour, baking powder and green tea.

Push four raspberries into the middle of the mixture. Cook in the microwave for 1 minute 40 seconds, or until risen and springy to the touch.

Decorate with the remaining raspberry. Allow to cool for 1 minute before eating.

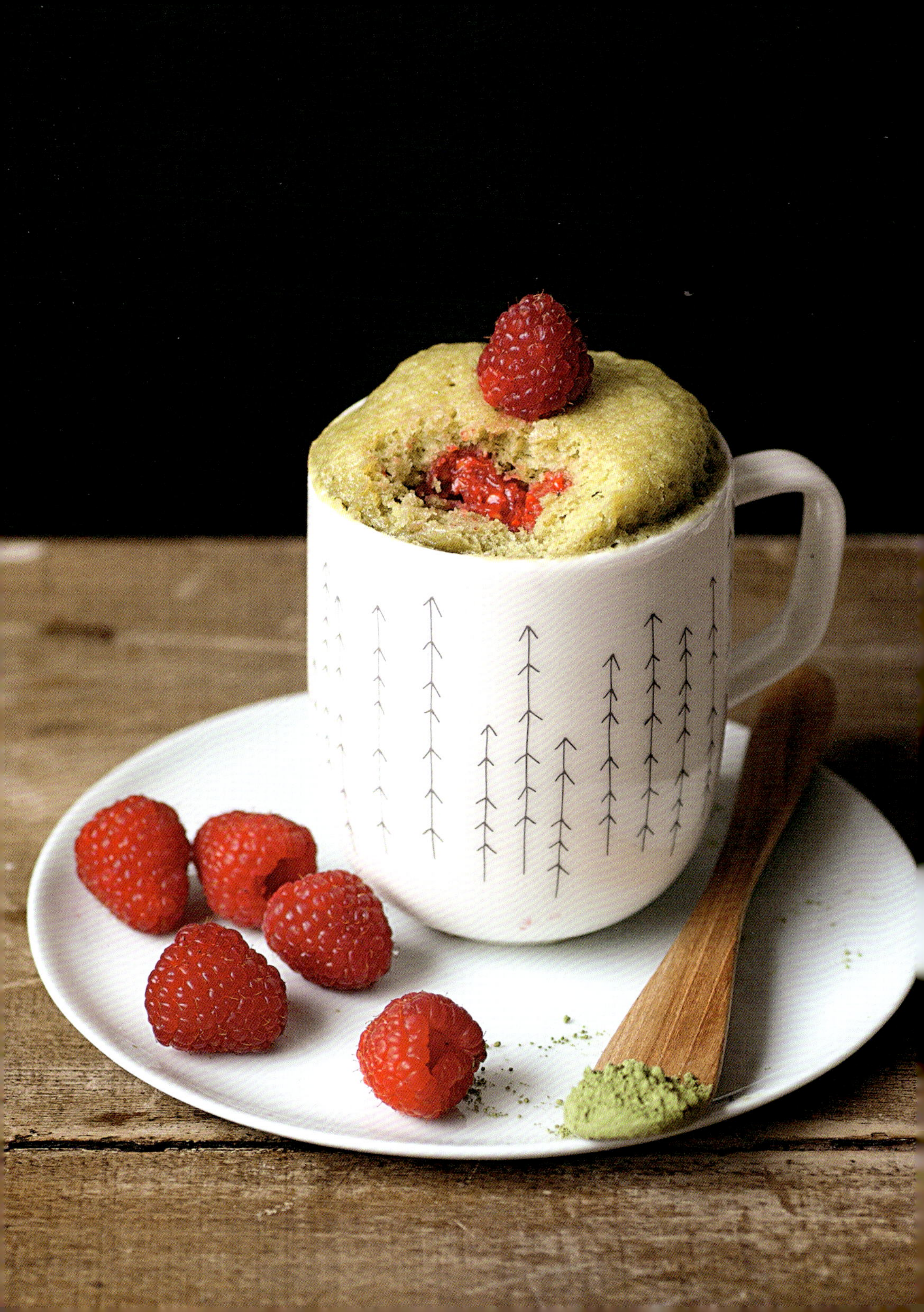

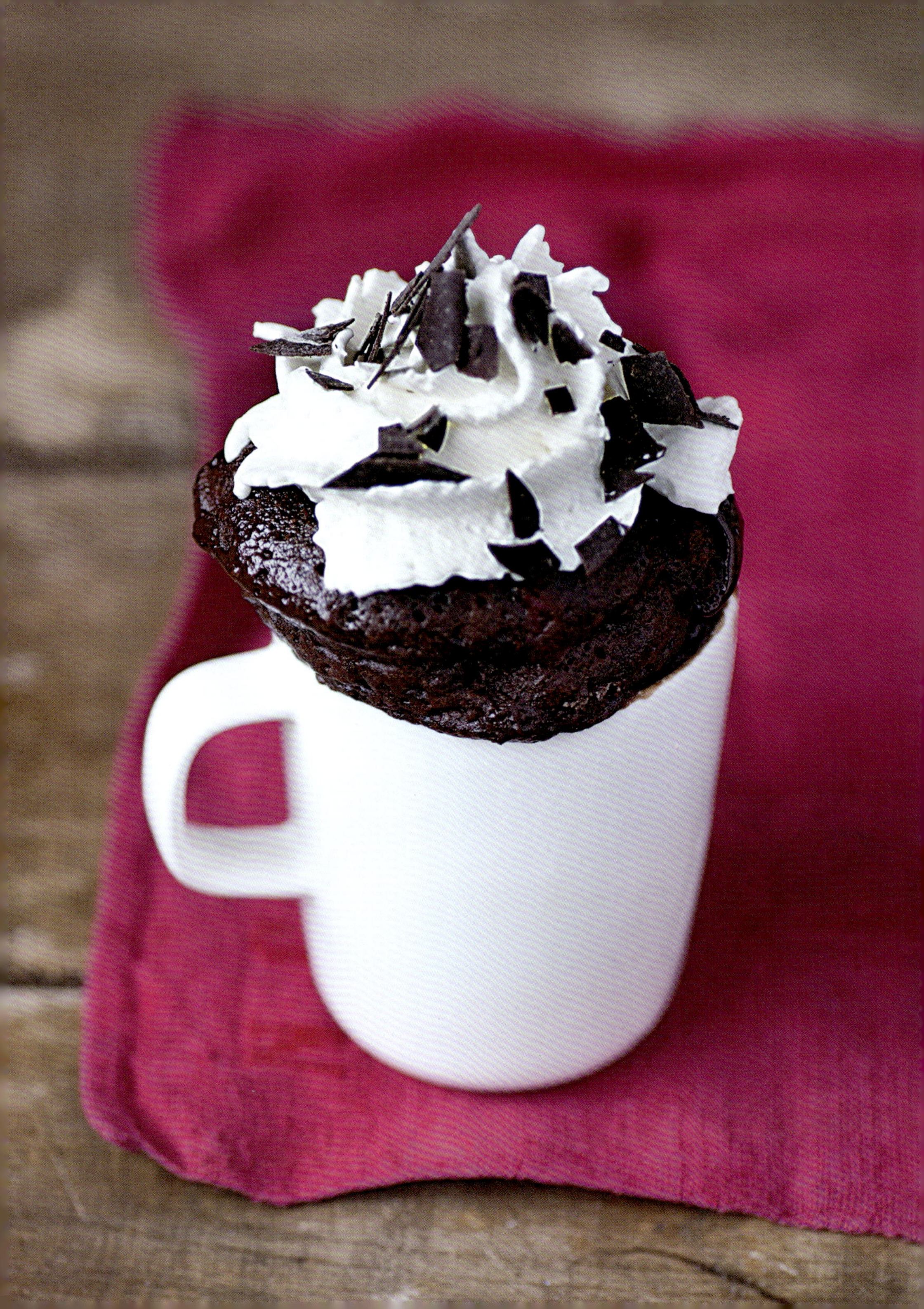

## Dark Chocolate
# Black Forest Cake

*This cake manages to squeeze a brilliant retro gateau into one mug – in no time at all. Rich chocolate sponge studded with sweet juicy cherries and all topped with a swirl of cream and a generous sprinkle of chocolate – unbeatable.*

**SERVES 1**

**TAKES 5 minutes**

1 slice of butter 1cm (½in) thick (30g/1oz)
6 squares of dark chocolate (30g/1oz)
1 egg
2 tablespoons soft brown sugar
5 tablespoons plain (all-purpose) flour, plus extra for sprinkling
½ teaspoon baking powder
30g/1oz drained pitted cherries in syrup

**Decoration**
whipped cream
1 tablespoon dark chocolate flakes

In a mug, melt the butter with the chocolate in the microwave for 30–40 seconds.

Beat the mixture until smooth, then allow it to cool slightly. One by one, whisk in the egg, sugar, flour and baking powder. Sprinkle the cherries with a little flour and add them to the mug without stirring too much. Cook in the microwave for 1 minute 20 seconds, or until risen and springy to the touch.

Allow to cool for 1 minute. Decorate with whipped cream and chocolate flakes. Eat immediately – the whipped cream melts very quickly!

## Right-Side-Up
# Pineapple Cake

*Truly sunny side up, this quick and fruity cake, based on the legendary dessert, is sure to put a smile on your face. The cute retro cocktail umbrellas are optional, but entirely encouraged.*

**SERVES 1**

**TAKES 4 minutes**

2 tablespoons sunflower oil
3 tablespoons golden caster (superfine) sugar
1 egg
1 teaspoon vanilla extract
4 tablespoons self-raising (self-rising) flour
1 canned pineapple ring, drained
1 glacé (candied) cherry
1 teaspoon pineapple syrup from the can

In a mug, mix together the oil, sugar, egg and vanilla using a fork until smooth. Add the flour and mix until just smooth.

Using a knife, make a cut in the pineapple ring so you can overlap it to make the ring fit your mug.

Microwave for 50 seconds, then place the pineapple and cherry on top and microwave for a further 40 seconds, or until risen and springy to the touch. Drizzle over the pineapple syrup, then dig in and enjoy.

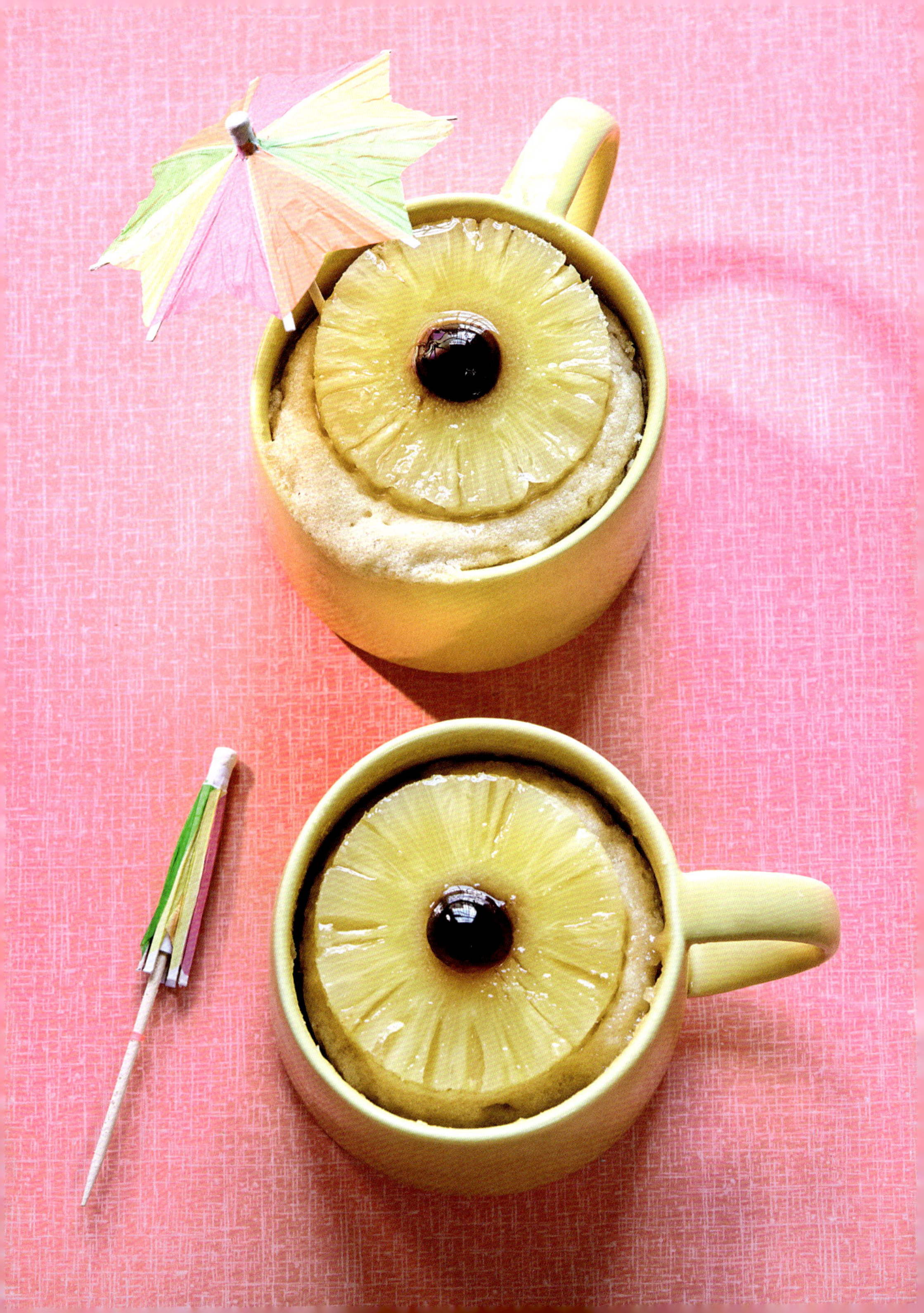

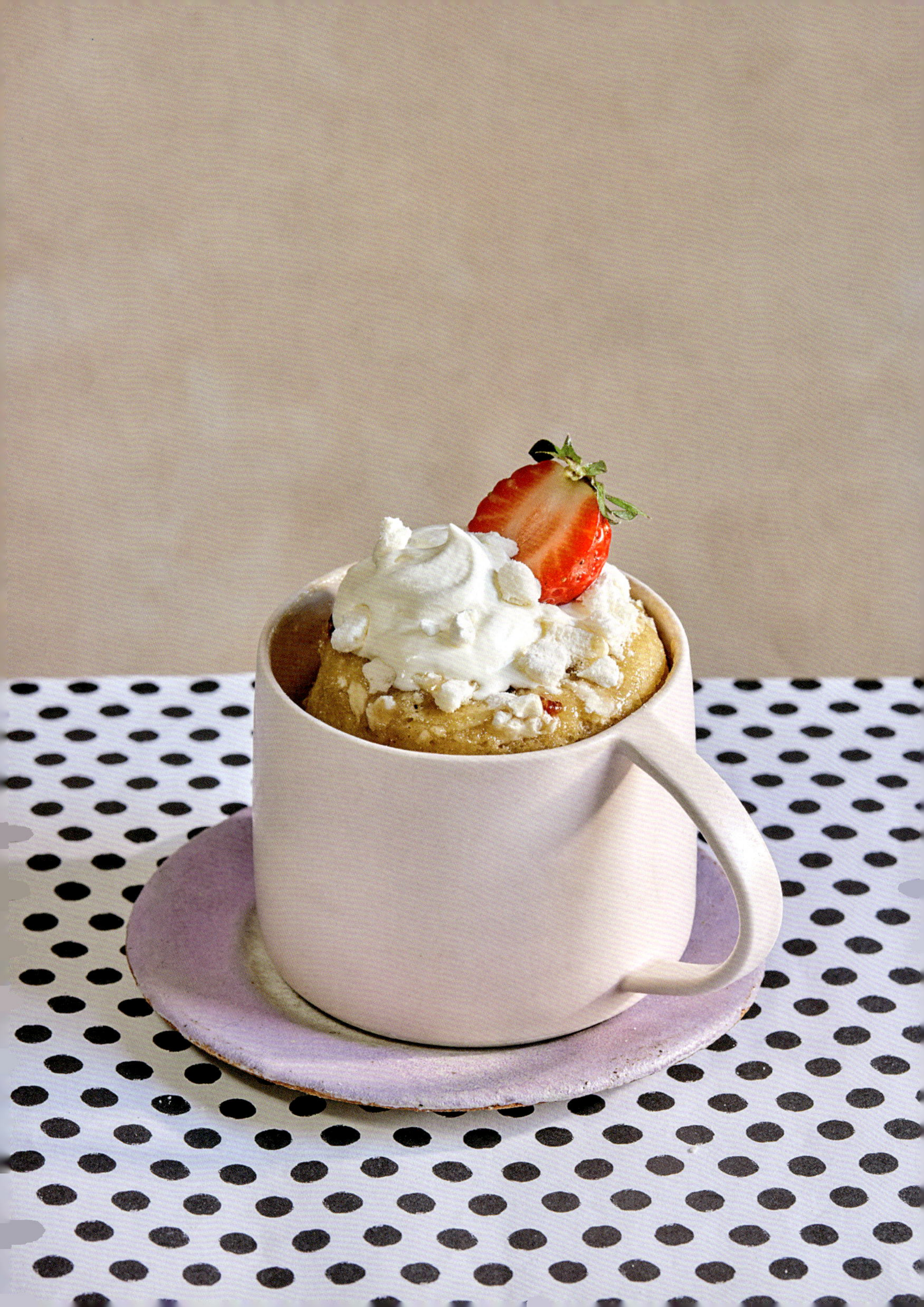

## Strawberry & Meringue
# Eton Mess Cake

*Ready-made meringue nests are the sort of ingredient that tend to languish for weeks at the back of kitchen cupboards, overlooked. This is especially true in the colder months, when chilled desserts give way to comforting warm puddings. This is the best of both worlds; a cake to warm you up whilst you remember sunnier days.*

**SERVES 1**

**TAKES 5 minutes, plus cooling**

2 tablespoons sunflower oil
3 tablespoons caster (superfine) sugar
1 egg
1 tablespoon double (heavy) cream, plus extra to decorate
1 teaspoon vanilla extract
4 tablespoons self-raising (self-rising) flour
1 heaped tablespoon strawberry jam
1 ready-made meringue nest, roughly crushed
strawberries, to decorate

In a mug, mix together the oil, sugar, egg, cream and vanilla using a fork until smooth. Add the flour, and mix until just smooth. Gently fold in the jam and most of the crushed meringue.

Microwave for 1 minute 30 seconds, or until risen and springy to the touch. Set aside to cool for 10 minutes.

For the topping, whip a few tablespoons of cream in a bowl until it forms soft peaks. Spoon the whipped cream over the cooled cake, then add a few strawberries and sprinkle with the remaining crushed meringue.

Dig in.

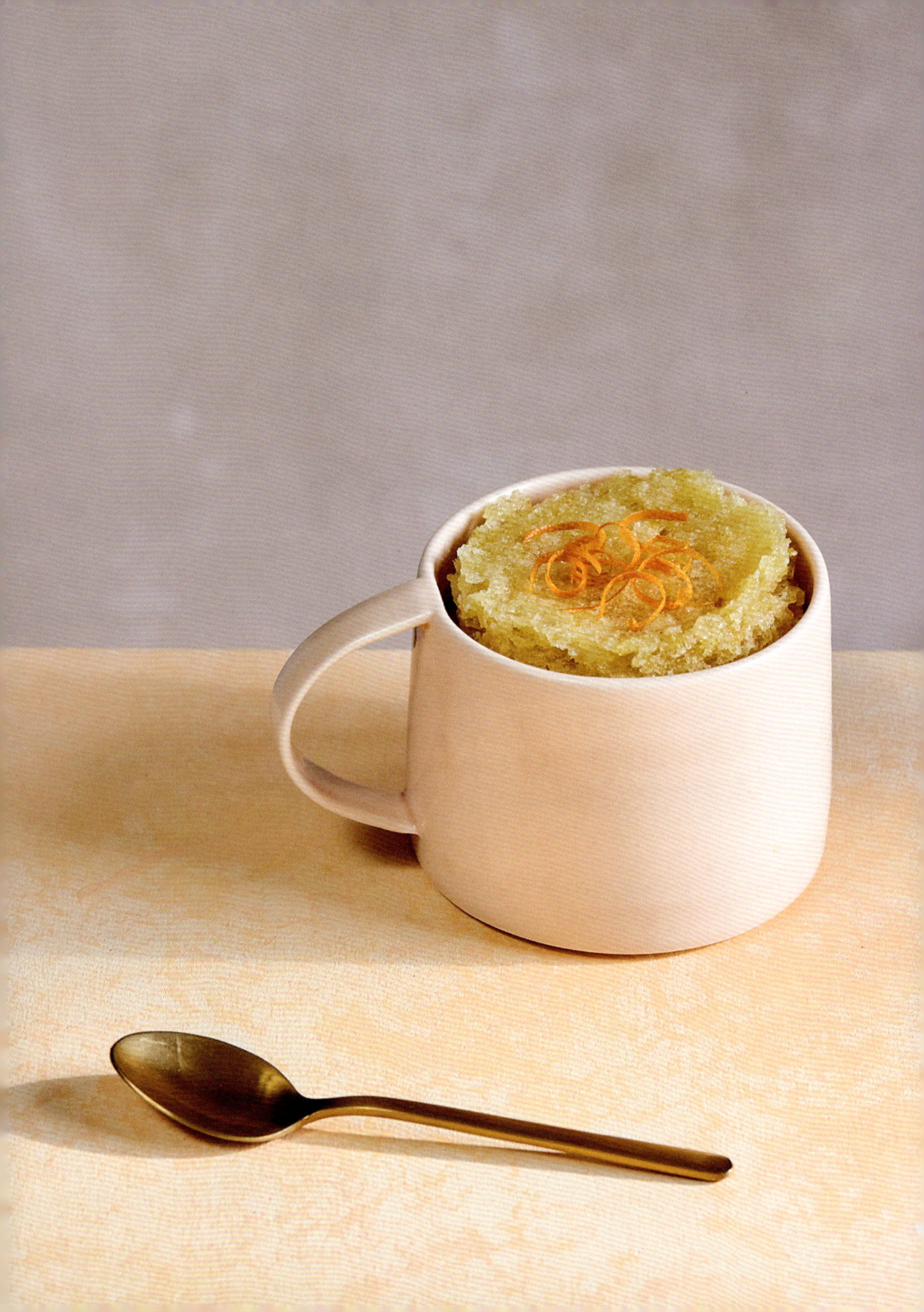

# Orange Zest & Almond Cake

*This super-simple cake swaps out flour for ground almonds, making it gluten-free (make sure you use GF baking powder, if necessary) and super moist, while the orange adds a zesty twist.*

**SERVES 1**

**TAKES 4 minutes**

2 tablespoons sunflower oil
3 tablespoons caster (superfine) sugar
1 egg
zest of 1 small orange, plus extra for decorating
4 tablespoons ground almonds
scant ½ teaspoon baking powder

In a mug, mix together the oil, sugar, egg and orange zest using a fork until smooth. Add the ground almonds and baking powder, and mix until just smooth.

Microwave for 1 minute 40 seconds, or until risen and springy to the touch. Decorate with extra orange zest and enjoy.

Chocolate
# Heaven
———

# Classic
# Cocoa Cake

*There's no need to complicate this classic, rich chocolate cake. It's one for purists; so simple, so chocolatey, so convenient for whipping up in 5 minutes flat when that chocolate craving strikes.*

**SERVES 1**

**TAKES 5 minutes**

1 slice of butter 1cm (½in) thick (30g/1oz)
1 egg
2 tablespoons caster (superfine) sugar
1 tablespoon vanilla sugar or 1 teaspoon vanilla extract
2 tablespoons unsweetened cocoa powder, plus extra to decorate
4 tablespoons plain (all-purpose) flour
½ teaspoon baking powder

In a mug, melt the butter in the microwave for 30 seconds.

One by one, whisk in the egg, sugar, vanilla sugar, cocoa, flour and baking powder. Cook in the microwave for 1 minute 20 seconds, or until risen and springy to the touch.

Dust with cocoa powder. Allow to cool for 1 minute before eating.

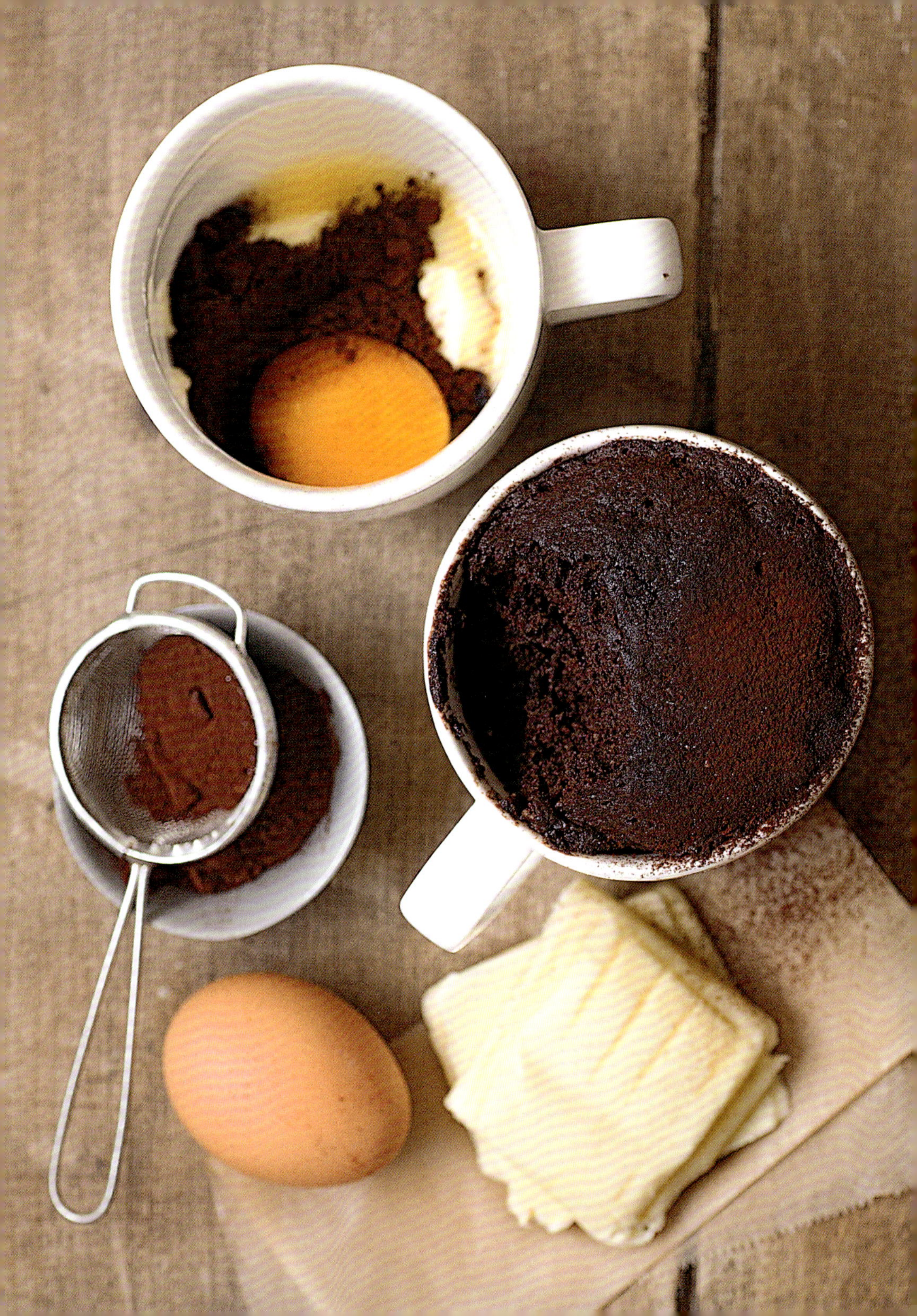

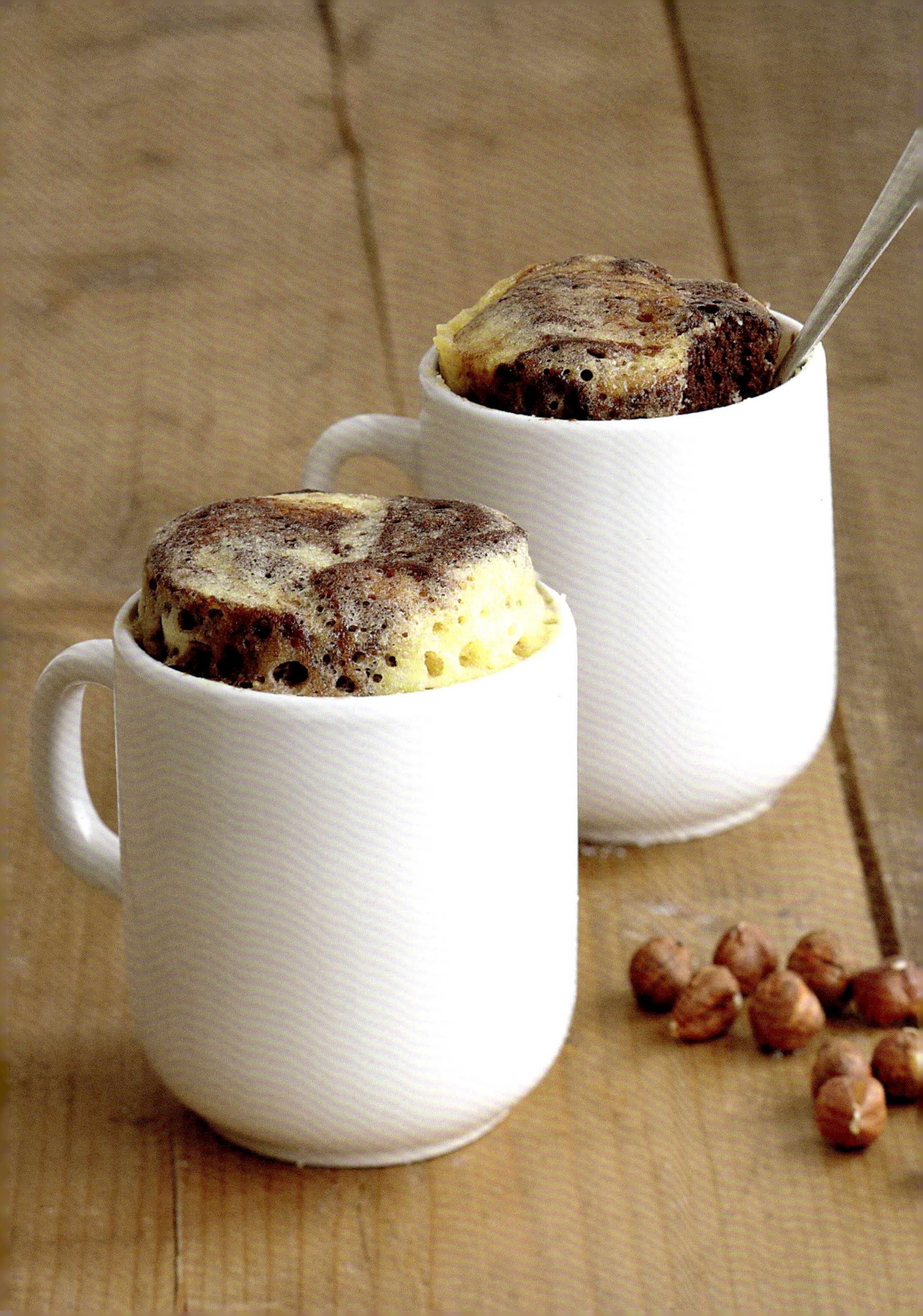

# Chocolate & Hazelnut
# Marble Cake

*Gianduja, praline, Nutella, Ferrero Rocher: there is a reason the chocolate-hazelnut flavour combo is so ubiquitous in our favourite desserts and confectionery. They just work, so marbling them together in this delicious mug cake honestly feels like a no-brainer.*

**SERVES 1**

**TAKES 6 minutes**

1 slice of butter 1cm (½in) thick (30g/1oz)
3 squares of dark chocolate (15g/½oz)
1 egg
3 tablespoons caster (superfine) sugar
½ teaspoon vanilla sugar
1 tablespoon single (light) cream
2 tablespoons ground hazelnuts
5 tablespoons plain (all-purpose) flour
½ teaspoon baking powder

Melt the butter in a bowl in the microwave for 20 seconds. In another bowl, melt the chocolate in the microwave for 1 minute 10 seconds.

In a third bowl, beat together the egg, sugar, vanilla sugar, cream, ground hazelnuts, flour, baking powder and melted butter.

Mix a third of the mixture into the melted chocolate.

In a mug, spoon in by turns the plain and chocolate mixtures. With a knife, draw a wave in the batter to create a marbled effect.

Cook in the microwave for 1 minute 40 seconds, or until risen and springy to the touch.

# Chocolate & Amaretto Cake

*If you're searching for a little Italian refinement from your mug cake, you've found it! A healthy glug of amaretto liqueur helps keep the sponge moist and soft, which is balanced perfectly with the crisp crunch of amaretti biscuits. Saluti!*

**SERVES 1**

**TAKES 4 minutes**

- 3 tablespoons self-raising (self-rising) flour
- 1 tablespoon unsweetened cocoa powder
- 3 tablespoons soft brown sugar
- 1 tablespoon ground almonds
- 2 tablespoons sunflower oil
- 1 egg
- 2 tablespoons amaretto (such as Disaronno)
- crushed amaretti biscuit (or mini amaretti), to decorate

In a mug, mix together the flour, cocoa, sugar and ground almonds using a fork until combined. Add the oil, egg and amaretto, and mix until just smooth.

Microwave for 1 minute 40 seconds, or until risen and springy to the touch. Top with the crushed amaretti biscuit, then dig in and enjoy.

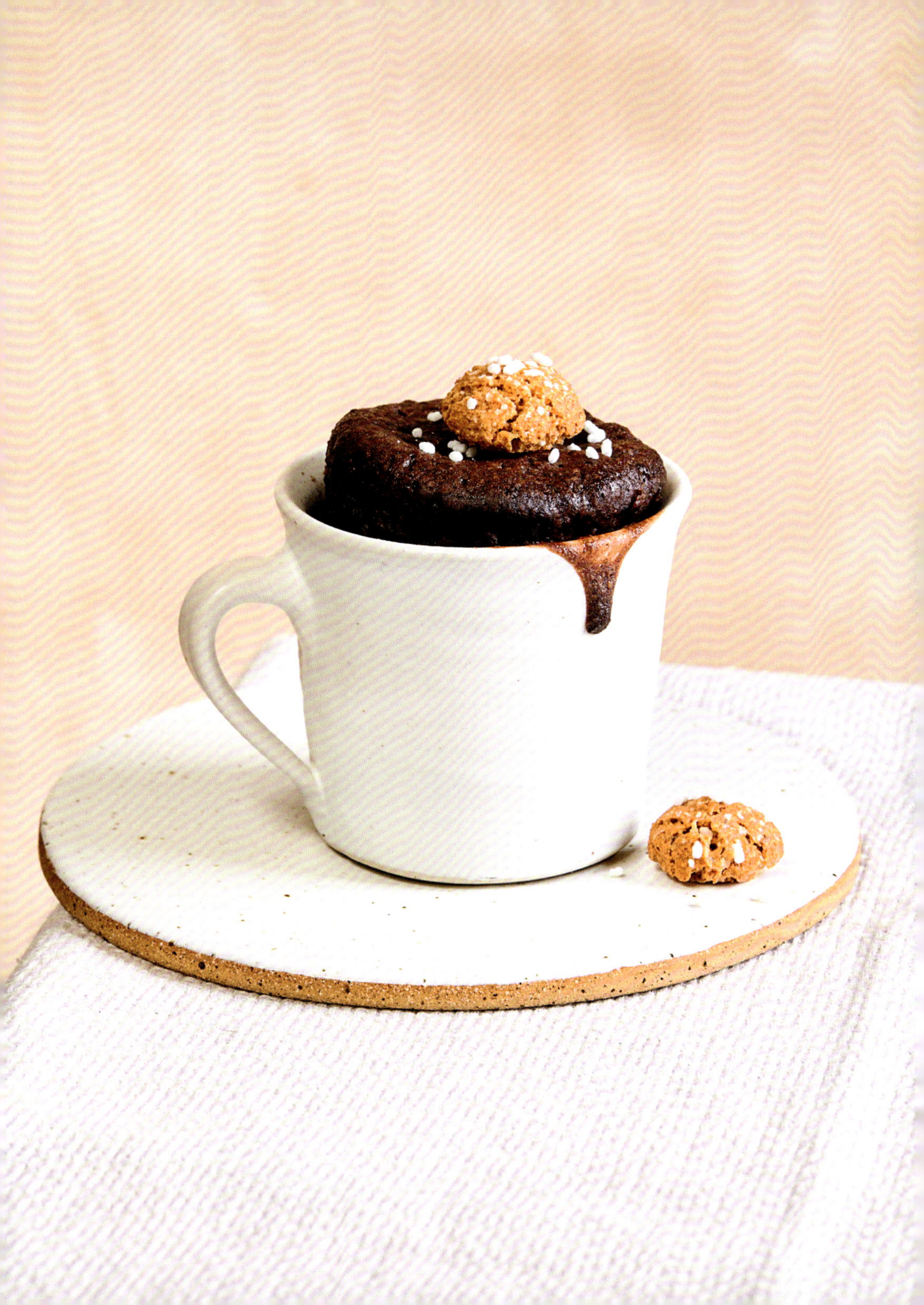

## Classic Mug Cake with
# Milk Chocolate

*Simple sweet indulgence, this cake is based on everyone's favourite creamy milk chocolate, with a bonus vanilla hit. They don't come much easier, or more comforting, than this.*

**SERVES 1**

**TAKES 5 minutes**

1 slice of butter 1cm (½in) thick (30g/1oz)
6 squares of milk chocolate (30g/1oz)
1 egg
2 tablespoons caster (superfine) sugar
1½ teaspoons vanilla sugar or ½ teaspoon vanilla extract
4½ tablespoons plain (all-purpose) flour
½ teaspoon baking powder

In a mug, melt the butter with the chocolate in the microwave for 30–40 seconds.

Beat the mixture until smooth, then allow it to cool slightly. One by one, whisk in the egg, sugar, vanilla sugar, flour and baking powder. Cook in the microwave for 1 minute 20 seconds, or until risen and springy to the touch.

Allow to cool for 1 minute before eating.

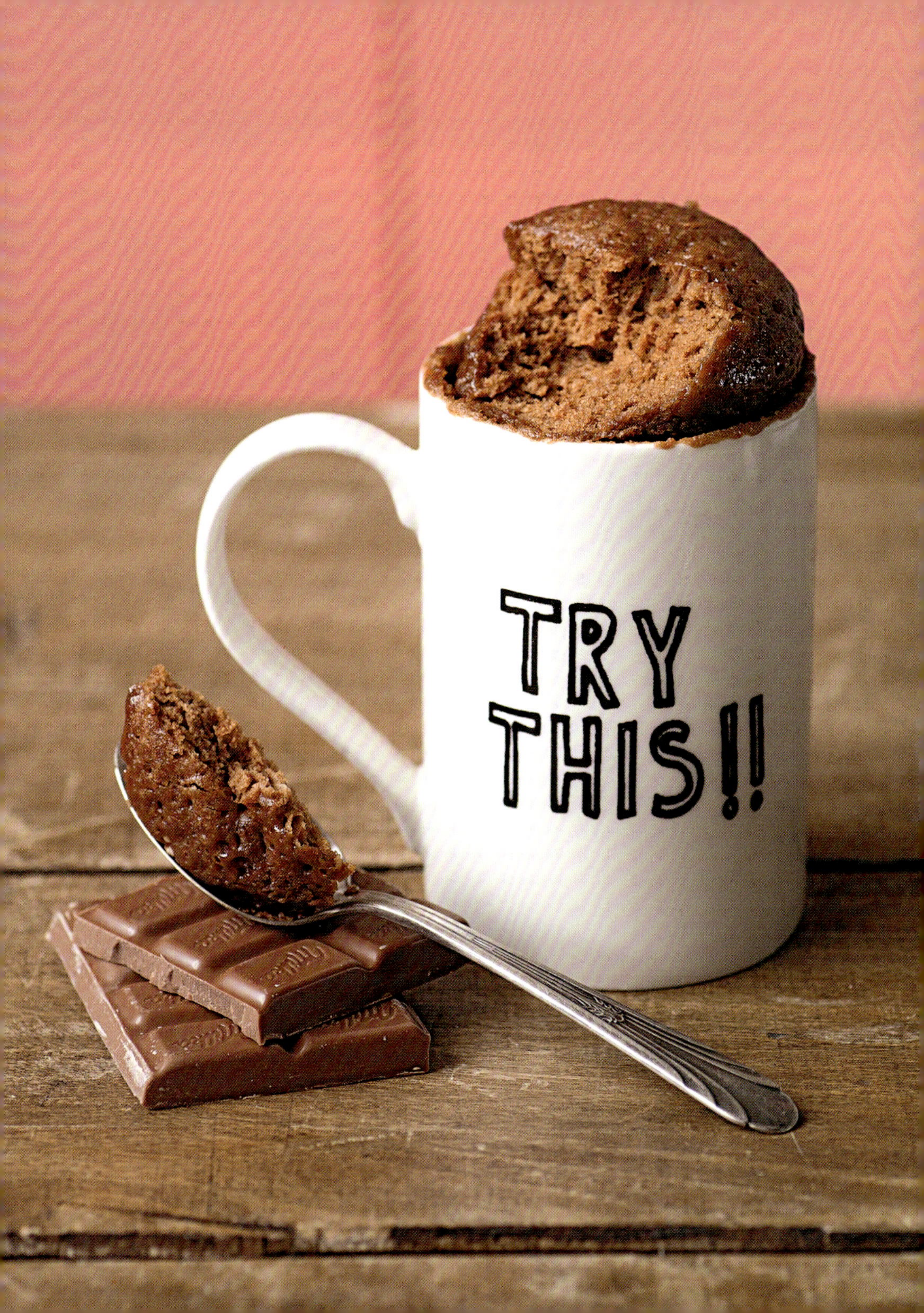
TRY
THIS!!

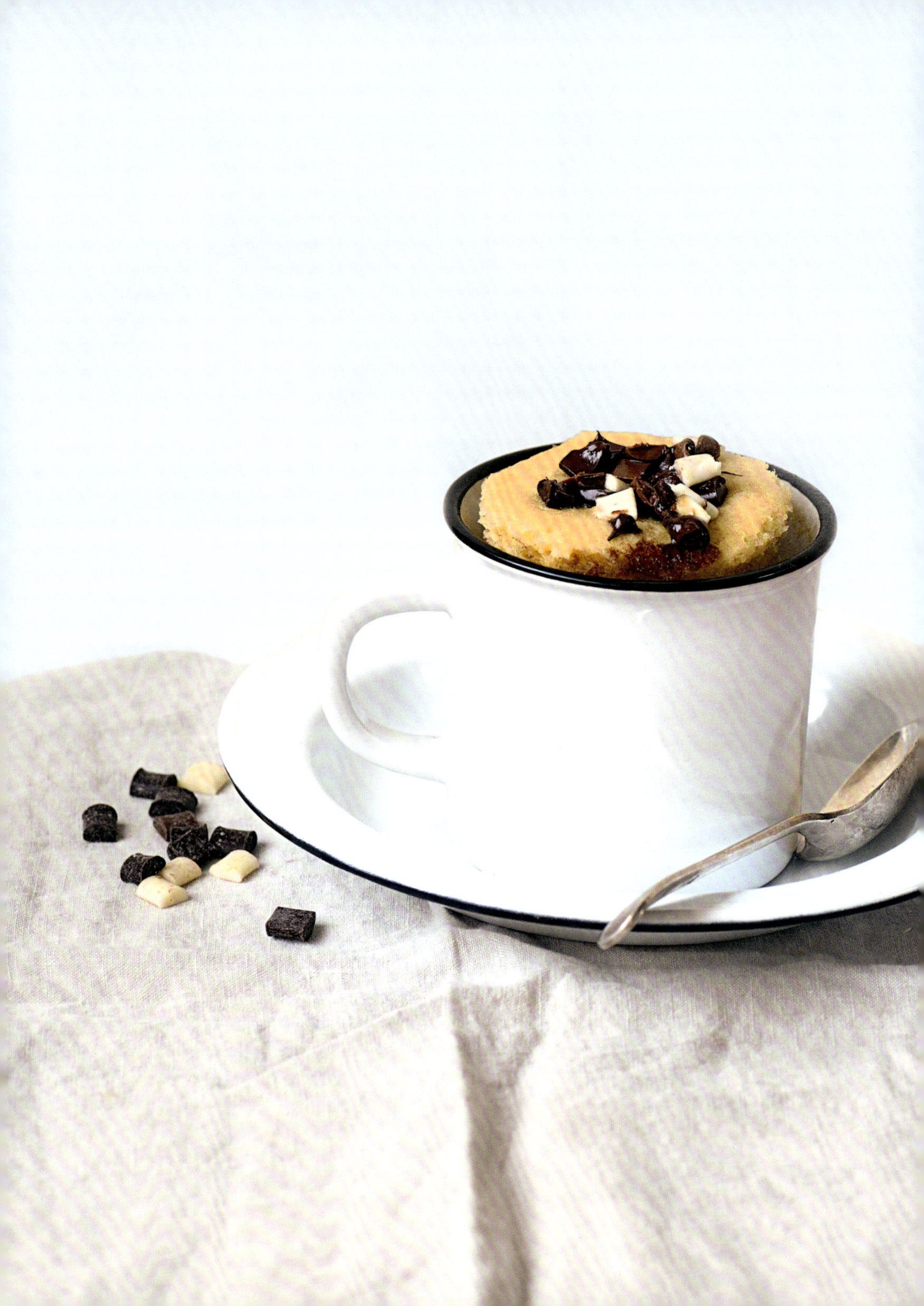

# Triple Chocolate & Vanilla Cake

*There's really no need to decide here which chocolate is best; we are giving you permission to throw them all in! Which makes this a great one for using up odds and ends of bags of chocolate drops which may be hiding at the backs of kitchen cupboards – you can adapt it to whatever chocolate you happen to have.*

**SERVES 1**

**TAKES 5 minutes**

- 1 slice of butter 1cm (½in) thick (30g/1oz)
- 1 egg
- 2 tablespoons soft brown sugar
- 1½ teaspoons vanilla sugar or ½ teaspoon vanilla extract
- 1 tablespoon single (light) cream
- 5 tablespoons plain (all-purpose) flour
- ½ teaspoon baking powder
- 2 tablespoons dark, milk and white chocolate chips (30–35g/1–1¼oz) or 3 squares each of dark, white and milk chocolate, chopped into chips, plus extra to decorate

In a mug, melt the butter in the microwave for 30 seconds.

One by one, beat in the egg, sugar, vanilla sugar, cream, flour and baking powder. Add the chocolate chips without stirring too much. Cook in the microwave for 1 minute 40 seconds until risen.

Decorate with a few mixed chocolate chips. Allow to cool for 1 minute before eating.

# Milk Chocolate & Oreo Cake

*Adding cookies to your mug cakes is a great way to add flavour and textural interest with minimum effort. The Oreos here provide an interesting crunch against the backdrop of soft sponge, as well as that distinctive monochrome stripe we all love.*

**SERVES 1**

**TAKES 5 minutes**

1 slice of butter 1cm (½in) thick (30g/1oz)
3 squares of milk chocolate (15g/½oz)
1 egg
2 tablespoons single (light) cream
1 teaspoon vanilla sugar or a few drops of vanilla extract
4 tablespoons plain (all-purpose) flour
½ teaspoon baking powder
3 broken Oreo biscuits (cookies), plus extra to decorate

In a mug, melt the butter with the chocolate in the microwave for 30–40 seconds.

Beat the mixture until smooth and allow it to cool slightly. One by one, whisk in the egg, cream, vanilla sugar, flour and baking powder. Add the broken Oreos without stirring too much.

Cook in the microwave for 1 minute 30 seconds, or until risen and springy to the touch. Decorate with the broken Oreo.

Allow to cool for 1 minute before eating.

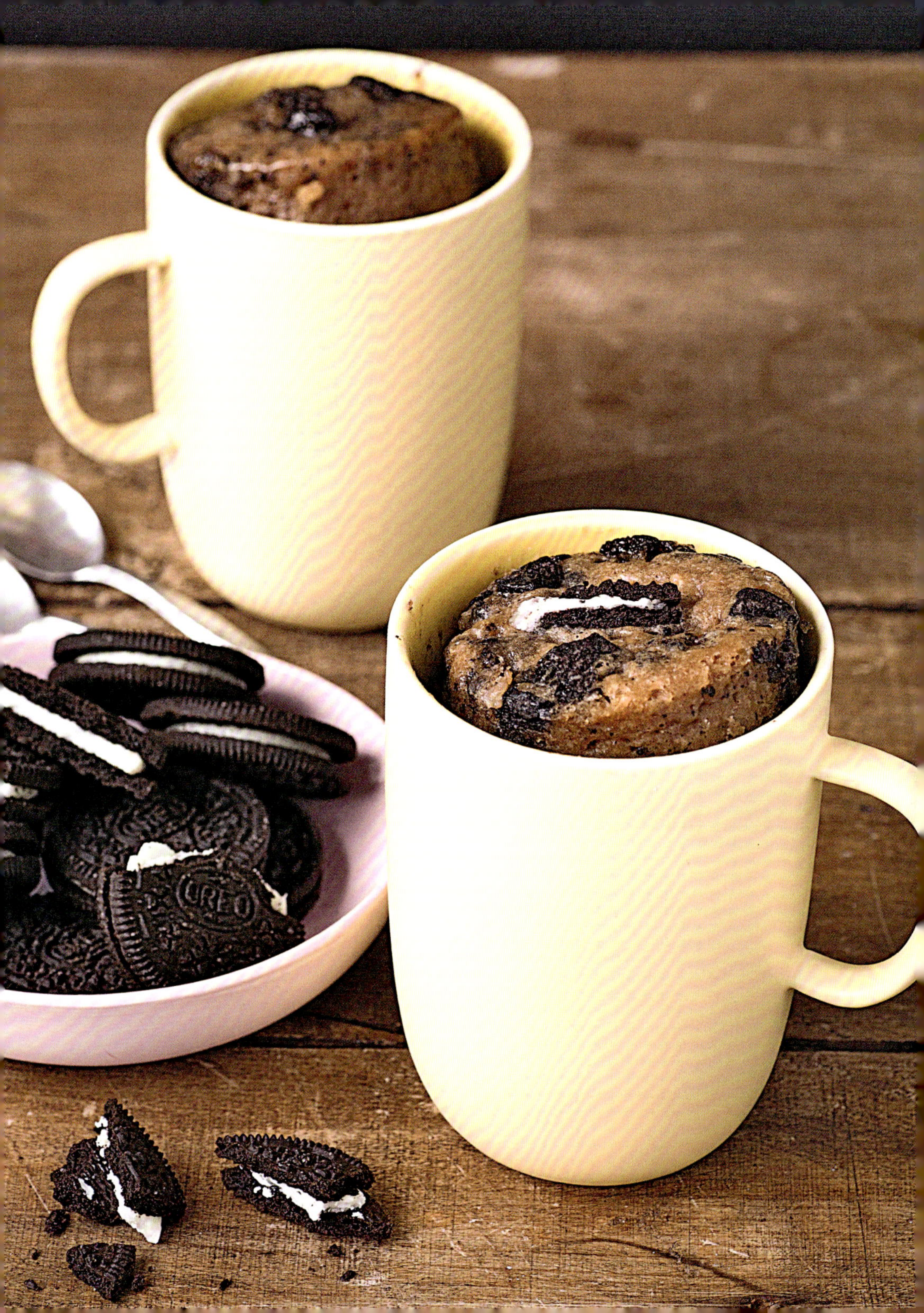
OREO

# Mug Cookie with
# M&M's

*So colourful, so fun, so easy! This mug cookie is irresistible with its bright and playful topping, which is guaranteed to delight kids and adults alike.*

**SERVES 1**

**TAKES 4 minutes**

1 slice of butter 5mm (¼in) thick (15g/½oz)
1 tablespoon soft brown sugar
1 teaspoon vanilla sugar
1 egg yolk
4 tablespoons plain (all-purpose) flour
4 M&M's, roughly chopped

In a mug, melt the butter in the microwave for 20 seconds. One by one, beat in the brown sugar, vanilla sugar, egg yolk and flour.

Add the M&M's to the top of the mixture.

Cook in the microwave for 1 minute, or until risen and springy to the touch.

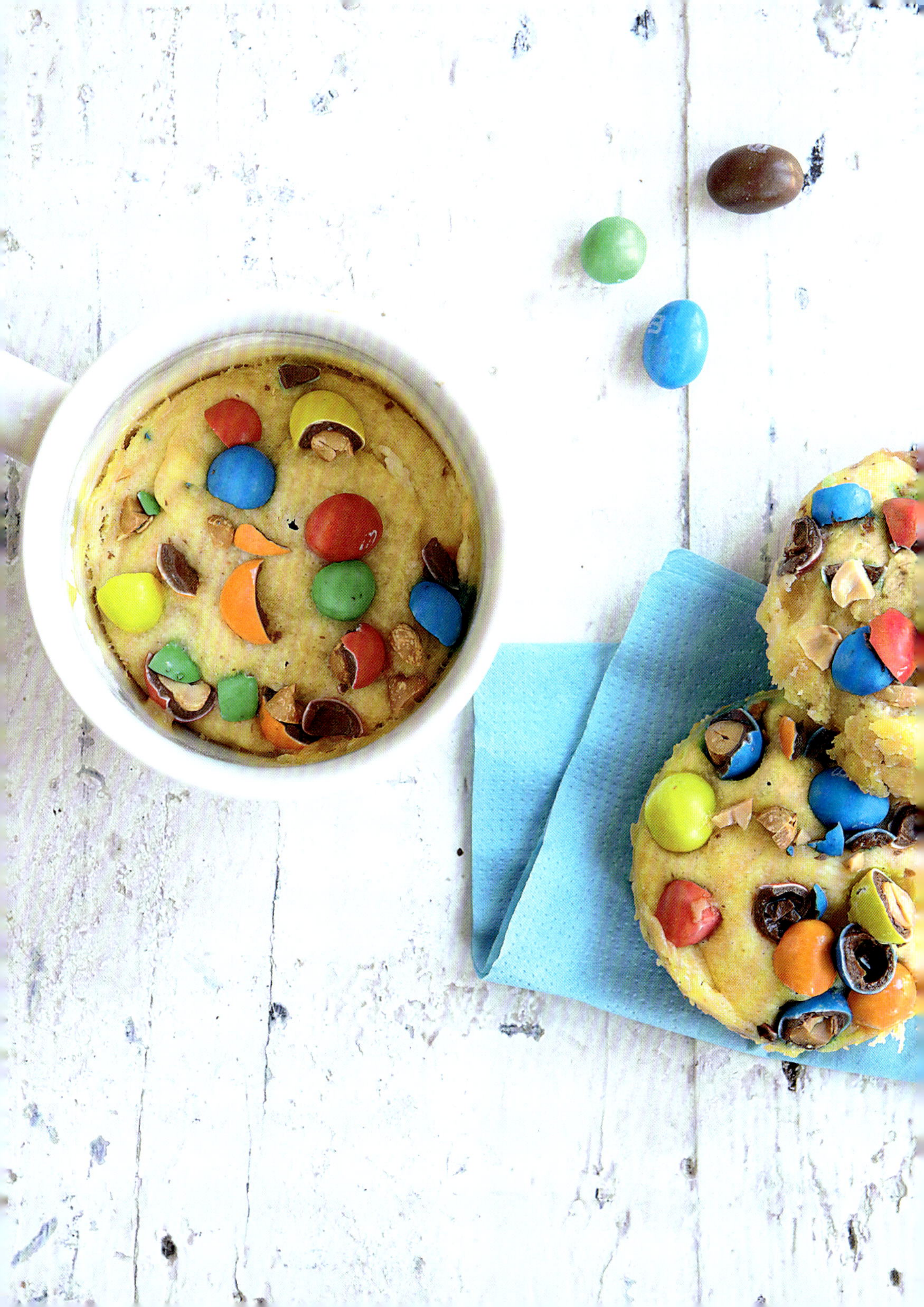

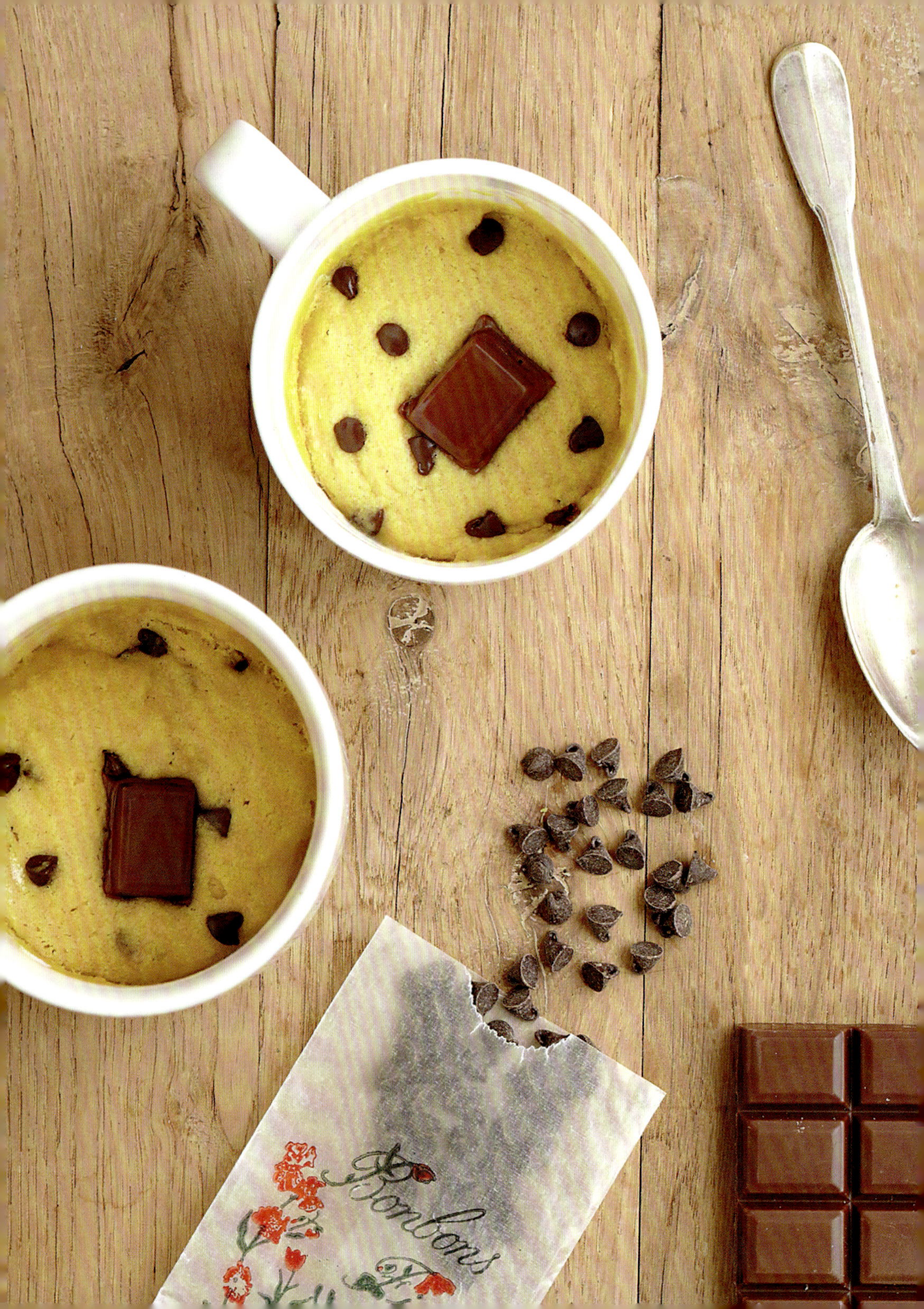
Bonbons

# Mug Cookie with
# Chocolate Chips

*Do you feel like a cake or a cookie? With chocolate chips or raisins? There really is no need to decide. Throw in some vanilla and caramel too, and you will have the best of all worlds.*

**SERVES 1**

**TAKES 4 minutes**

1 slice of butter 5mm (¼in) thick (15g/½oz)
1½ tablespoons soft brown sugar
½ teaspoon vanilla sugar
1 egg yolk
4 tablespoons plain (all-purpose) flour
2 teaspoons chocolate chips
1 teaspoon raisins
1 square of caramel chocolate (5g/¼oz)

In a mug, melt the butter in the microwave for 20 seconds.

One by one, beat in the brown sugar, vanilla sugar, egg yolk, flour, chocolate chips and raisins.

Add the square of caramel chocolate to the top of the mixture.

Cook in the microwave for 1 minute, or until risen and springy to the touch.

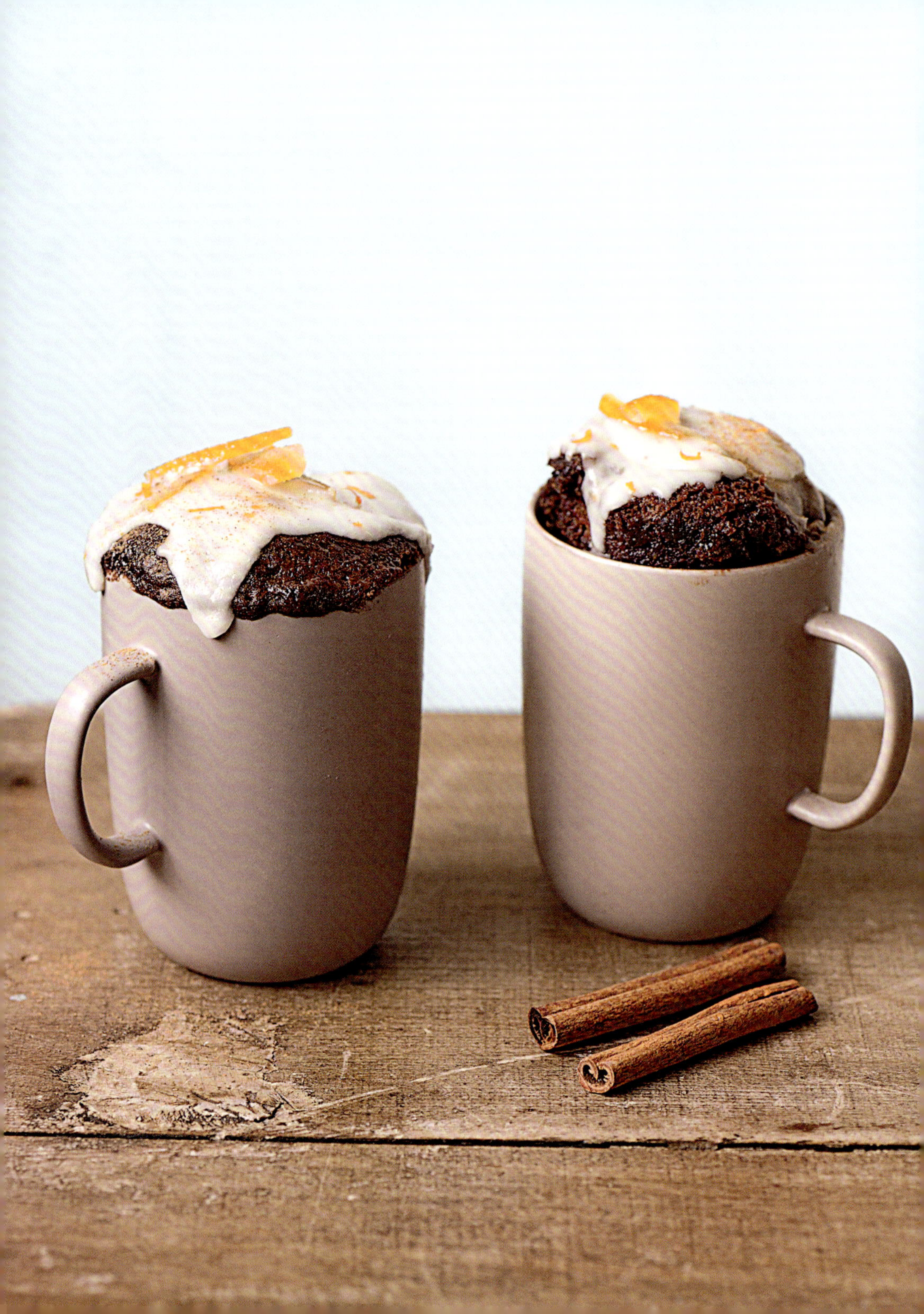

# Chocolate Mug Cake with
# Orange & Cinnamon

*For a mug cake with a touch of the Aztec sophistication, try this treat which combines rich dark chocolate with zesty orange and a hint of aromatic cinnamon.*

**SERVES 1**

**TAKES 5 minutes**

1 slice of butter 1cm (½in) thick (30g/1oz)
6 squares of dark chocolate (30g/1oz)
1 egg
2 tablespoons soft brown sugar
5 tablespoons plain (all-purpose) flour
½ teaspoon baking powder
1 tablespoon orange marmalade

**Icing (Frosting)**
2 tablespoons icing (confectioners') sugar
a few drops of orange juice
1 teaspoon orange zest

**Decoration**
a generous pinch of ground cinnamon
2 pieces of candied orange peel

In a mug, melt the butter with the chocolate in the microwave for 30–40 seconds.

Beat the mixture until smooth, then allow it to cool slightly. One by one, whisk in the egg, sugar, flour and baking powder. Add the marmalade without stirring. Cook in the microwave for 1 minute 30 seconds, or until risen and springy to the touch.

Allow to cool for 1 minute.

For the icing, mix all the ingredients to make a thick, but pourable icing, then ice the mug cake. Sprinkle with cinnamon and decorate with candied orange peel.

# Dark Chocolate &
# Cream Cheese Swirl

*If ever there was a quick way to raise your mug cake game, it's including a generous, decadent swirl of cream cheese alongside that bitter dark chocolate for a proper grown-up treat.*

**SERVES 1**

**TAKES 5 minutes**

2 tablespoons (30g/1oz) cream cheese
1 tablespoon milk
1 slice of butter 1cm (½in) thick (30g/1oz)
6 squares of dark chocolate (30g/1oz)
1 egg
2 tablespoons caster (superfine) sugar
4 tablespoons plain (all-purpose) flour
½ teaspoon baking powder

In a bowl, mix the cream cheese and milk together with a mini whisk.

In a mug, melt the butter with the chocolate in the microwave for 30–40 seconds.

Beat the chocolate mixture until smooth, then allow it to cool slightly. One by one, whisk in the egg, sugar, flour and baking powder. Add the cream cheese without mixing too much, so you can still see a swirl in the batter. Cook in the microwave for 1 minute 30 seconds, or until risen and springy to the touch.

Allow to cool for 1 minute before eating.

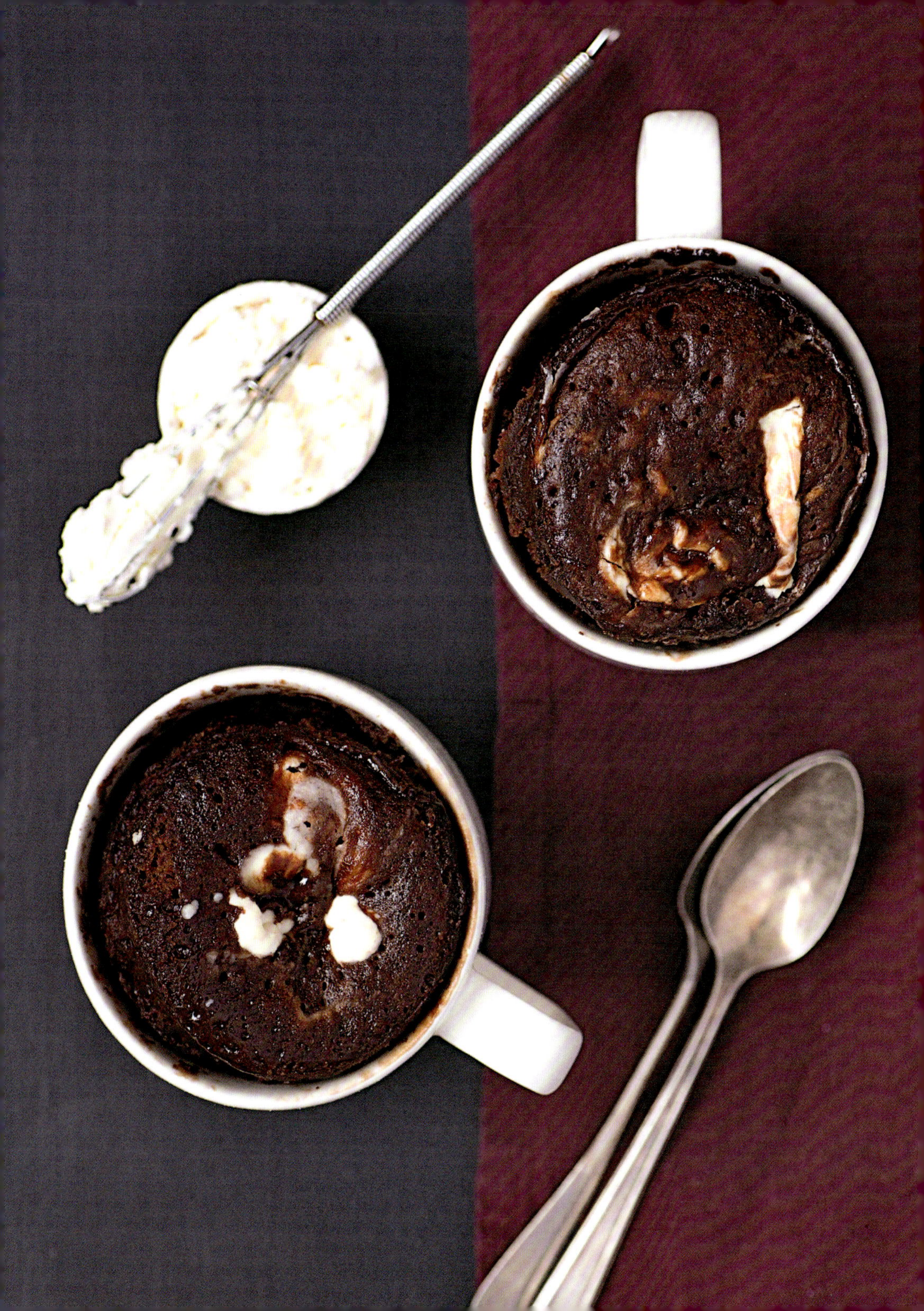

# Chocolate Mug Cake with
# Double-Choc Chips

*For those who like some chocolate with their chocolate, do the double (or triple if you count the cocoa in the sponge) and whip up this chocoholic's dream.*

**SERVES 1**

**TAKES 4 minutes**

2 tablespoons caster (superfine) sugar
3 tablespoons plain (all-purpose) flour
1 tablespoon unsweetened cocoa powder
¼ teaspoon baking powder
1 egg
½ teaspoon vanilla extract
1 tablespoon milk
2 tablespoons sunflower oil
1 tablespoon milk chocolate chips, plus extra to decorate
1 tablespoon white chocolate chips or chunks, plus extra to decorate

In a mug, mix together the sugar, flour, cocoa and baking powder using a fork. Add the egg, vanilla extract, milk and oil, and mix until just smooth. Gently stir the chocolate chips into the top half of the batter.

Microwave for 1 minute 40 seconds, or until risen and springy to the touch. Sprinkle a few extra chocolate chips over the top and dig in.

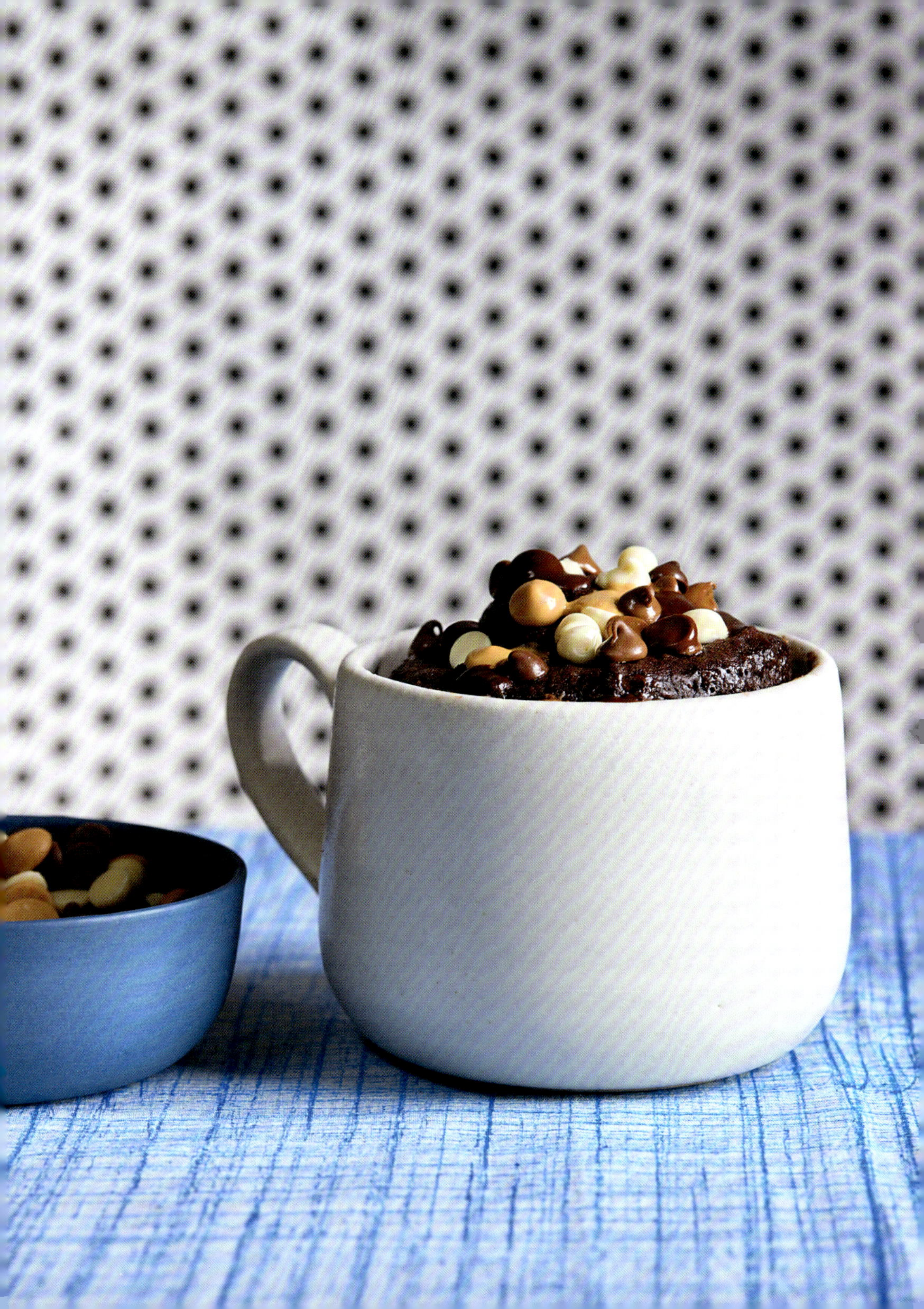

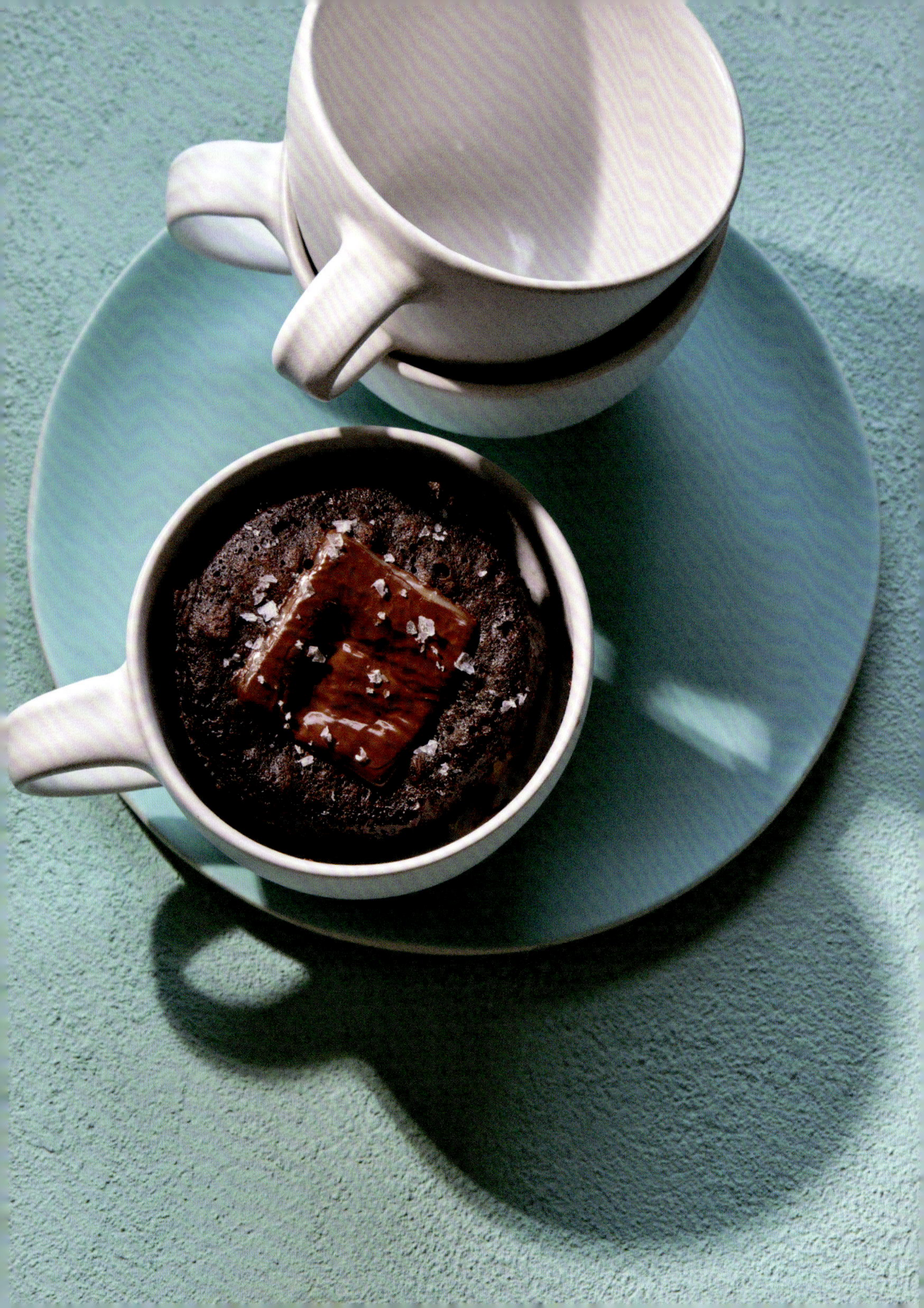

## After-Dinner
# Mint-Choc Mug Cake

*Before you treat your dinner party guests to those unmistakable little black-enveloped chocolate mints, make sure you squirrel a few of them away for making these delicious mug cakes. Future you will thank you.*

**SERVES 1**

**TAKES 4 minutes**

2 tablespoons caster (superfine) sugar
2 tablespoons plain (all-purpose) flour
1 tablespoon unsweetened cocoa powder
¼ teaspoon baking powder
1 egg
½ teaspoon vanilla extract
1 tablespoon milk
2 tablespoons sunflower oil
2 mint chocolate thins (such as After Eights)
sea salt, to decorate

In a mug, mix together the sugar, flour, cocoa and baking powder using a fork. Add the egg, vanilla extract, milk and oil, and mix until just smooth. Add one mint chocolate thin, lying flat on top of the batter.

Microwave for 1 minute 20 seconds, or until risen and springy to the touch. Remove from the microwave and add another mint chocolate thin on top. It will start to melt within seconds. Sprinkle with salt before diving in.

Utterly
# Nutty
───────────

# Coconut Mug Cake with
# Chocolate Sauce

*OK, not technically a nut, but I think we can all agree that coconut is always a welcome addition to cakes, keeping the sponge tender and moist and bringing serious flavour. Cover it with chocolate sauce and you have a warm Bounty bar in a mug.*

**SERVES 1**

**TAKES 5 minutes**

1 slice of butter 1cm (½in) thick (30g/1oz)
1 egg
2 tablespoons caster (superfine) sugar
½ teaspoon vanilla sugar
1 tablespoon single (light) cream
6 tablespoons plain (all-purpose) flour
½ teaspoon baking powder
4 tablespoons dessicated (dried shredded) coconut, plus 1 teaspoon to decorate

**Chocolate Sauce**
5 squares of dark chocolate (25g/1oz)
1 teaspoon neutral oil

Melt the butter in a bowl in the microwave for 20 seconds.

In a mug, beat in one by one the egg, sugar, vanilla sugar, cream, flour, baking powder, melted butter and coconut.

Cook in the microwave for 1 minute 40 seconds, until risen and slightly springy to the touch.

To make the chocolate sauce, put the chocolate in a separate mug and melt in the microwave for 30 seconds. Add the neutral oil and stir well: the mixture should be nice and smooth.

Top the mug cake with chocolate sauce and dessicated coconut.

*Utterly Nutty*

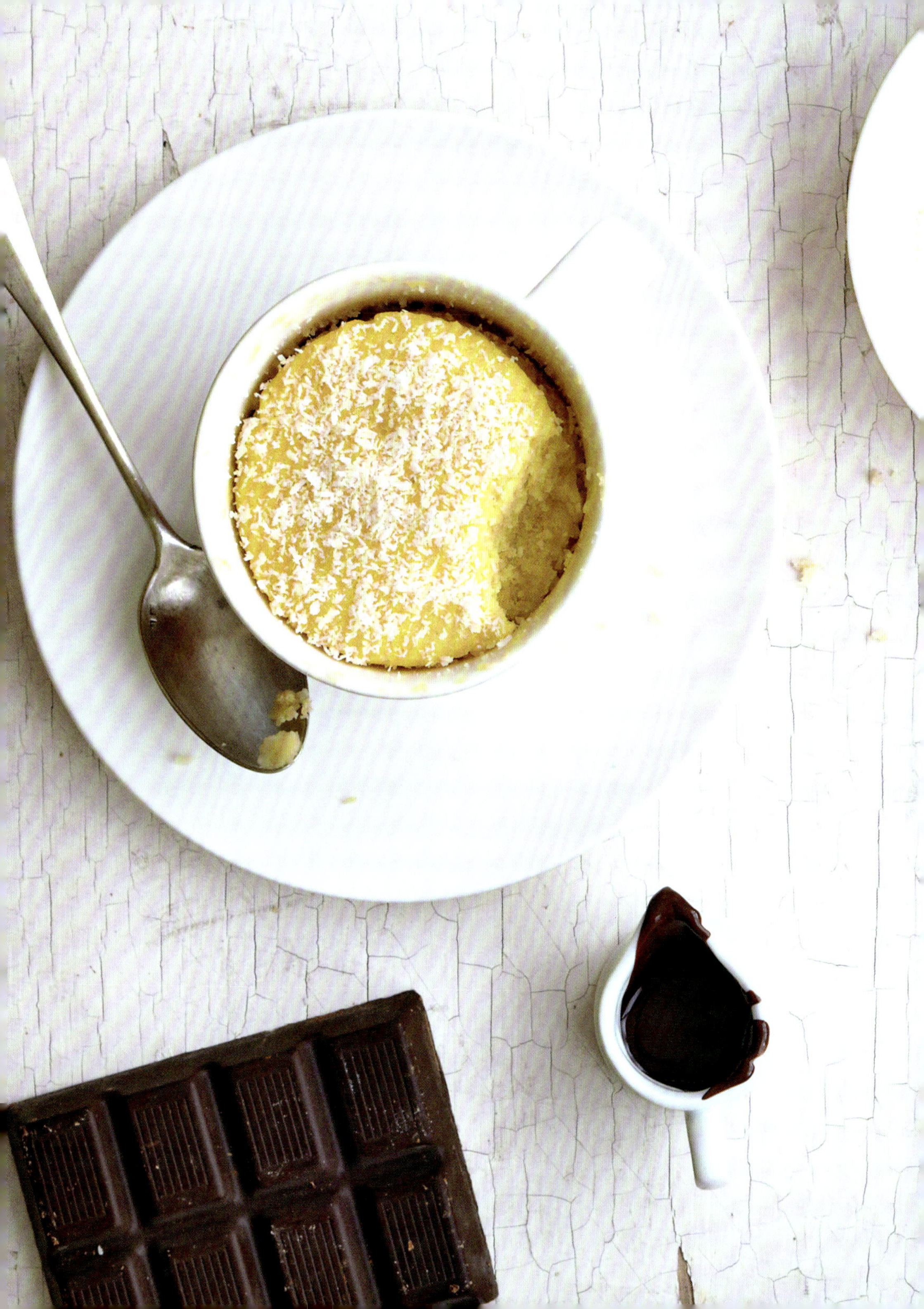

# Almond Mug Cake with
# Frangipane & Custard

*This is most definitely a more sophisticated type of mug cake! A triple almond treat, the ground almonds give the sponge a great texture, while the extract provides a flavour punch and the splash of Amaretto brings the party.*

**SERVES 1**

**TAKES 5 minutes**

1 slice of butter 1cm (½in) thick (30g/1oz)
1 egg
4 tablespoons caster (superfine) sugar
½ teaspoon vanilla sugar
2 teaspoons single (light) cream
½ teaspoon French bitter almond extract
6 tablespoons plain (all-purpose) flour
½ teaspoon baking powder
2 tablespoons ground almonds
2 tablespoons raisins
1 tablespoon Amaretto (or other liqueur)
custard, to serve

Melt the butter in a bowl in the microwave for 20 seconds.

In a mug, beat in one by one the egg, sugar, vanilla sugar, cream, almond extract, flour, baking powder, ground almonds, melted butter, raisins and Amaretto.

Cook in the microwave for 1 minute 50 seconds, or until risen and springy to the touch.

Serve with custard.

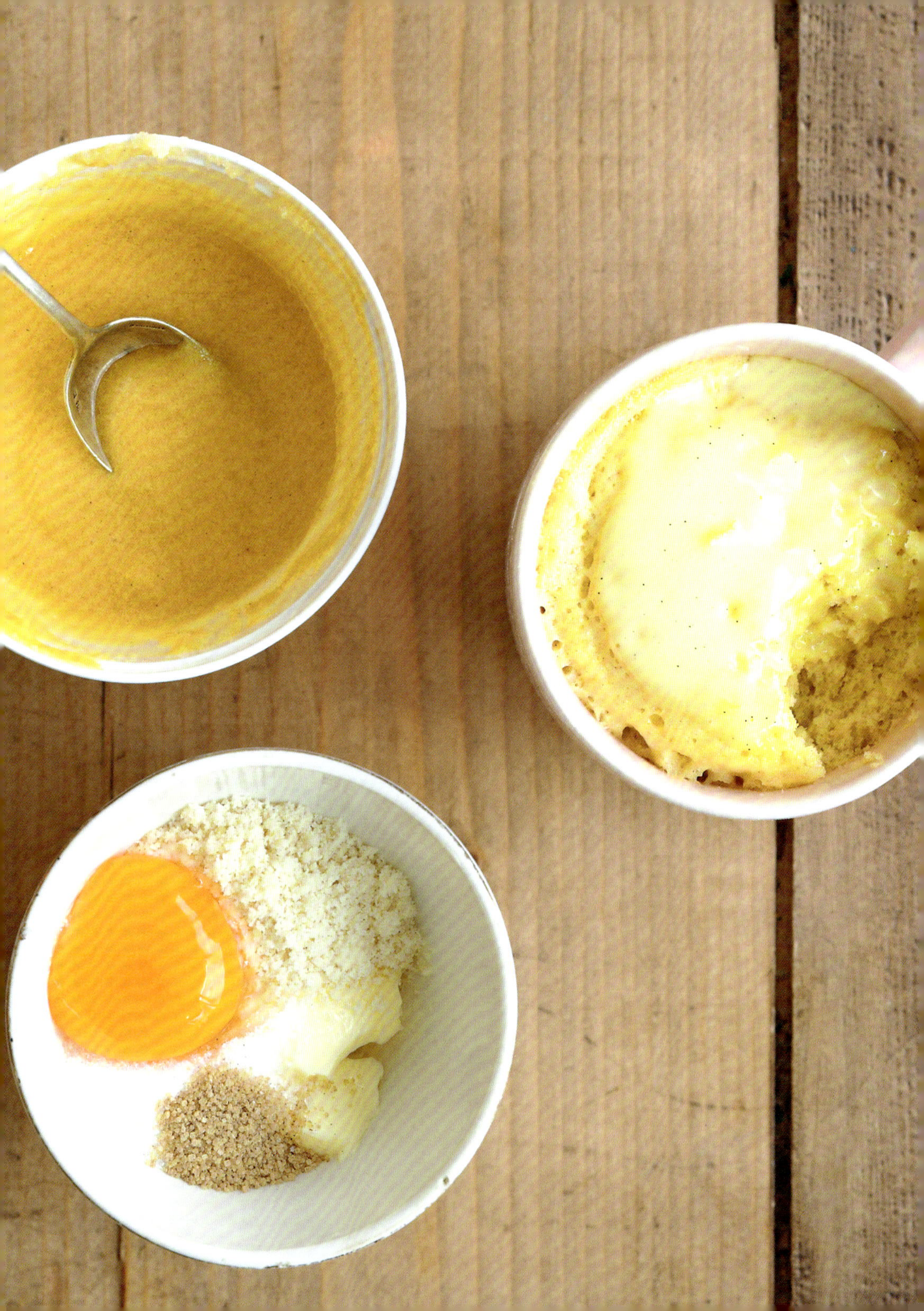

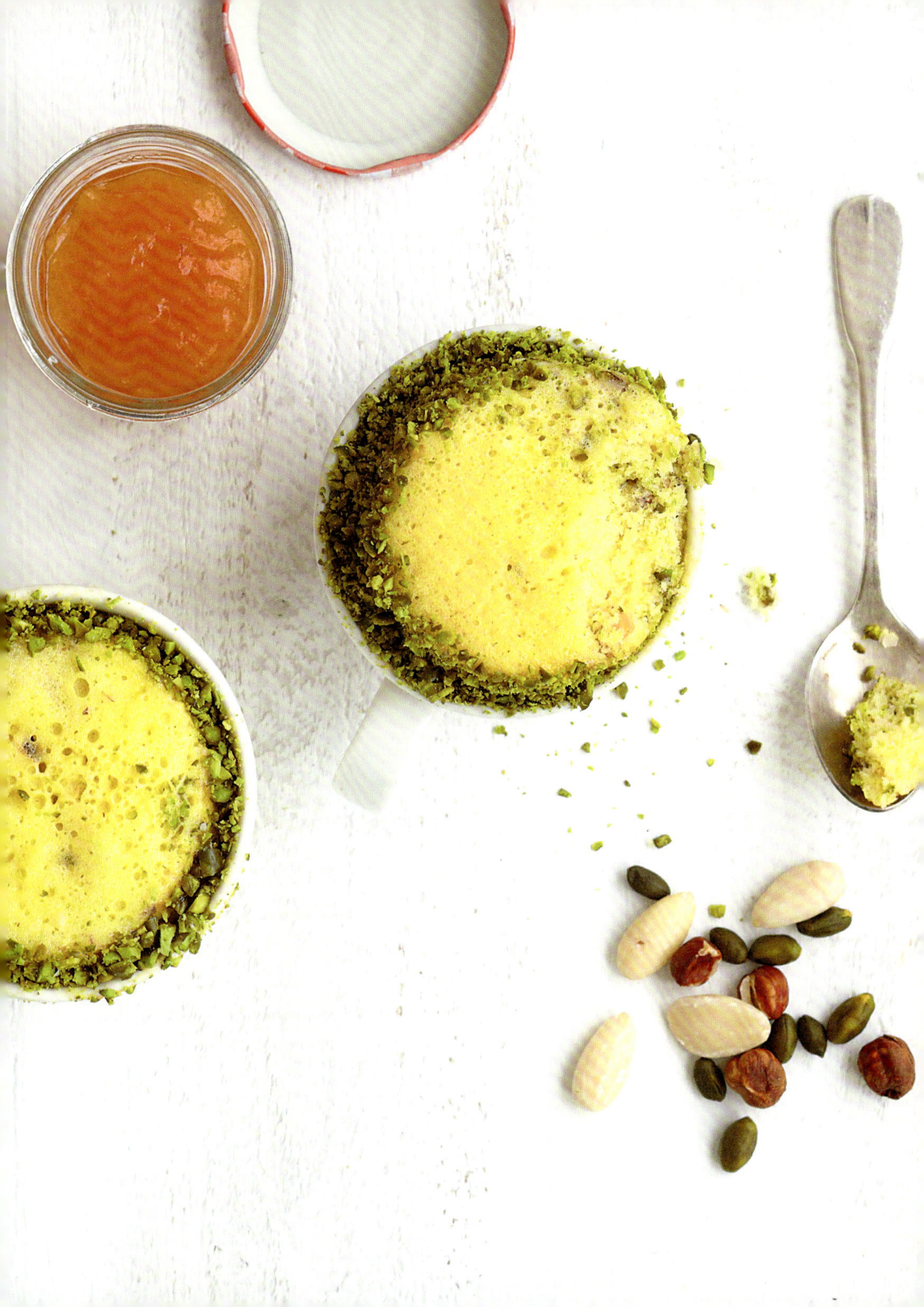

# Hazelnut, Almond & Pistachio Cake

*If you're truly nuts about nuts, head straight for this cake with its great combination of three favourites. And if you're going to the trouble of adding the pistachio decoration, seek out the greenest ones you can find – Middle Eastern shops are often the best choice for this.*

**SERVES 4**

**TAKES 5 minutes**

1 slice of butter 1cm (½in) thick (30g/1oz)
1 egg
2 tablespoons caster (superfine) sugar
½ teaspoon vanilla sugar
1 tablespoon single (light) cream
1 tablespoon apricot jam
5 tablespoons plain (all-purpose) flour
½ teaspoon baking powder
1 tablespoon hazelnuts, chopped
1 tablespoon almonds, chopped
1½ tablespoons pistachios, chopped

**Decoration**
½ teaspoon jam (jelly)
1 tablespoon finely chopped pistachios

Melt the butter in a bowl for 20 seconds.

In a mug, beat in one by one the egg, sugar, vanilla sugar, cream, apricot jam, flour, baking powder, melted butter, chopped hazelnuts, almonds and pistachios.

Cook in the microwave for 1 minute 40 seconds, or until risen and springy to the touch.

Spread a thin layer of jam on the outside edge and stick the remaining pistachio pieces onto it.

# Peanut Butter & Sesame Mug Cookie

*If you're a real peanut butter fan, chances are you enjoy the taste of sesame too – they both share that nutty toasty flavour. Team them up here in this mug cookie, which is simple perfection. For extra flavour, toast the sesame seeds gently in a dry frying pan first until lightly golden.*

**SERVES 1**

**TAKES 4 minutes**

1 slice of butter 5mm (¼in) thick (15g/½oz)
1 tablespoon caster (superfine) sugar
1 egg yolk
1 tablespoon smooth peanut butter
4 tablespoons plain (all-purpose) flour
½ teaspoon sesame seeds

In a mug, melt the butter in the microwave for 20 seconds. One by one, beat in the sugar, egg yolk, peanut butter, flour and sesame seeds.

Cook in the microwave for 1 minute, or until risen and springy to the touch.

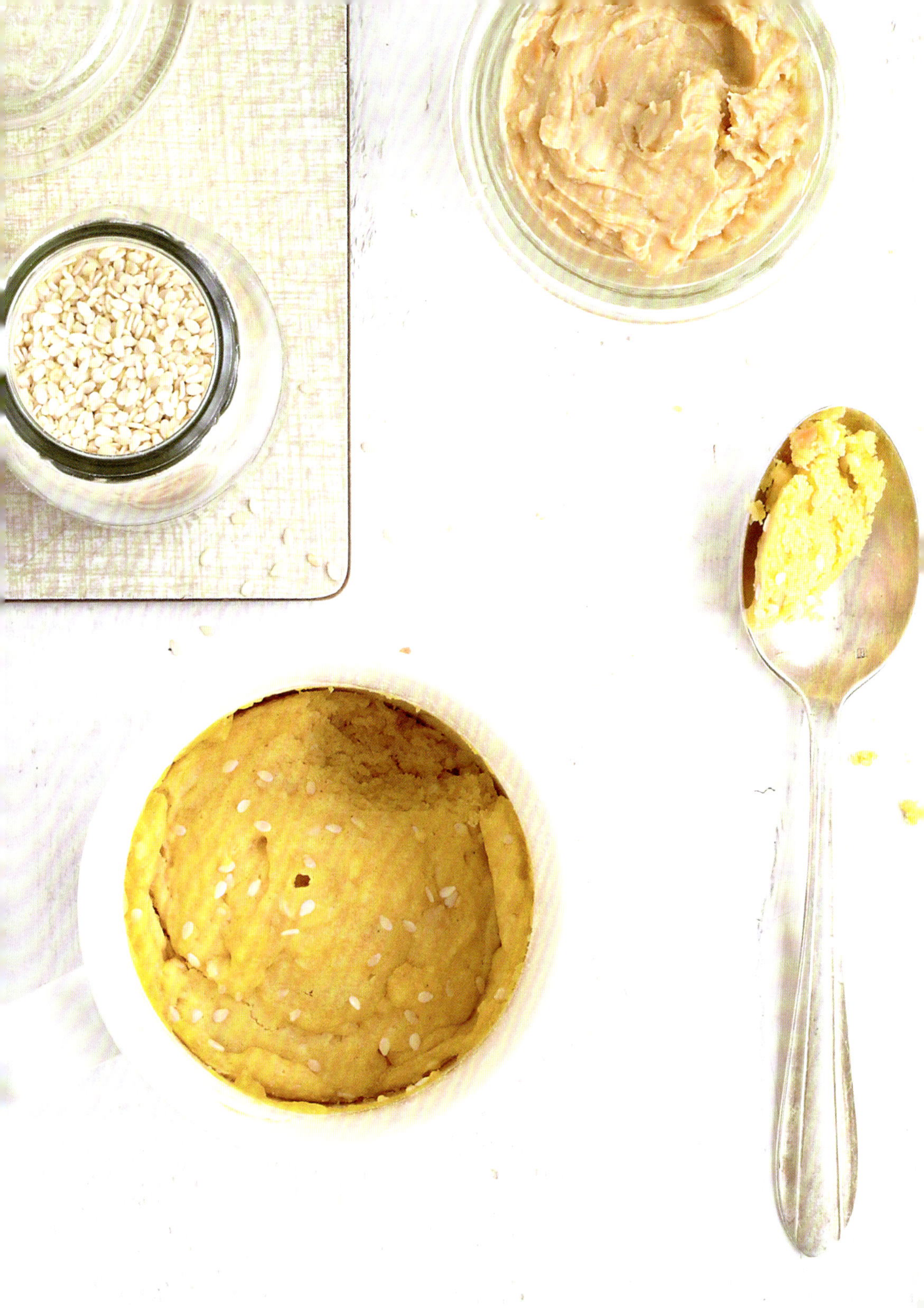

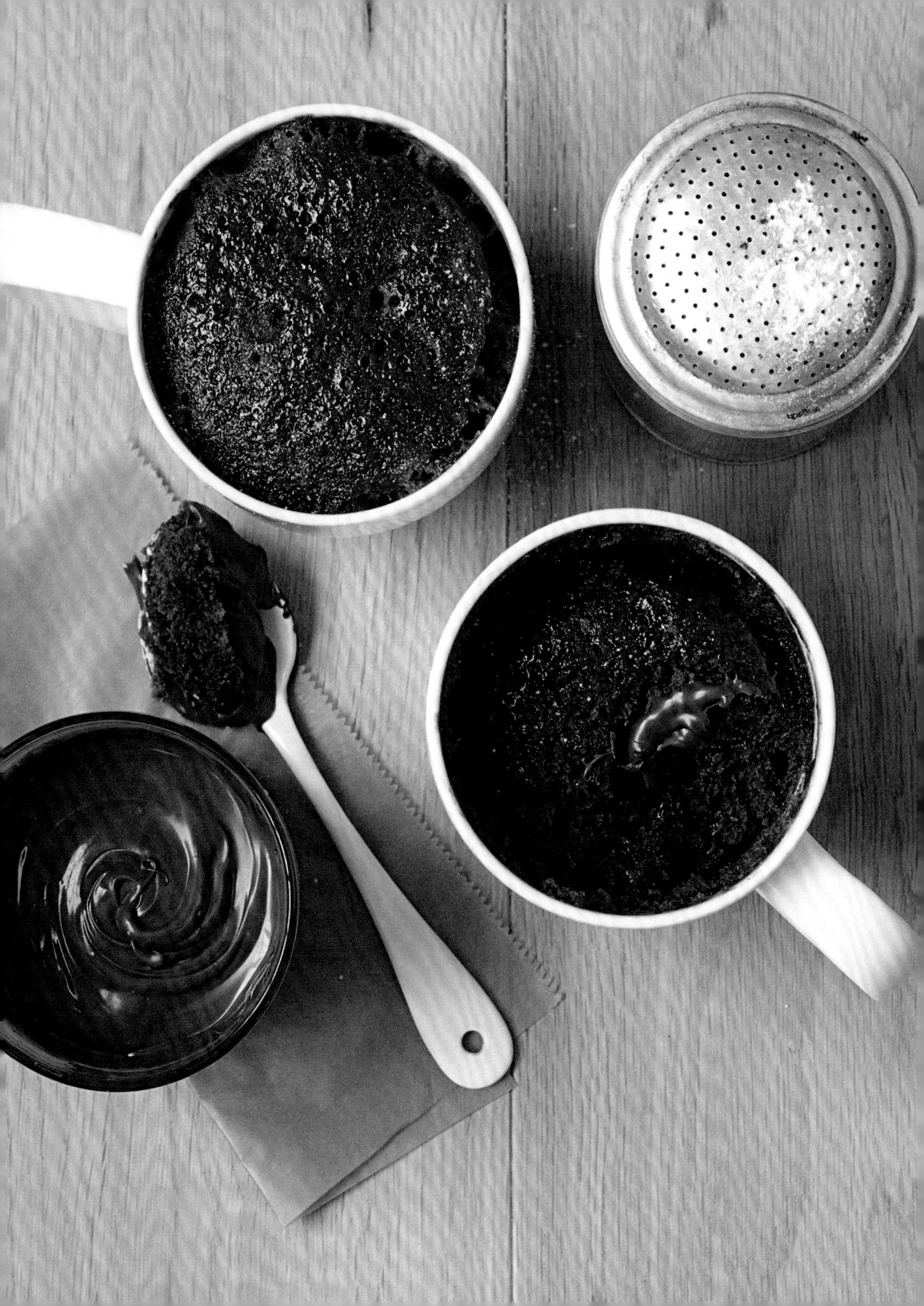

## Molten Centre
# Nutella Cake

*If you happen to have a jar of chocolate hazelnut spread in the pantry, you are only minutes away from this decadent molten middle pudding. Pure indulgence, with just simple store-cupboard staples.*

**SERVES 1**

**TAKES 5 minutes**

1 slice of butter 1cm (½in) thick (30g/1oz)
3 tablespoons chocolate and hazelnut spread (such as Nutella), plus 1 teaspoon for the middle
1 egg
3 tablespoons soft brown sugar
4 tablespoons plain (all-purpose) flour
½ teaspoon baking powder

In a mug, melt the butter with the chocolate and hazelnut spread in the microwave for 30 seconds.

Beat the mixture until smooth, then allow it to cool slightly. One by one, whisk in the egg, sugar, flour and baking powder. Cook in the microwave for 40 seconds. Spoon the extra teaspoon of chocolate and hazelnut spread into the middle and cook for a further 40 seconds, or until the sponge is risen but the middle is still gooey.

Allow to cool for 1 minute before eating.

# Chocolate & Hazelnut
# Praline Cake

*The pleasure factor of this mug cake just keeps on rising. As if the fluffy chocolate and hazelnut sponge wasn't enough, dig in and you'll find a creamy chocolate praline centre, all topped off with the complimentary crunch of praline and nuts.*

**SERVES 1**

**TAKES 5 minutes**

1 slice of butter 5mm (¼in) thick (15g/½oz)
6 squares of praline chocolate (30g/1oz)
1 egg
2 tablespoons soft brown sugar
2 tablespoons milk
5 tablespoons plain (all-purpose) flour
¼ teaspoon baking powder
2 tablespoons ground hazelnuts

**Middle & Decoration**
1 square of praline chocolate (5g/¼oz)
2 teaspoons chopped hazelnuts

In a mug, melt the butter with the praline chocolate in the microwave for 30–40 seconds.

Beat the mixture until smooth, then allow it to cool slightly. One by one, whisk in the egg, brown sugar, milk, flour, baking powder and ground hazelnuts. Cook in the microwave for 1 minute, or until risen and springy to the touch. Push the extra square of praline chocolate into the middle of the mixture and cook for a further 30 seconds.

Sprinkle with praline and chopped hazelnuts. Allow to cool for 1 minute before eating.

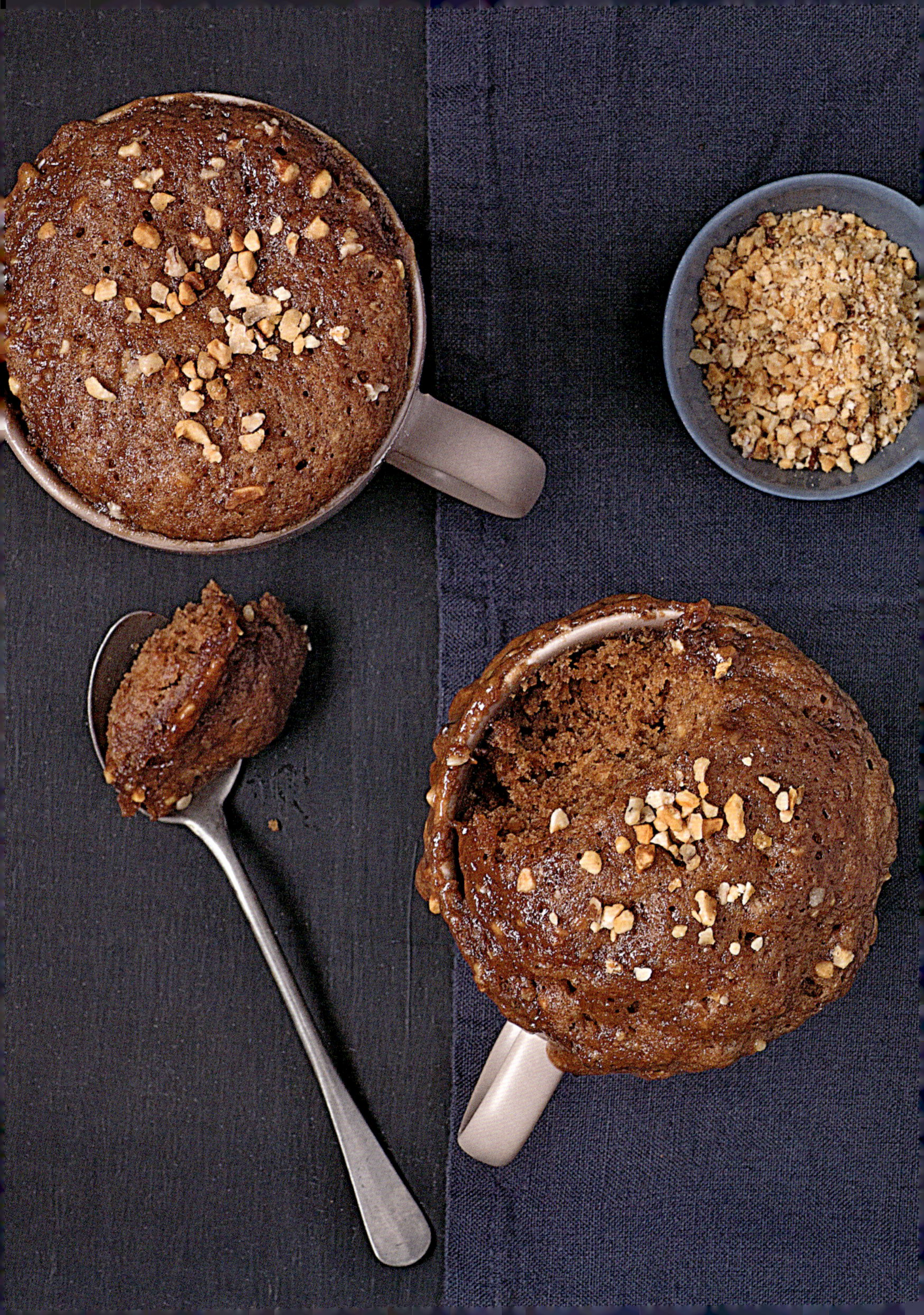

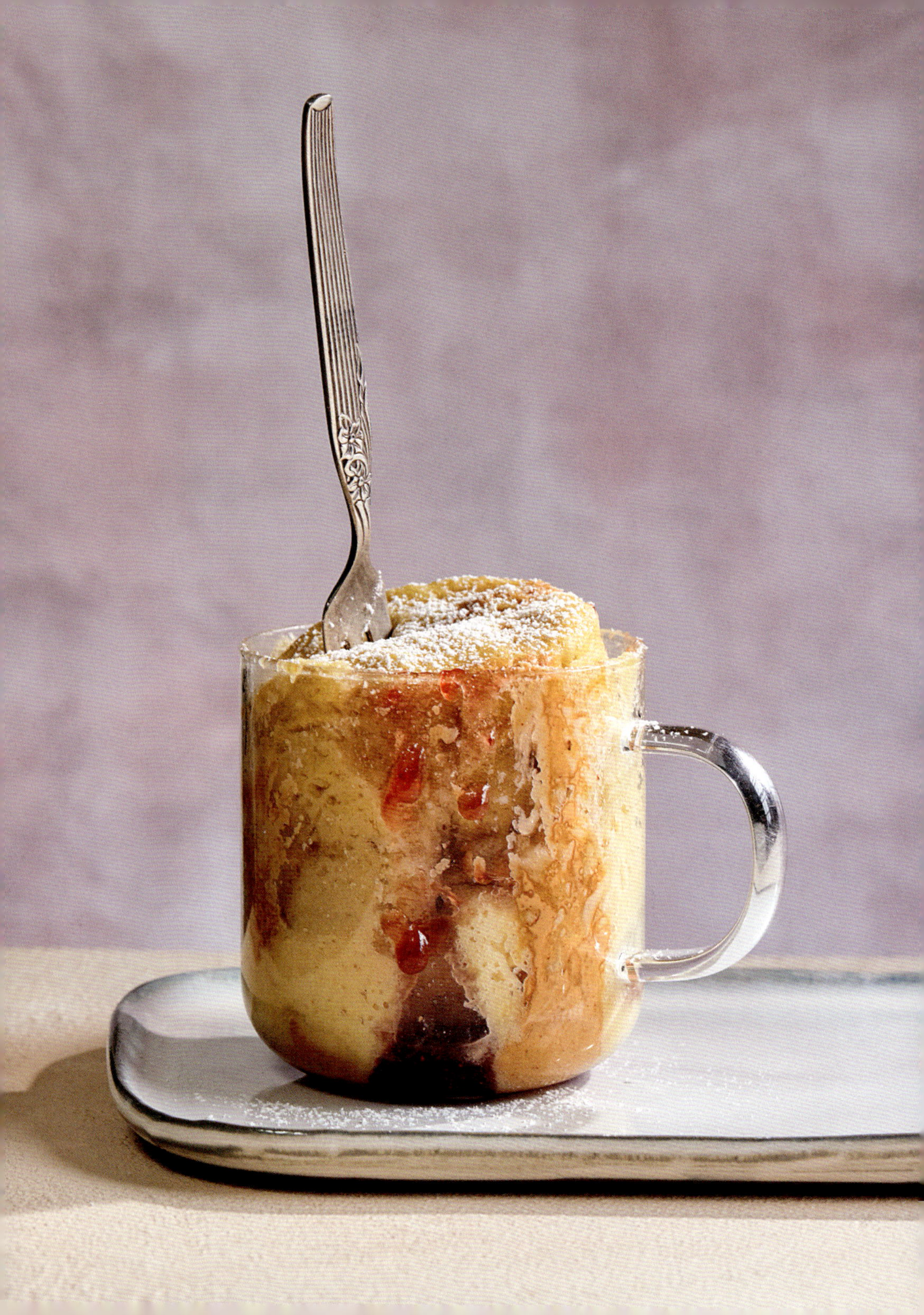

## Sweet & Salty
# PB&J Cake

*So classic, the combination of peanut butter and jam is a success in pretty much whatever format you try it – and mug cakes are no exception. Go for a peanut butter with a really deep roast and don't forget to add a pinch of salt to amp up the flavour even more.*

**SERVES 1**

**TAKES 4 minutes**

1 tablespoon sunflower oil
3 tablespoons soft brown sugar
1 egg
1 tablespoon milk
½ teaspoon vanilla extract
4 tablespoons self-raising (self-rising) flour
1 heaped tablespoon crunchy peanut butter
1 heaped tablespoon raspberry or strawberry jam

**Decoration**
icing (confectioner's) sugar
a generous pinch of flaked sea salt

In a mug, mix together the oil, sugar, egg, milk and vanilla using a fork until smooth. Add the flour and mix until just smooth. Add the crunchy peanut butter and jam, and gently swirl into the top half of the batter.

Microwave for 1 minute 40 seconds, or until risen and springy to the touch. Dust with icing sugar, sprinkle over the salt, and dig in.

# Toasted Coconut & Cherry Cake

*There's something wonderfully nostalgic about coconut bakes studded with bright red glacé cherries. Toasting the coconut for the topping gives it a huge flavour bump, so if you can't find it ready-toasted, pop the flakes in the oven for a few minutes first.*

**SERVES 1**

**TAKES 4 minutes**

2 tablespoons sunflower oil
3 tablespoons caster (superfine) sugar
1 egg
½ teaspoon vanilla extract
2 tablespoons glacé (candied) cherries (about 6), rinsed, dried and halved
4 tablespoons self-raising (self-rising) flour
2 tablespoons desiccated (dried shredded) coconut
a pinch of salt

**Decoration**
icing (confectioner's) sugar
toasted coconut flakes

In a mug, mix together the oil, sugar, egg and vanilla using a fork until smooth.

In a small bowl, toss the cherries in the flour to coat them, then add the cherries and flour to the mug along with the desiccated coconut and salt. Mix until just smooth.

Microwave for 1 minute 40 seconds, or until risen and springy to the touch. Dust with a little icing sugar and sprinkle on a few coconut flakes, then enjoy.

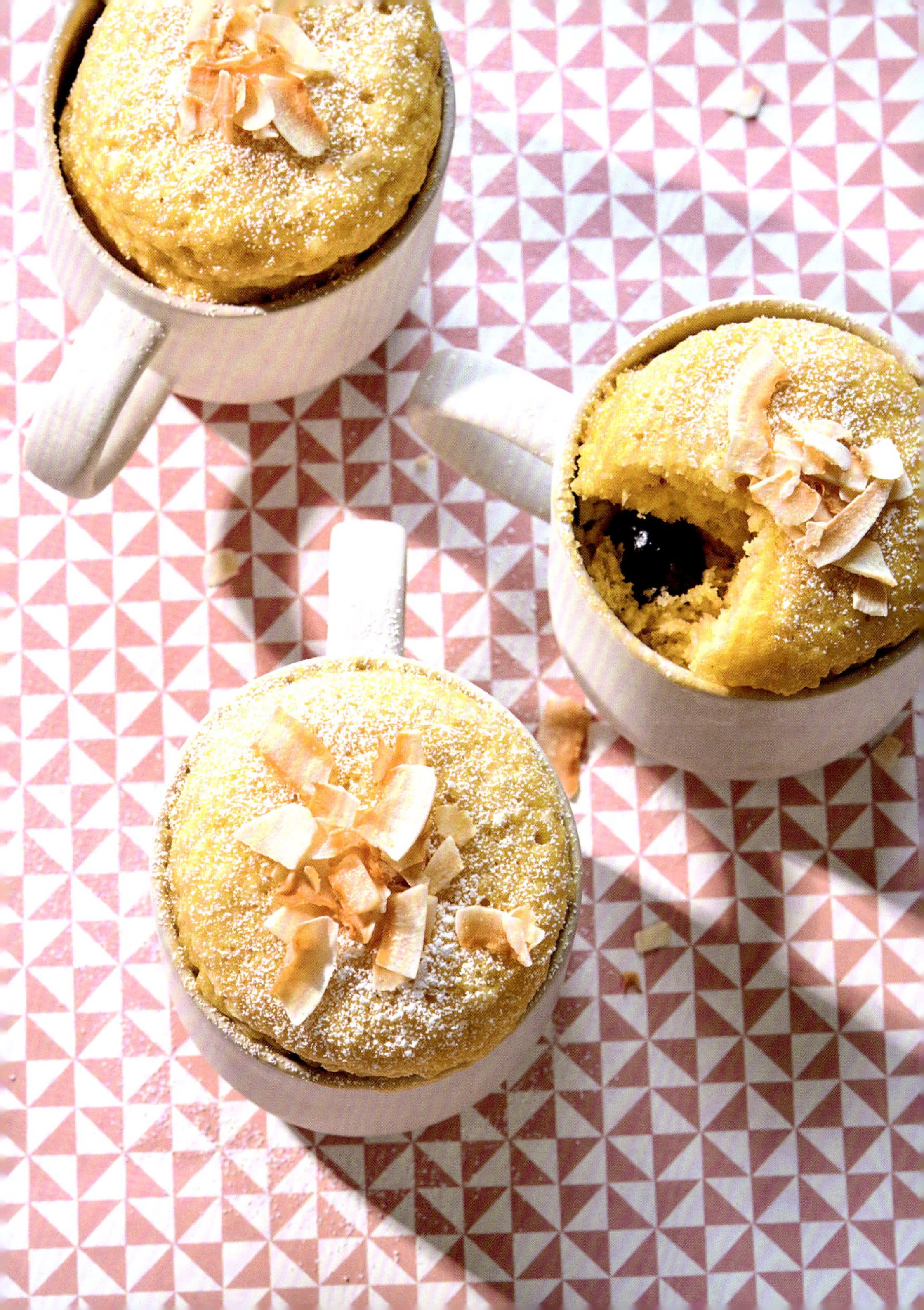

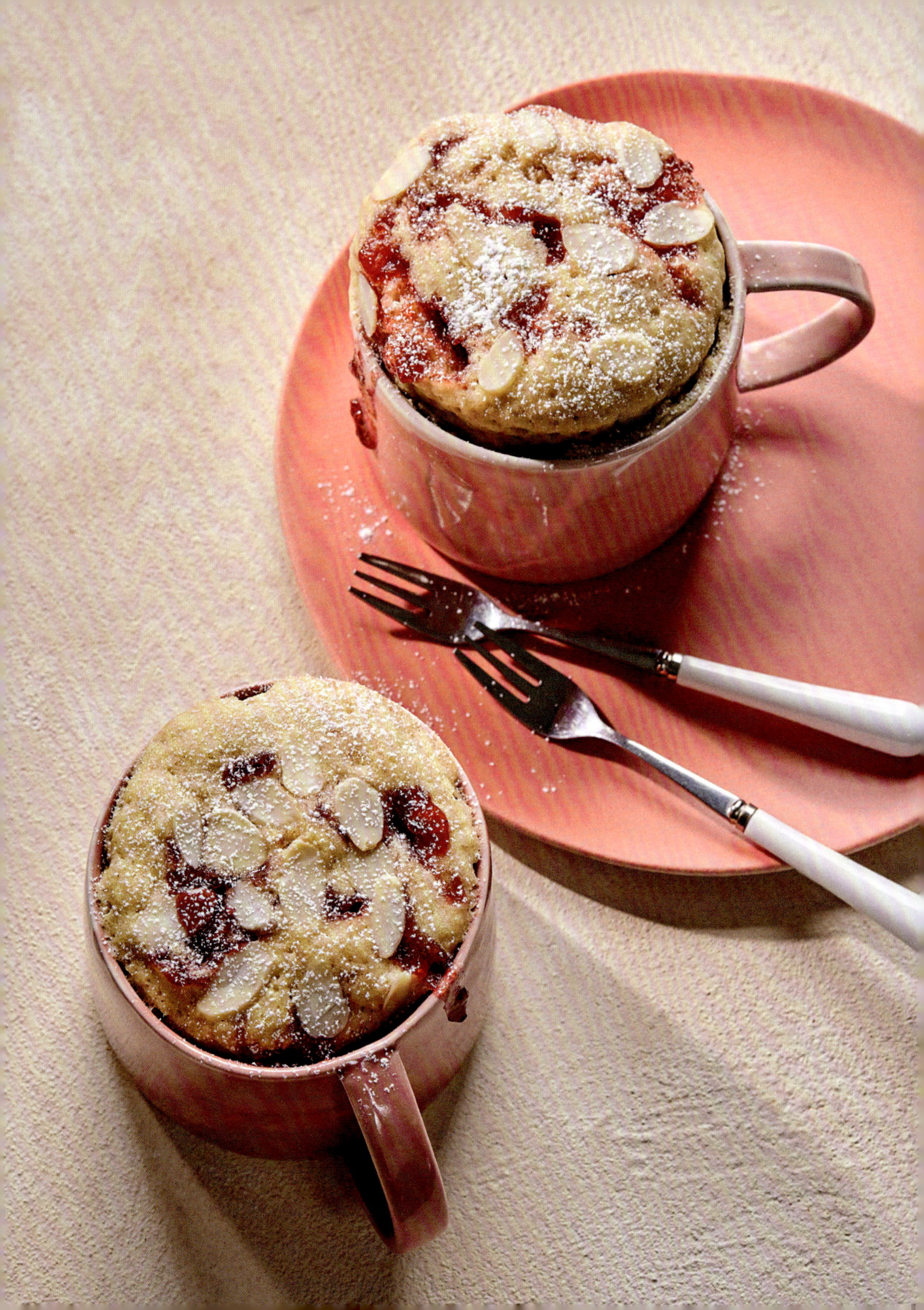

## Raspberry & Almond
# Bakewell

*This is retro home baking at its quickest, tastiest and most convenient. This mug cake gives the classic English tart, with its almond and raspberry flavour base, a truly modern makeover.*

**SERVES 1**

**TAKES 5 minutes**

2 tablespoons raspberry jam
2 tablespoons sunflower oil
3 tablespoons soft brown sugar
1 egg
½ teaspoon almond extract
4 tablespoons self-raising (self-rising) flour
1 heaped tablespoon ground almonds
1 heaped teaspoon flaked (slivered) almonds
icing (confectioner's) sugar, to decorate

Evenly spread 1 tablespoon of the jam in the bottom of a mug.

In a small bowl, mix together the oil, sugar, egg and almond extract using a fork until smooth. Add the flour and ground almonds, and mix until just smooth. Pour the batter into your mug. Add the remaining tablespoon of jam and gently swirl it in. Sprinkle over the flaked almonds.

Microwave for 1 minute 30 seconds, or until risen and springy to the touch. Dust with icing sugar and enjoy.

# Marshmallow & Chocolate
# Rocky Road

*Yes it's nutty, thanks to the pecans, but it's also biscuity, marshmallowy and chocolatey: the ultimate mug cake for those who can't quite decide which treat they want to eat, but they want it in a hurry nonetheless.*

**SERVES 1**

**TAKES 4 minutes**

- 2 tablespoons sunflower oil
- 3 tablespoons soft brown sugar
- 1 egg
- ½ teaspoon vanilla extract
- 3 tablespoons self-raising (self-rising) flour
- 1 tablespoon unsweetened cocoa powder
- 1 heaped tablespoon mini marshmallows
- 1 digestive biscuit (graham cracker), broken into small pieces
- 1 tablespoon pecan nuts, chopped

In a mug, mix together the oil, sugar, egg and vanilla using a fork. Add the flour and cocoa, and mix until just smooth. Finally, gently fold in the marshmallows, half of the biscuit pieces and all the chopped nuts. Do not overmix.

Microwave for 1 minute 30 seconds, or until risen and springy to the touch. Sprinkle over the remaining biscuit pieces and dig in.

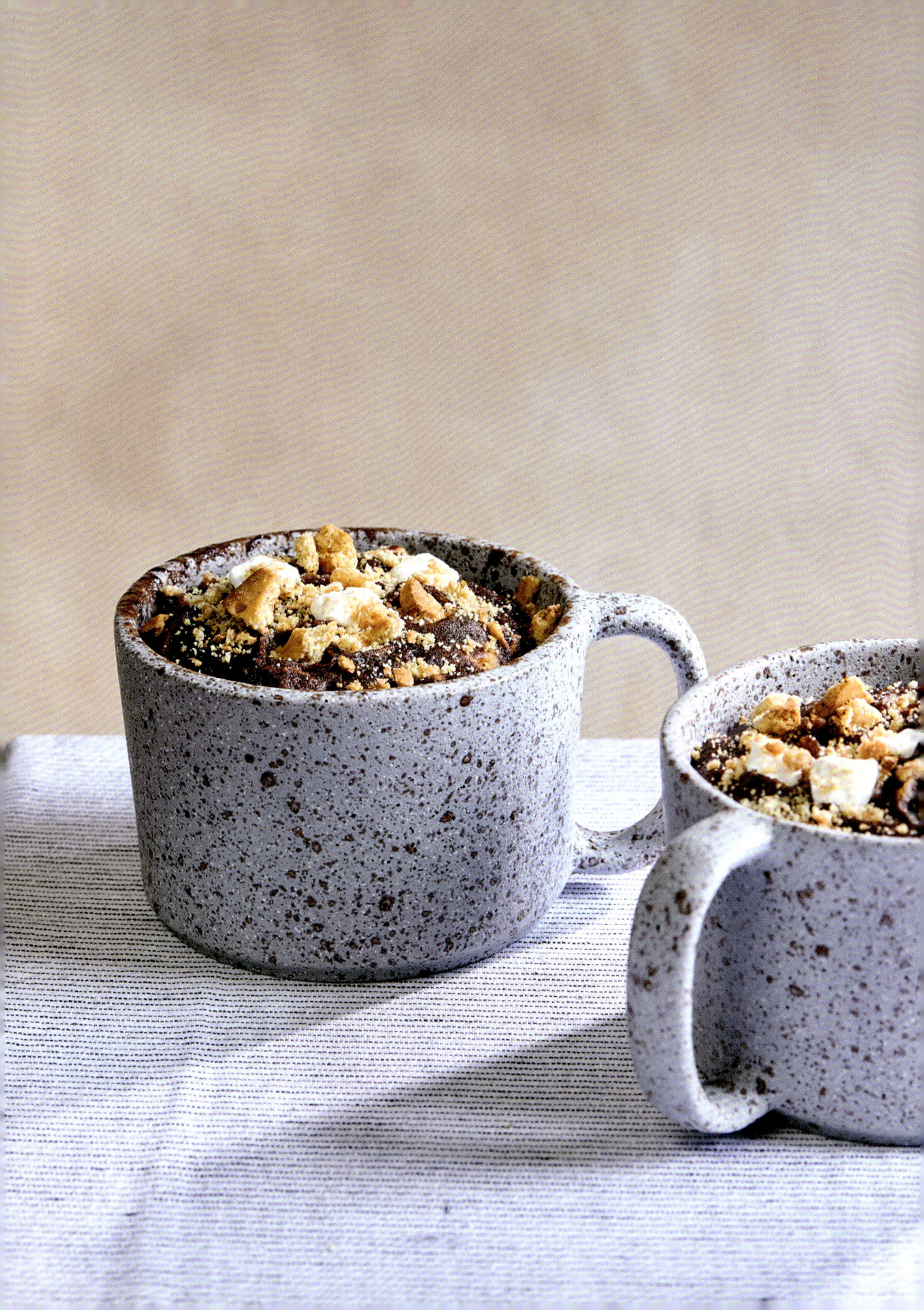

Caramel &
# Coffee
———

## Caramel & Chocolate
# Truffle Cake

*Put the last couple of truffles in the box to good use and raise your mug cake to new heights. A simple chocolate mug cake can be easily made to feel extra special by melting a couple of these in the middle and finishing with dusting of pleasurably bitter cocoa.*

**SERVES 1**

**TAKES 4 minutes**

2 tablespoons caster (superfine) sugar
3 tablespoons plain (all-purpose) flour
1 tablespoon unsweetened cocoa powder, plus extra to decorate
¼ teaspoon baking powder
1 egg
½ teaspoon vanilla extract
1 tablespoon milk
2 tablespoons sunflower oil
2 salted caramel or butterscotch cocoa-dusted truffles

In a mug, mix together the sugar, flour, cocoa and baking powder using a fork. Add the egg, vanilla extract, milk and oil, and mix until just smooth. Put the truffles into the centre of the batter, one after another, so they are stacked on top of each another. The top half of the top truffle should be sticking out of the batter.

Microwave for 1 minute 20 seconds, or until risen and springy to the touch. Dust with cocoa powder and dig in.

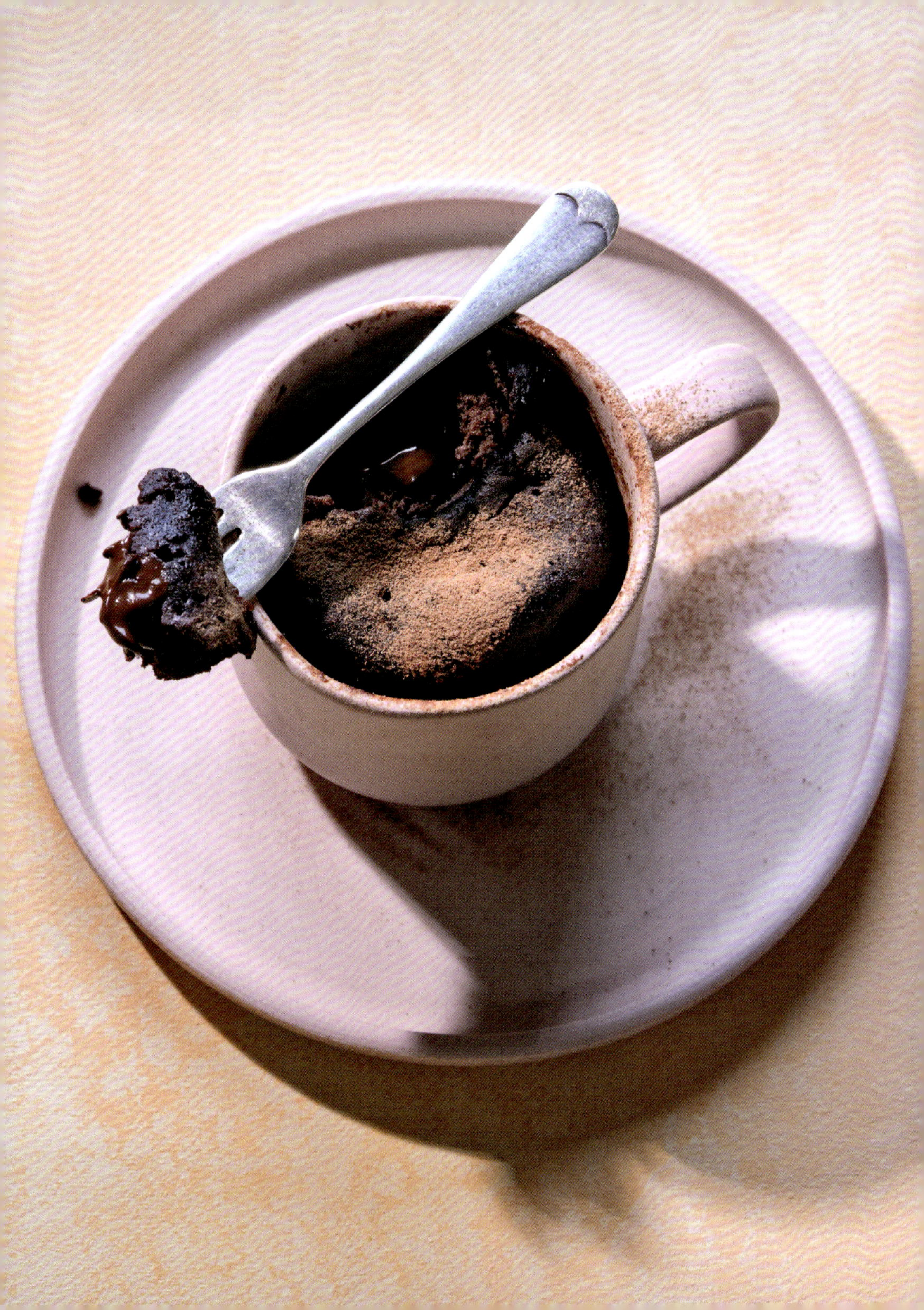

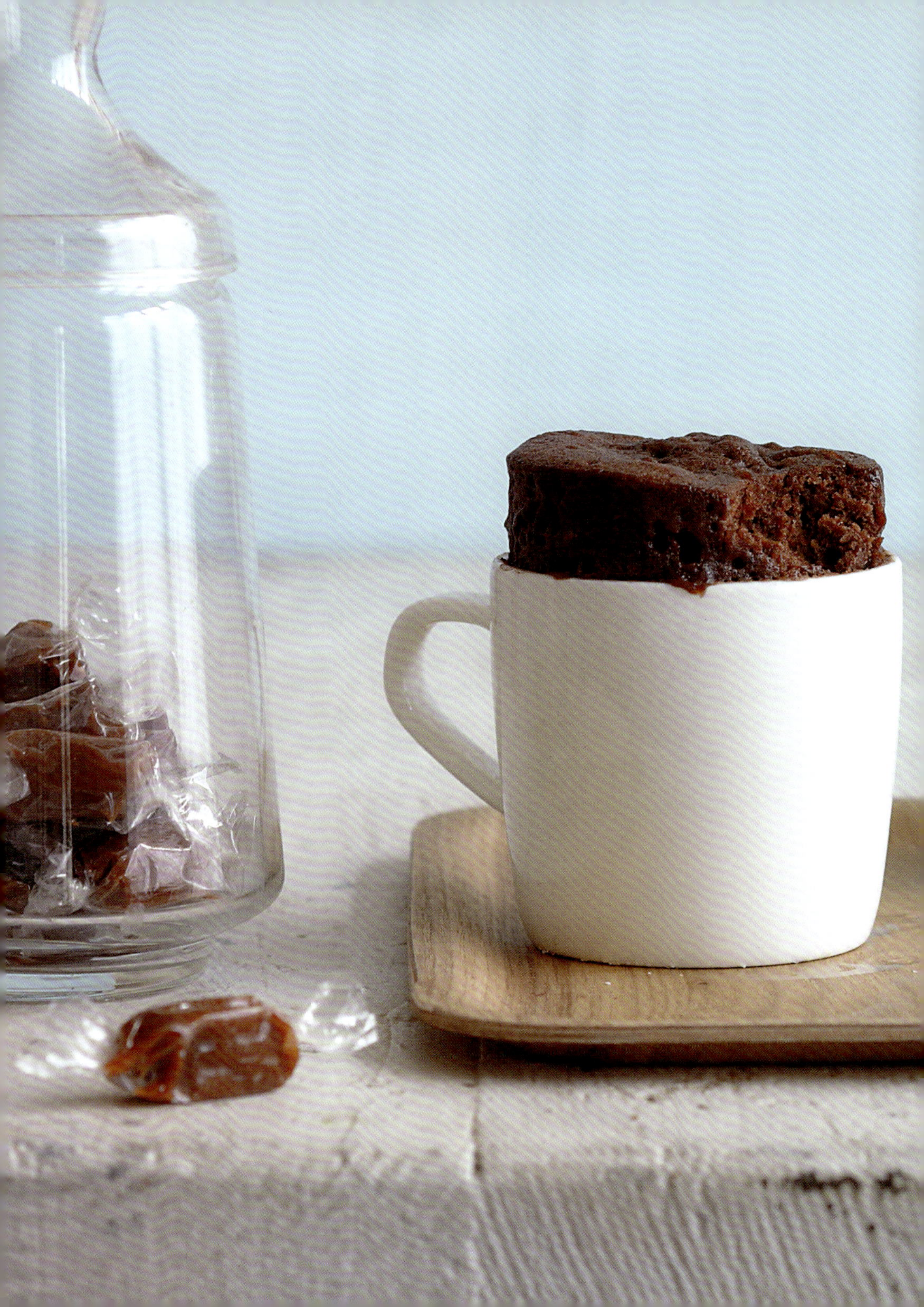

# Salted Butter Caramel Cake

*There is nothing more moreish than a sweet and salty combination, and so from planting a couple of salted caramels into the centre of this mug cake can seriously irresistible things grow.*

**SERVES 1**

**TAKES 5 minutes**

1 slice of butter 1cm (½in) thick (30g/1oz)
1 egg
3 tablespoons caster (superfine) sugar
1 tablespoon single (light) cream
2 tablespoons unsweetened cocoa powder
6 tablespoons plain (all-purpose) flour
½ teaspoon baking powder
3 salted butter caramels, cut into small pieces

Melt the butter in a bowl in the microwave for 20 seconds.

In a mug, whisk together the egg, sugar, cream, cocoa, flour, baking powder, melted butter and the chopped salted butter caramels.

Cook in the microwave for 1 minute 20 seconds, or until risen and springy to the touch.

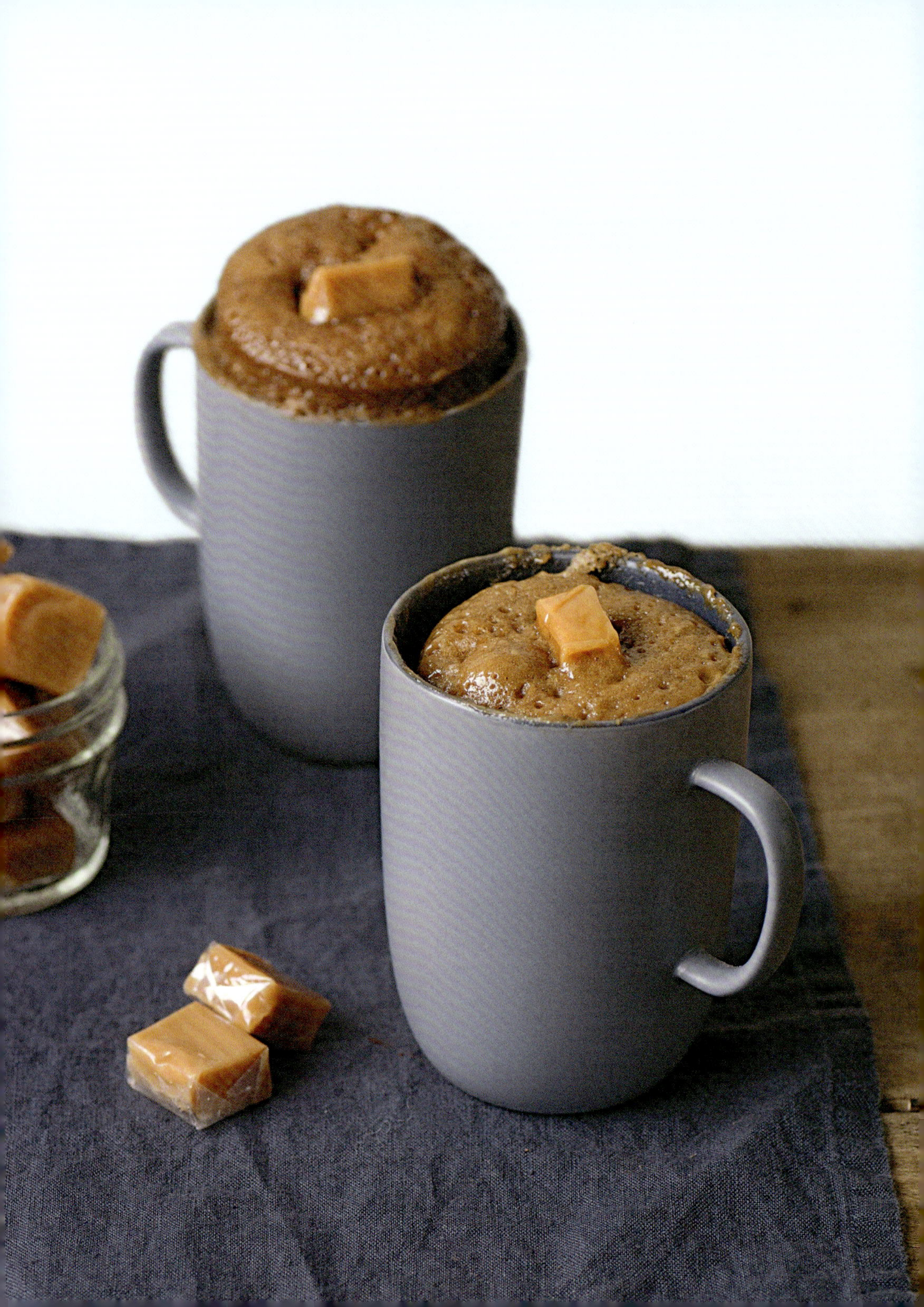

# Chocolate, Caramel &
# Coffee Cake

*Caramel and coffee: as if the title of this chapter doesn't already sound appealing enough, this cake promises even more by throwing chocolate into the mix. A seriously indulgent treat, this one is sure to become a favourite.*

**SERVES 1**

**TAKES 5 minutes**

1 slice of butter 1cm (½in) thick (30g/1oz)
8 squares of milk chocolate (40g/1½oz)
1 teaspoon coffee extract
1 egg
2 tablespoons soft brown sugar
5 tablespoons plain (all-purpose) flour
½ teaspoon baking powder
1 soft caramel

In a mug, melt the butter with the chocolate in the microwave for 30–40 seconds.

Beat the mixture until smooth, add the coffee extract, then allow it to cool slightly. One by one, whisk in the egg, sugar, flour and baking powder. Cook in the microwave for 40 seconds. Gently push the soft caramel into the middle and cook for a further 50 seconds, or until risen and springy to the touch.

Allow to cool for 1 minute before eating.

# Dark Chocolate Cake with a
# **Biscoff Middle**

*Caramelized biscuits languished for years as the old-fashioned individually-wrapped freebies, often left abandoned on saucers at cafés. Until some genius put them into a spread format. Move aside chocolate lava pudding – the melting Biscoff centre is here to stay!*

**SERVES 1**

**TAKES 5 minutes**

1 slice of butter 5mm (¼in) thick (15g/½oz)
6 squares of dark chocolate (30g/1oz)
1 egg
1 teaspoon single (light) cream
2 tablespoons soft brown sugar
2 tablespoons crushed Lotus or other caramelized biscuits (cookies), plus 1 teaspoon to decorate
5 tablespoons plain (all-purpose) flour
½ teaspoon baking powder
1 teaspoon Biscoff spread (or make your own by mixing melted butter, crushed caramelized biscuits (cookies) and condensed milk)

In a mug, melt the butter with the chocolate in the microwave for 30–40 seconds.

Beat the mixture until smooth, then allow it to cool slightly. One by one, whisk in the egg, cream, sugar, crushed biscuits, flour and baking powder. Cook in the microwave for 50 seconds. Push the Biscoff spread into the middle and cook for a further 40 seconds, or until the sponge is risen but the spread is still gooey.

Allow to cool for 1 minute. Sprinkle with the crushed biscuit before eating.

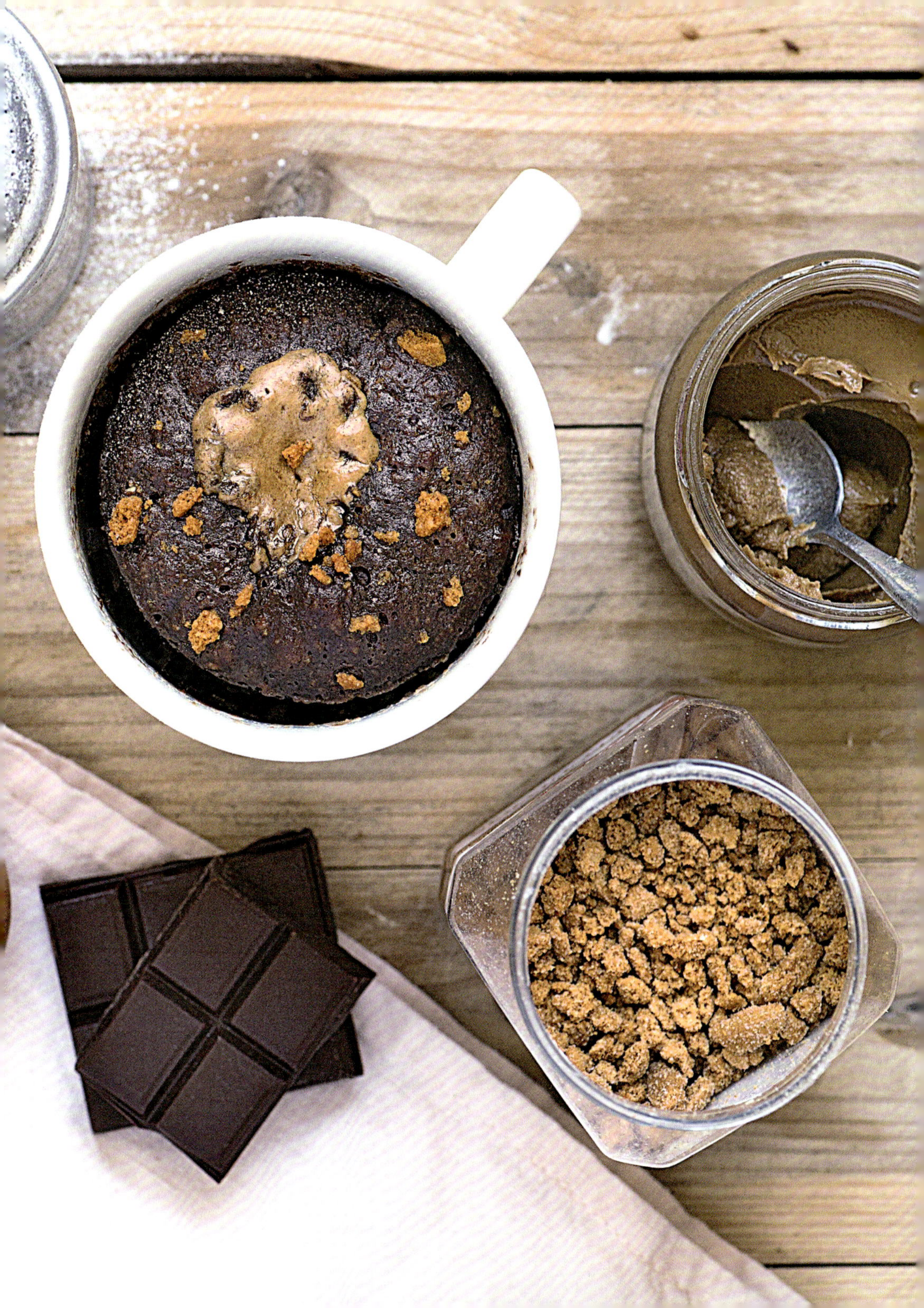

# Mocha Mug Cake with
# Coffee Cream

*Ideally you'd use a good espresso for this (if you have a machine), but mug cakes aren't really about labouring through tradition, so failing that, a strong coffee made with good instant coffee powder will be almost as satisfying.*

**SERVES 1**

**TAKES 5 minutes, plus cooling**

2 tablespoons soft brown sugar
2 tablespoons plain (all-purpose) flour
1 tablespoon unsweetened cocoa powder
¼ teaspoon baking powder
1 egg
2 tablespoons sunflower oil
2 tablespoons espresso or double-strength coffee, cooled to room temperature
1 tablespoon chocolate chips

**Coffee Cream**

1 tablespoon espresso or double-strength coffee, cooled to room temperature
½ teaspoon icing (confectioner's) sugar
3 tablespoons double (heavy) cream

In a mug, mix together the sugar, flour, cocoa and baking powder using a fork. Add the egg, oil and coffee, and mix until just smooth. Gently stir the chocolate chips into the top half of the batter.

Microwave for 1 minute 30 seconds, or until risen and springy to the touch. Set aside to cool for 10 minutes.

In a small bowl, combine all the ingredients for the coffee cream, and whisk until the cream forms soft peaks. Dollop a large spoonful of the coffee cream onto your cake and enjoy.

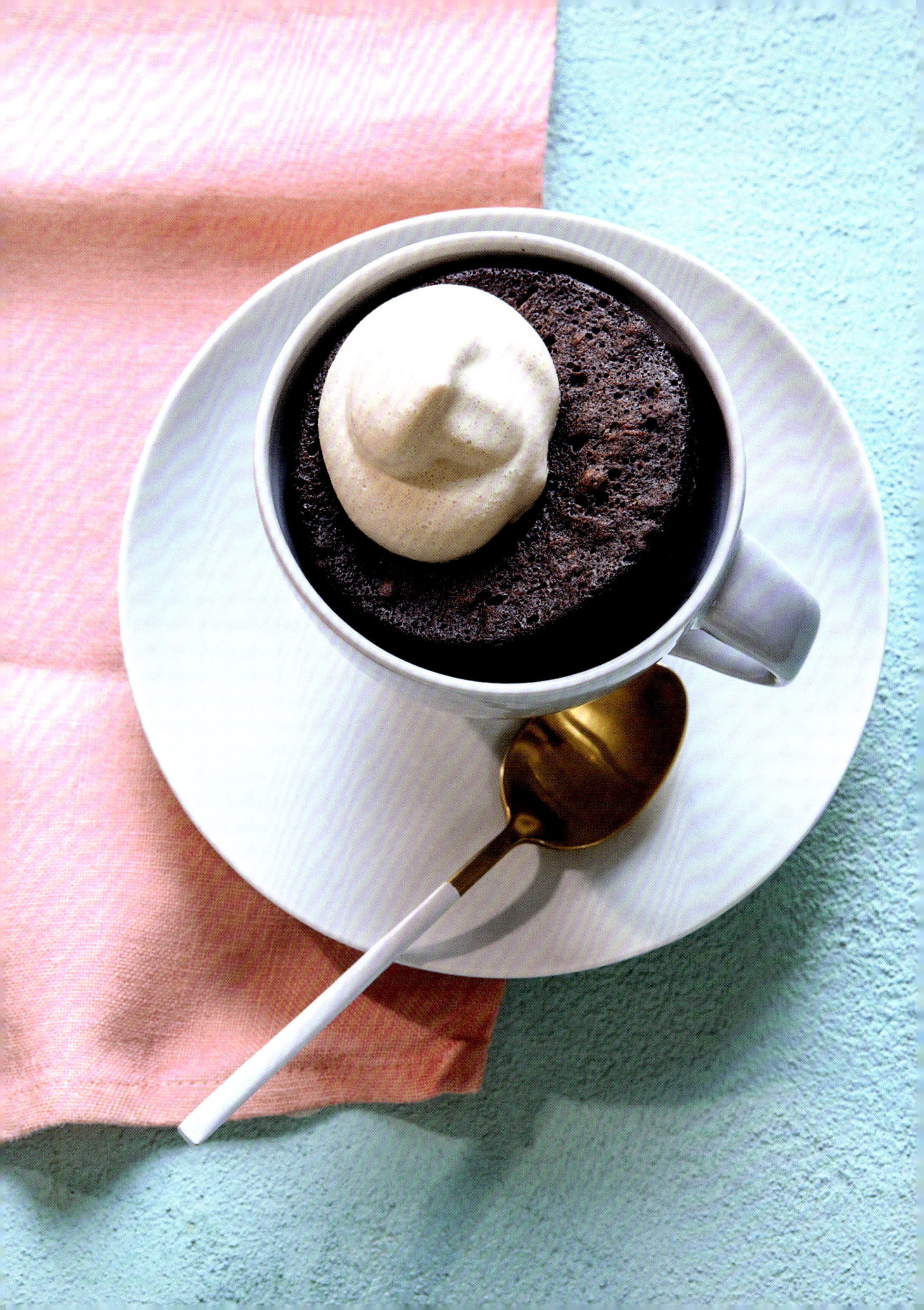

# Whipped Cream Cappuccino Cake

*If you're after a dessert and a caffeine boost in one hit, look no further. A light coffee sponge topped with a creamy swirl – it's your favourite beverage in cake form, ready in an instant.*

**SERVES 1**

**TAKES 5 minutes**

1 slice of butter 1cm (½in) thick (30g/1oz)
6 squares of dark chocolate (30g/1oz)
1 egg
2 tablespoons caster (superfine) sugar
5 tablespoons plain (all-purpose) flour
½ teaspoon baking powder
1 tablespoon instant coffee
1 tablespoon single (light) cream
1 drop of coffee extract

**Decoration**
whipped cream
1 teaspoon unsweetened cocoa powder

In a mug, melt the butter with the chocolate in the microwave for 30–40 seconds.

Beat the mixture until smooth, then allow it to cool slightly. One by one, whisk in the egg, sugar, flour, baking powder, instant coffee and cream. Add the drop of coffee extract and draw a spiral with the tip of a knife. Cook in the microwave for 1 minute 30 seconds, or until risen and springy to the touch.

Allow to cool for 1 minute. Decorate with whipped cream and cocoa powder. Eat straight away – the whipped cream melts quickly!

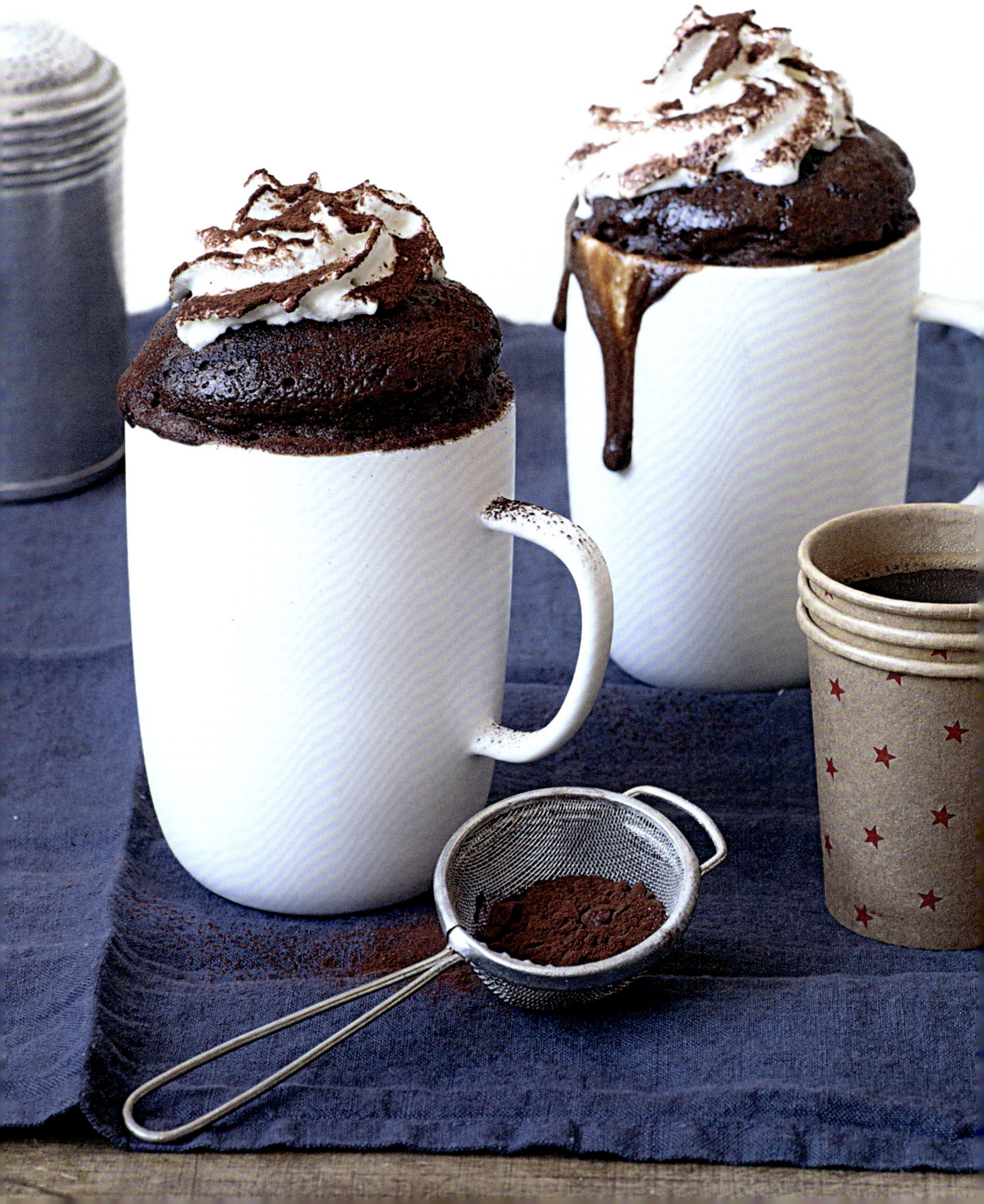

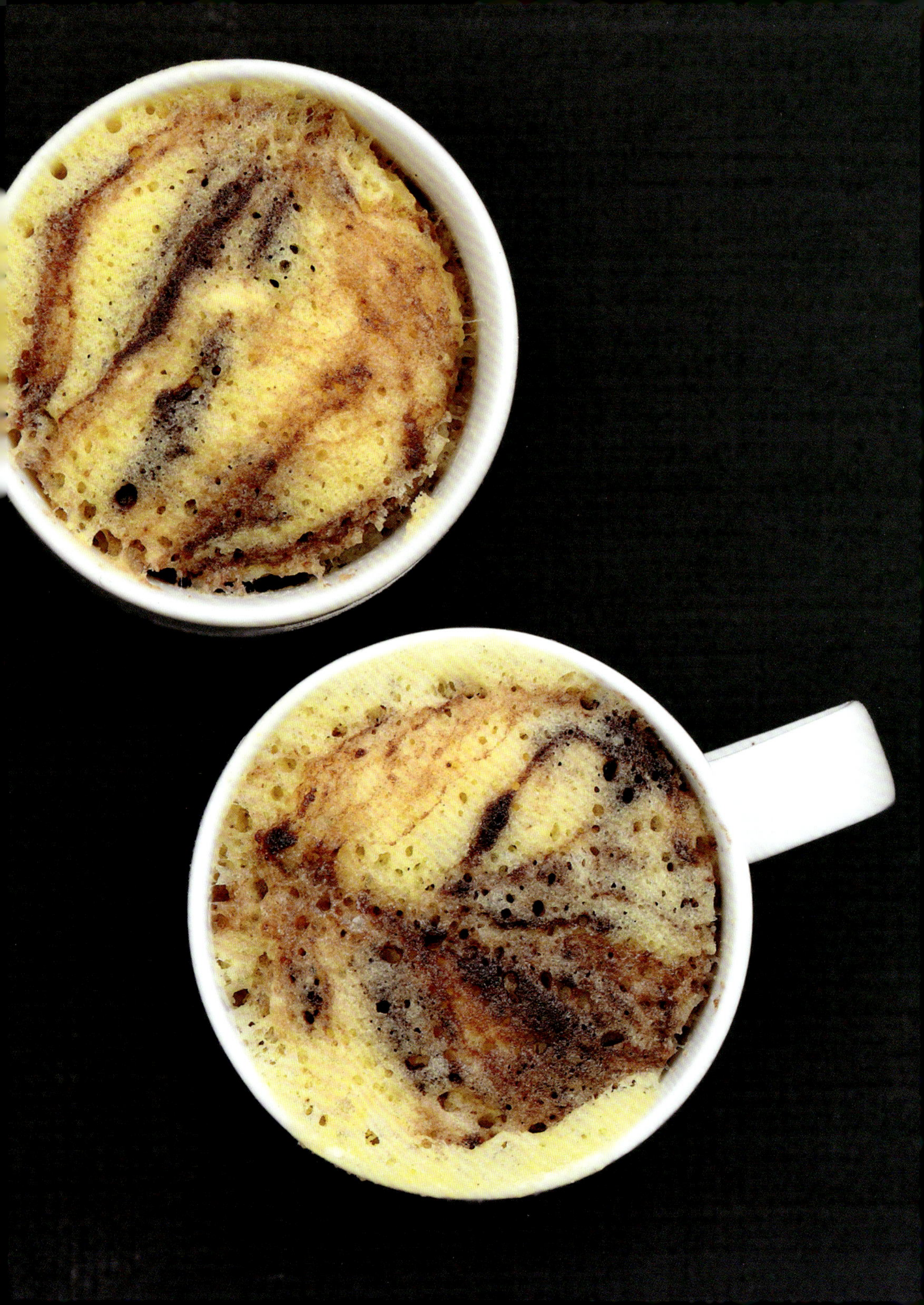

# Marble Mug Cake with
# Coffee & Chocolate

*Marble mug cakes are so fun to make. Simply split your batter and colour one half with chocolate, then layer them back into the mug and swirl with a knife. Less than two minutes in the microwave and you can marvel at your own artwork – and then enjoy consuming it.*

**SERVES 1**

**TAKES 6 minutes**

- 1 slice of butter 1cm (½in) thick (30g/1oz)
- 3 squares of dark chocolate (15g/½oz)
- 1 egg
- 2 tablespoons caster (superfine) sugar
- 1 teaspoon vanilla sugar
- 4 teaspoons single (light) cream
- 5 tablespoons plain (all-purpose) flour
- ½ teaspoon baking powder
- 1 teaspoon instant coffee

Melt the butter in a bowl in the microwave for 20 seconds. Melt the dark chocolate in another bowl in the microwave for 1 minute 10 seconds.

In a third bowl, beat in one by one the egg, sugar, vanilla sugar, cream, flour, baking powder and melted butter.

Transfer half of the batter to the bowl with the melted chocolate, add the instant coffee and mix together.

In a mug, spoon in by turns the plain and coffee/chocolate mixtures. With a knife, draw a wave in the mixture to create a marbled effect.

Cook in the microwave for 1 minute 40 seconds, or until risen and springy to the touch.

## Pick-Me-Up
# Espresso Martini

*One for the grown-ups, cake meets the cocktail hour in this deliciously boozy treat. With all the usual suspects there – coffee, Kahlúa, vodka, and a decadently creamy top – it really is the pick-me-up promised.*

**SERVES 1**

**TAKES 4 minutes**

2 tablespoons soft brown sugar
2 tablespoons plain (all-purpose) flour
1 tablespoon unsweetened cocoa powder
¼ teaspoon baking powder
1 egg
2 tablespoons sunflower oil
1 tablespoon espresso or double-strength coffee, cooled to room temperature
1 tablespoon coffee-flavoured liqueur (such as Kahlúa)
1 tablespoon vodka
mascarpone, to serve

In a mug, mix together the sugar, flour, cocoa and baking powder with a fork until combined. Add the egg, oil, coffee, coffee liqueur and vodka, and mix until just smooth.

Microwave for 1 minute 40 seconds, or until risen and springy to the touch. This cake has a big rise in the microwave, but then sinks to become gorgeous and fudgy. Serve with a dollop of mascarpone and enjoy.

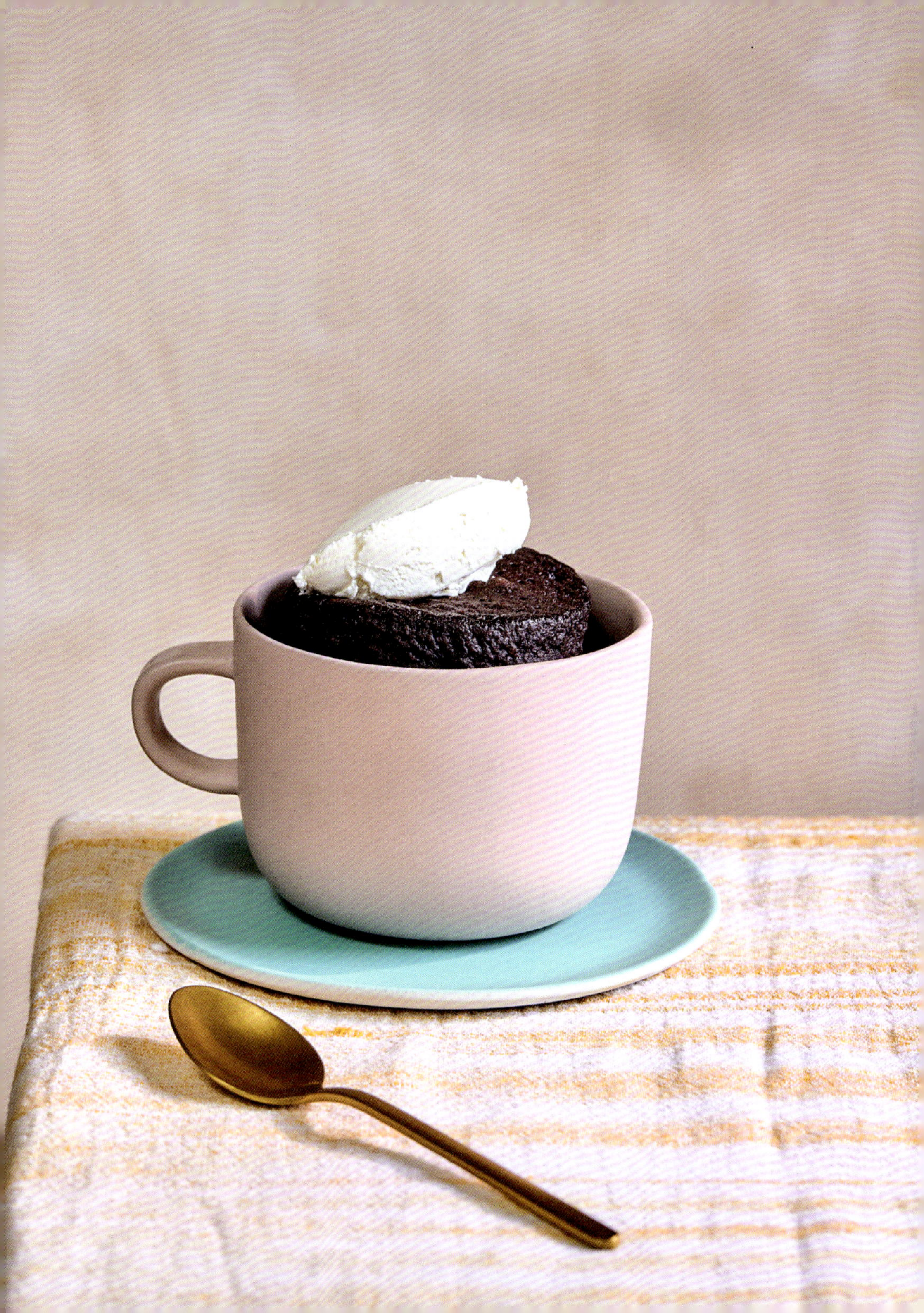

# Mug
# Crumbles
---

# Classic
# Apple Crumble

*The classic comfort food; the OG, but this one's all for you! A single-serve mug of sweet cinnamon-spiced apples with a buttery crumbly topping and a hint of toasty almonds, ready in mere moments.*

**SERVES 1**

**TAKES 8 minutes**

½ apple, peeled and diced
1 teaspoon lemon juice
1 teaspoon vanilla sugar or maple syrup
a pinch of ground cinnamon

**Crumble**
1 slice of butter 5mm (¼in) thick (15g/½oz), chilled
1 tablespoon fine oat flakes
4 tablespoons plain (all-purpose) flour
2 tablespoons sugar
2 blanched almonds, chopped

To make the crumble, mix the butter, oat flakes, flour, sugar and almonds, rubbing everything together with your fingertips until it resembles coarse breadcrumbs. .

In a mug, mix together the apple, lemon juice, vanilla sugar or maple syrup, cinnamon and 1 tablespoon of water.

Cook in the microwave for 3 minutes.

Add the crumble to the top of the mixture. Cook in the microwave for 2 minutes 30 seconds.

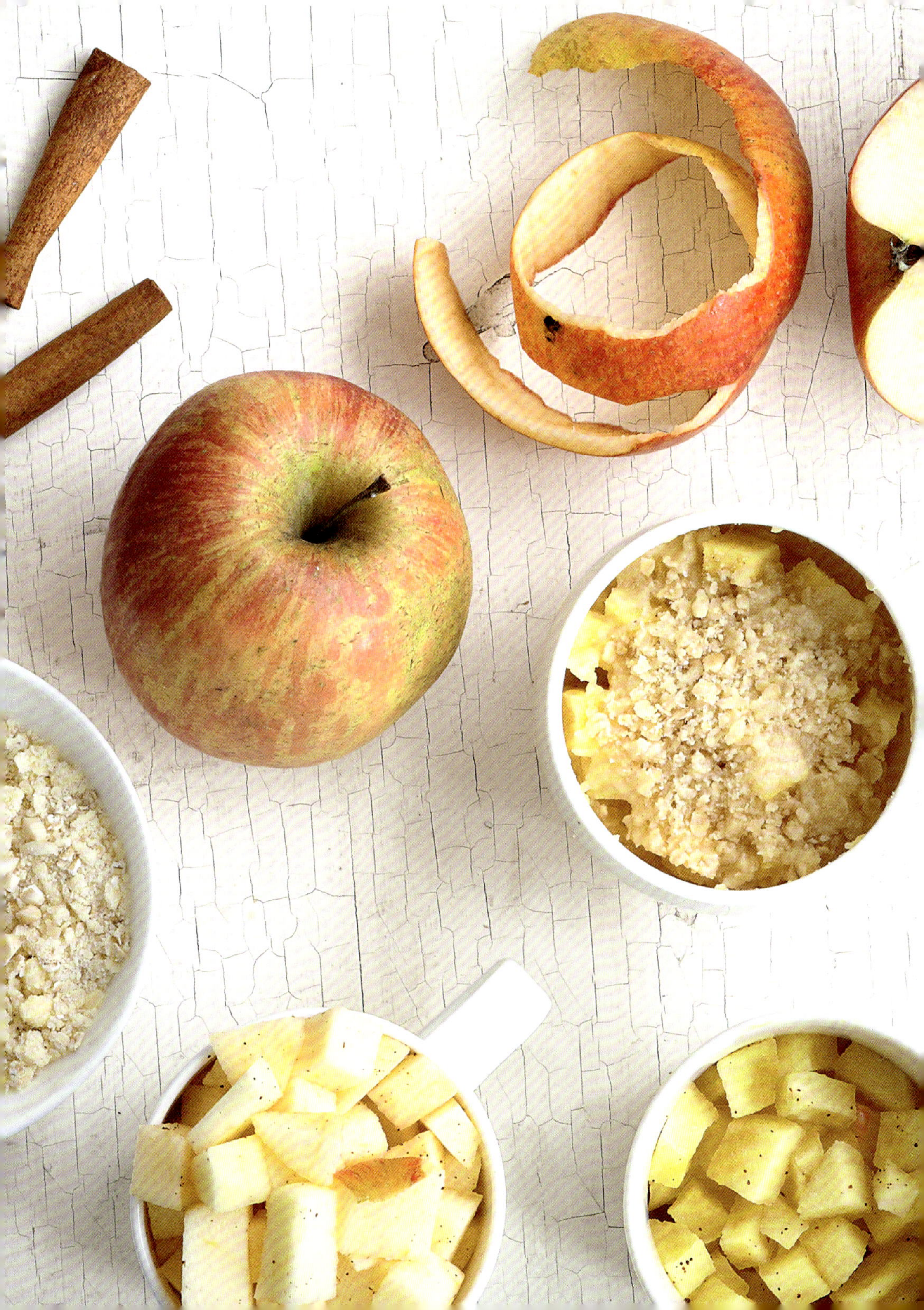

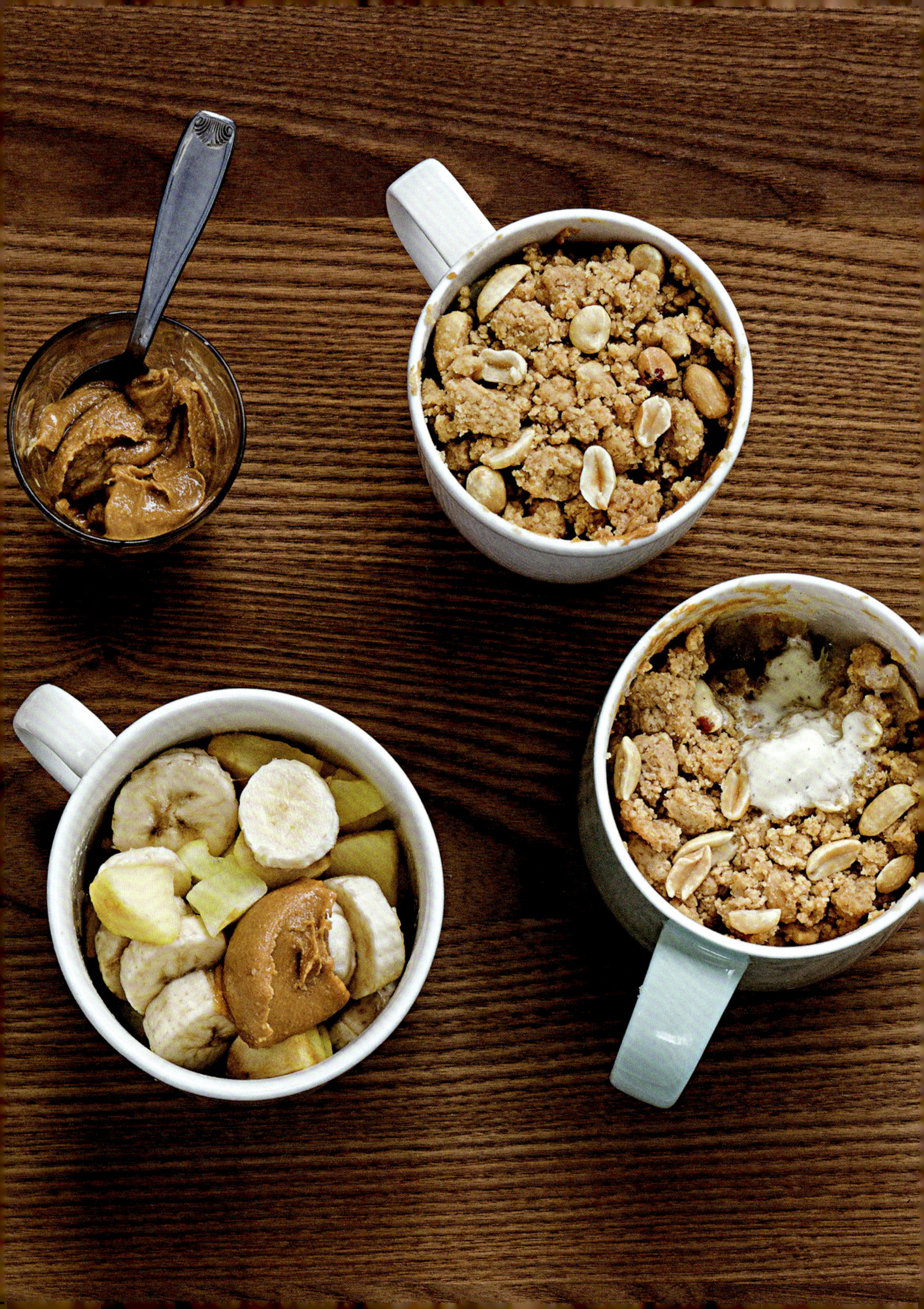

# Banana, Apple & Peanut Crumble

*Bananas don't get added to crumbles nearly enough. Nor, for that matter, does peanut butter. This quirky crumble is a true mash-up of favourite flavours and desserts – definitely one to try.*

**SERVES 1**

**TAKES 6 minutes**

1 apple, peeled, cored and diced
1 tablespoon caster (superfine) sugar
½ banana, sliced into rounds
1 heaped tablespoon peanut butter

**Crumble**
1 slice of butter 5mm (¼in) thick (15g/½oz)
1 tablespoon soft brown sugar
2 heaped tablespoons peanut butter
2 heaped tablespoons plain (all-purpose) flour
1 tablespoon chopped roasted and salted peanuts

In a mug, mix the apple with the sugar. Cover the mug with cling film (plastic wrap) and pierce it several times.

Cook in the microwave for 1 minute. Pour off any excess liquid. Add the banana and the peanut butter and stir.

In a bowl, mix the butter, brown sugar, peanut butter, flour and peanuts with your fingertips to form a coarse breadcrumb-like consistency.

Crumble it into the mug and cook in the microwave for 1 minute. Let it cool a little before eating.

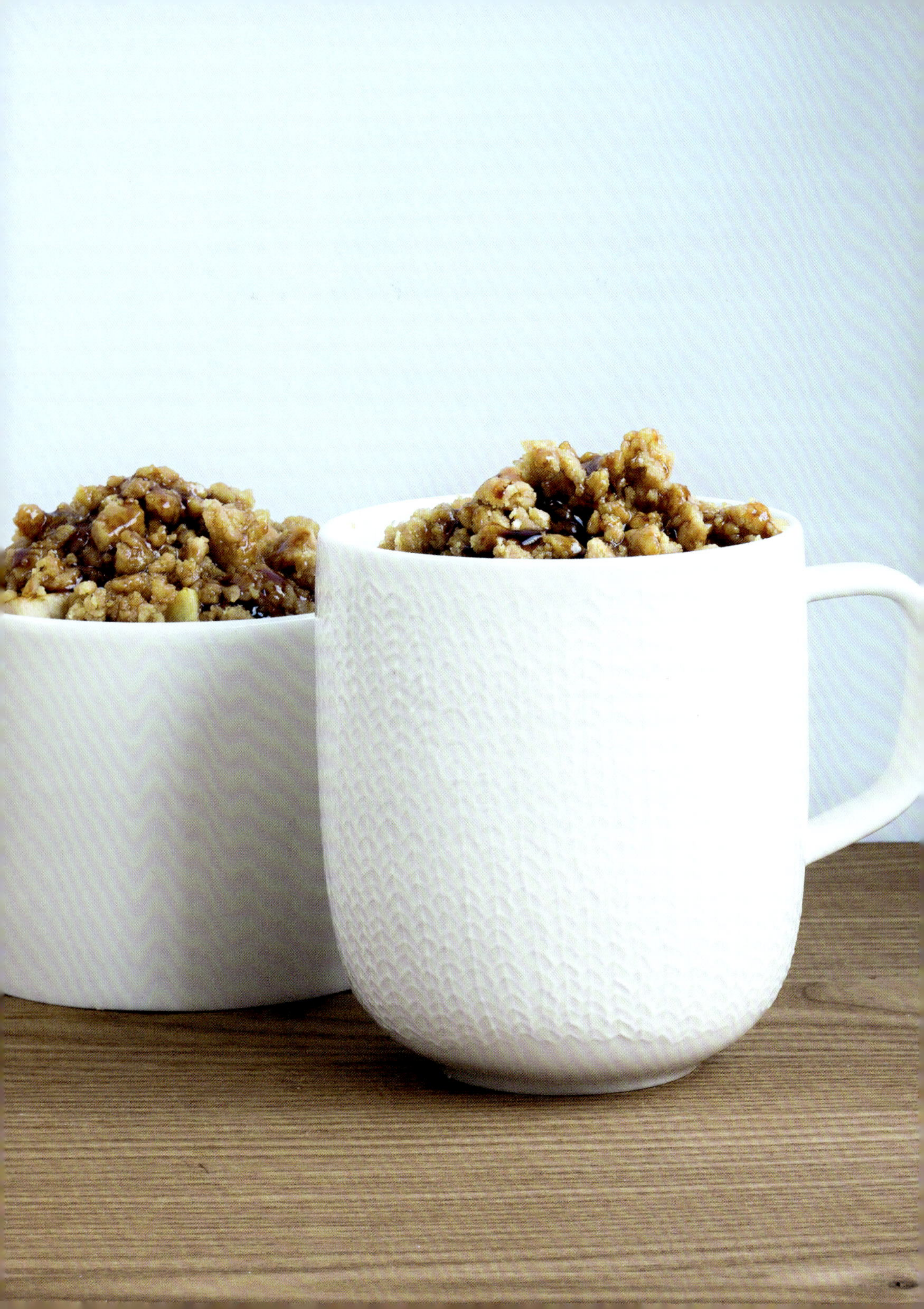

# Apple & Caramel Crumble

While they certainly pack in the wholesome fresh fruit, crumbles have never really been about abstinence. Even more so when you're pouring caramel – that liquid gold – over the top. But if you can get your hands on a jar of dulce de leche, it really will take it to new heights.

**SERVES 1**

**TAKES 6 minutes**

2 apples, peeled, cored and diced
1 tablespoon caster (superfine) sugar
1 teaspoon natural vanilla extract
a knob of butter

**Crumble**
1 slice of butter 5mm (¼in) thick (15g/½oz)
1 tablespoon soft brown sugar
2 tablespoons liquid caramel or 1 tablespoon of dulce de leche (caramelized milk)
3 heaped tablespoons plain (all-purpose) flour
a pinch of salt

In a mug, mix the apples with the sugar, vanilla and butter. Cover the mug with cling film (plastic wrap) and pierce it several times.

Cook in the microwave for 1 minute. Pour off any excess liquid and stir again.

In a bowl, mix the butter, soft brown sugar, half the caramel, the flour and salt with your fingertips to form a coarse breadcrumb-like texture.

Crumble it into the mug and cook in the microwave for 2 minutes. Pour the remaining caramel over the crumble before eating.

# Apple & Pecan Crumble

*A perfect cosy treat as the weather cools down – sweet apples, toasty pecans and that bonus gorgeous hit of maple. If you don't have a fireside to enjoy it by, a radiator will work too – you'll be far too focused on the crumble to notice anyway!*

**SERVES 1**

**TAKES 6 minutes**

2 apples, peeled, cored and diced
1 tablespoon caster (superfine) sugar
a knob of butter
2 tablespoons maple syrup

**Crumble**
1 slice of butter 5mm (¼in) thick (15g/½oz)
1 tablespoon soft brown sugar
1 tablespoon chopped pecan nuts
3 heaped tablespoons plain (all-purpose) flour
a pinch of salt

In a mug, mix the apple with the sugar and butter. Cover the mug with cling film (plastic wrap) and pierce it several times.

Cook in the microwave for 1 minute. Pour off any excess liquid. Add the maple syrup and stir again.

In a bowl, mix the butter, soft brown sugar, pecan nuts, flour and salt with your fingertips to form a coarse breadcrumb-like texture.

Crumble it into the mug and cook in the microwave for 2 minutes. Pour the maple syrup over the crumble before eating.

*Tip: For an even tastier mug crumble, dry toast the pecans in a frying pan for about 5 minutes.*

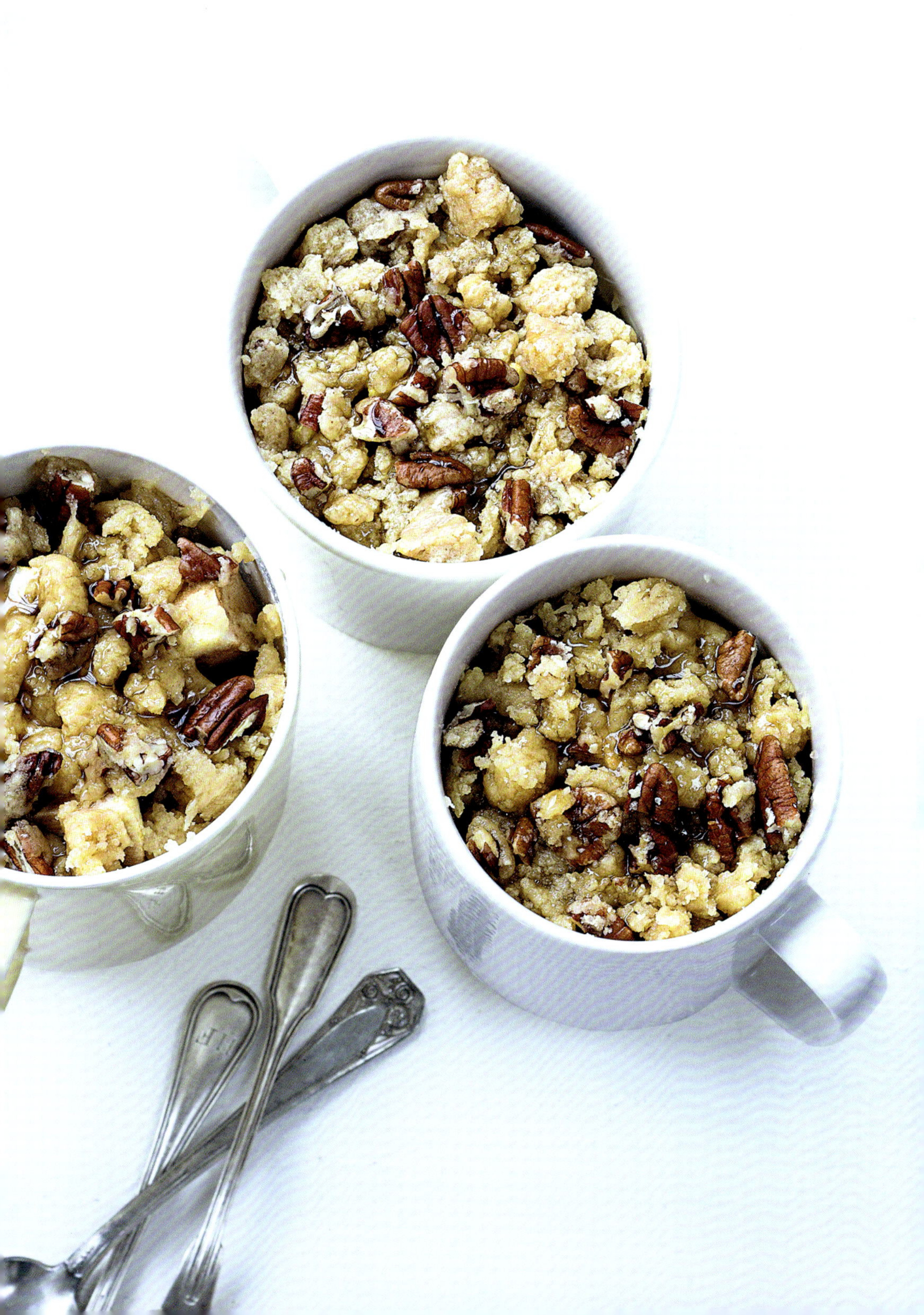

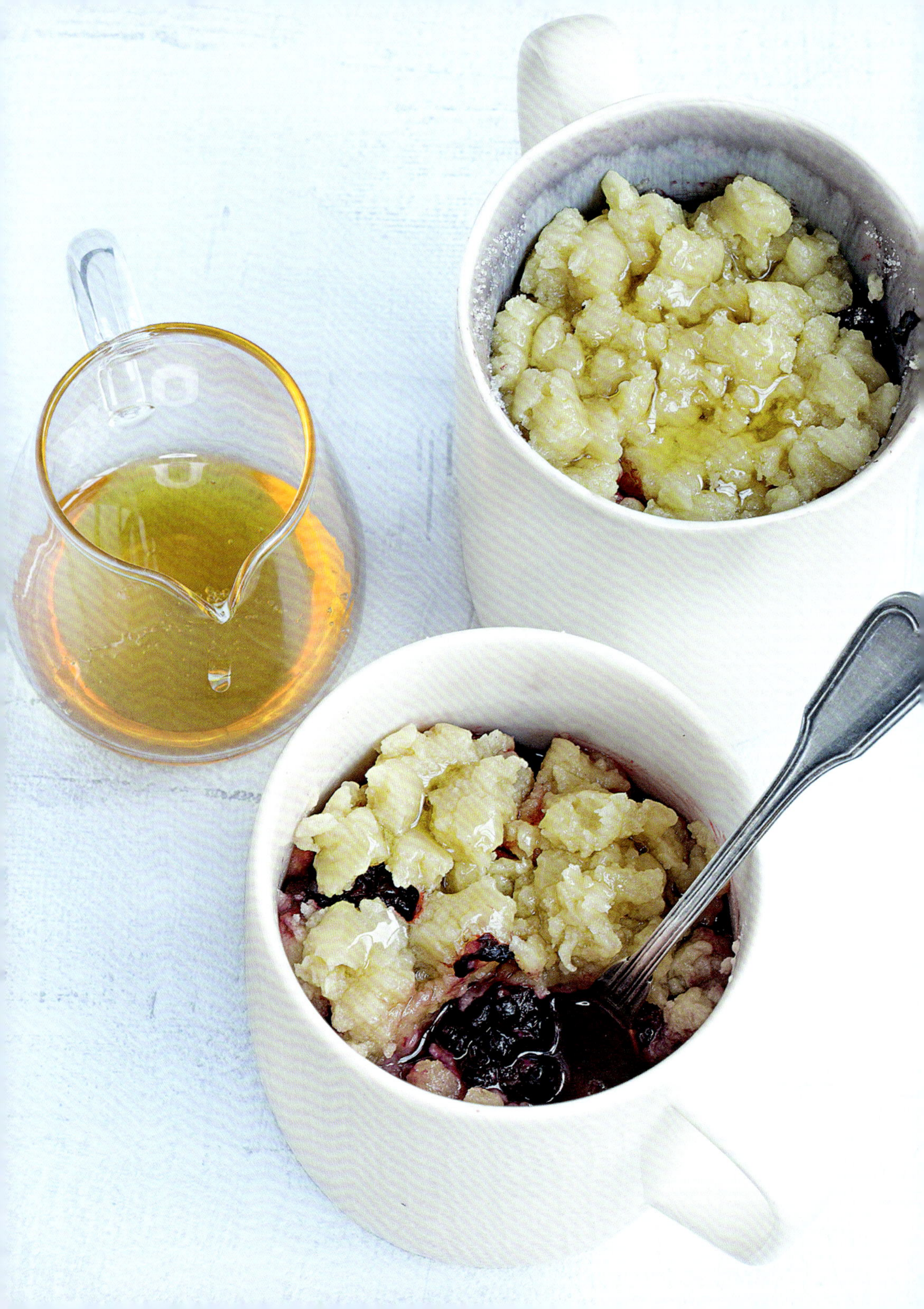

# Apple & Blackberry Crumble

*It's not just a happy accident that apples and blackberries are so content in each other's company – it's a rule of nature. As tree branches begin to droop with the weight of juicy apples, so too do blackberry brambles offer up their autumnal crop. Make this crumble with them both; it would be rude not to.*

**SERVES 1**

**TAKES 6 minutes**

1 apple, peeled, cored and diced
1 heaped tablespoon caster (superfine) sugar
a knob of butter
generous ½ cup (80g/3oz) blackberries

**Crumble**
1 slice of butter 5mm (¼in) thick (15g/½oz)
1 teaspoon soft brown sugar
2 tablespoons runny honey
2 heaped tablespoons plain (all-purpose) flour
a pinch of salt

In a mug, mix the apple with the sugar and butter. Cover the mug with cling film (plastic wrap) and pierce it several times.

Cook in the microwave for 1 minute. Pour off any excess liquid. Add the blackberries and stir again.

In a bowl, mix the butter, sugar, 1 tablespoon of the honey, the flour and salt with your fingertips to form a coarse breadcrumb-like consistency.

Crumble it into the mug and cook in the microwave for 1 minutes. Pour the remaining honey over the crumble and let it cool a little before eating.

# Apple, Chocolate & Nut Crumble

This classic quick-fix dessert has a secret ingredient – adding a little cream to the fruit mixture helps make it all feel much more luxurious and satisfying. The trio of favourite nuts finishes it off, but if you don't have all three on hand, feel free to make up the quantity with any combination of these.

**SERVES 1**

**TAKES 6 minutes**

1 apple, peeled, cored and diced
1 tablespoon caster (superfine) sugar
6 squares of milk chocolate, chopped (30g/1oz)
1 tablespoon single (light) cream

**Crumble**
1 slice of butter 5mm (¼in) thick (15g/½oz)
1 tablespoon soft brown sugar
1 heaped tablespoon plain (all-purpose) flour
1 tablespoon chopped pecan nuts
1 tablespoon chopped walnuts
1 tablespoon chopped hazelnuts
a pinch of salt

In a mug, mix the apple with the sugar. Cover the mug with cling film (plastic wrap) and pierce it several times.

Cook in the microwave for 1 minute. Pour off any excess liquid. Add the chocolate and cream and stir. Cover with cling film again and cook for a further 30 seconds. Stir.

In a bowl, mix the butter, soft brown sugar, flour, the trio of nuts and salt with your fingertips to form a coarse breadcrumb-like consistency.

Crumble it into the mug and cook in the microwave for 1 minute. Let it cool a little before eating.

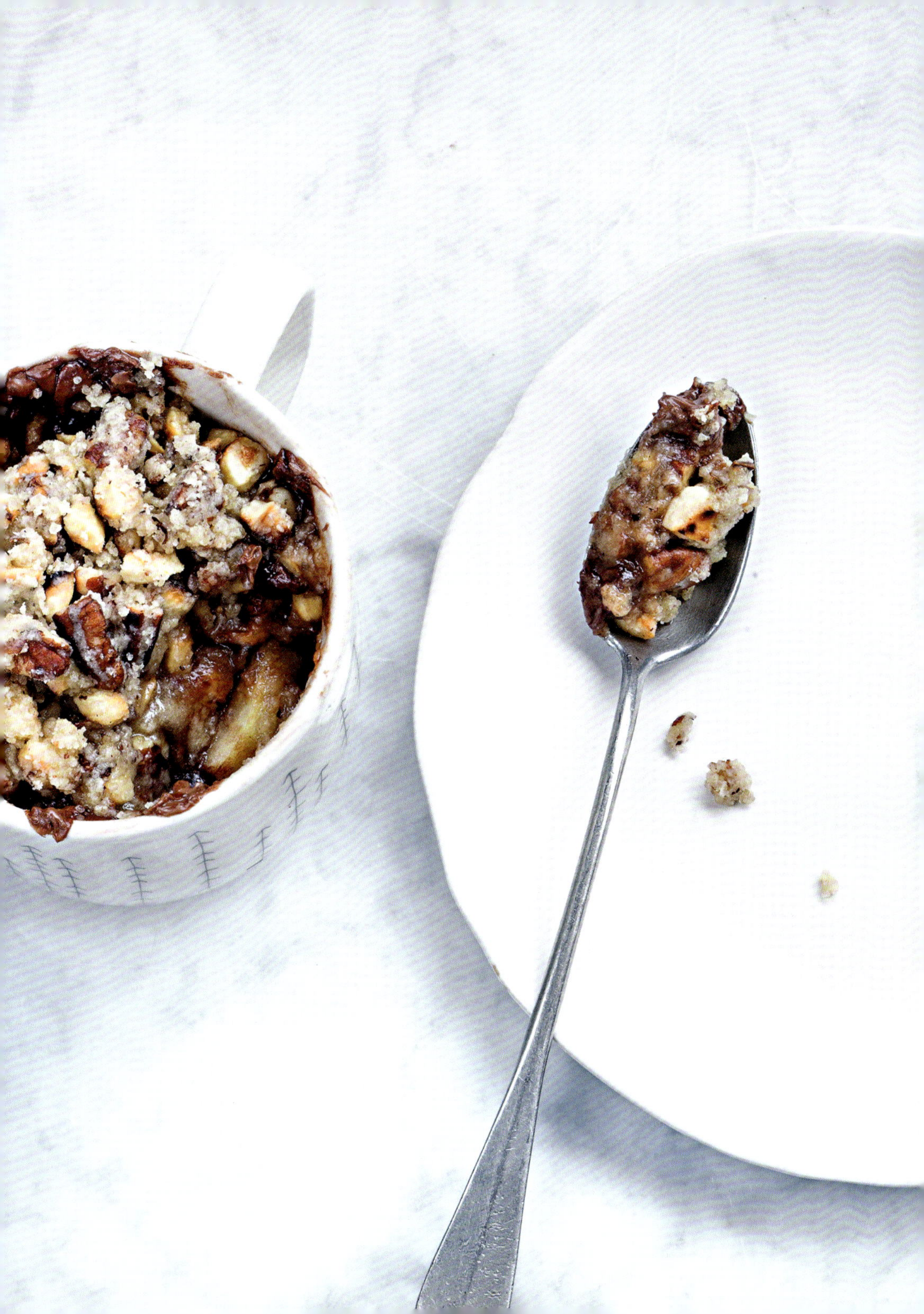

# Apple, White Chocolate &
# Raspberry Crumble

*White chocolate and raspberries are such a lovely summery combination. In berry season, those lovely tangy pink pearls add sharpness to the molten pockets of sweet white chocolate, while the apple helps balance it all out.*

**SERVES 1**

**TAKES 6 minutes**

1 apple, peeled, cored and diced
1 tablespoon caster (superfine) sugar
a knob of butter
generous ⅓ cup (50g/2oz) raspberries

**Crumble**
1 slice of butter 5mm (¼in) thick (15g/½oz)
1 tablespoon soft brown sugar
2 heaped tablespoons plain (all-purpose) flour
1 tablespoon white chocolate chips
a pinch of salt

In a mug, mix the apple with the sugar and butter. Cover the mug with cling film (plastic wrap) and pierce it several times.

Cook in the microwave for 1 minute. Pour off any excess liquid, add the raspberries and stir again.

In a bowl, mix the butter, brown sugar, flour, chocolate chips and salt with your fingertips to form a coarse breadcrumb-like consistency.

Crumble it into the mug and cook in the microwave for 1 minute.

Let it cool a little before eating.

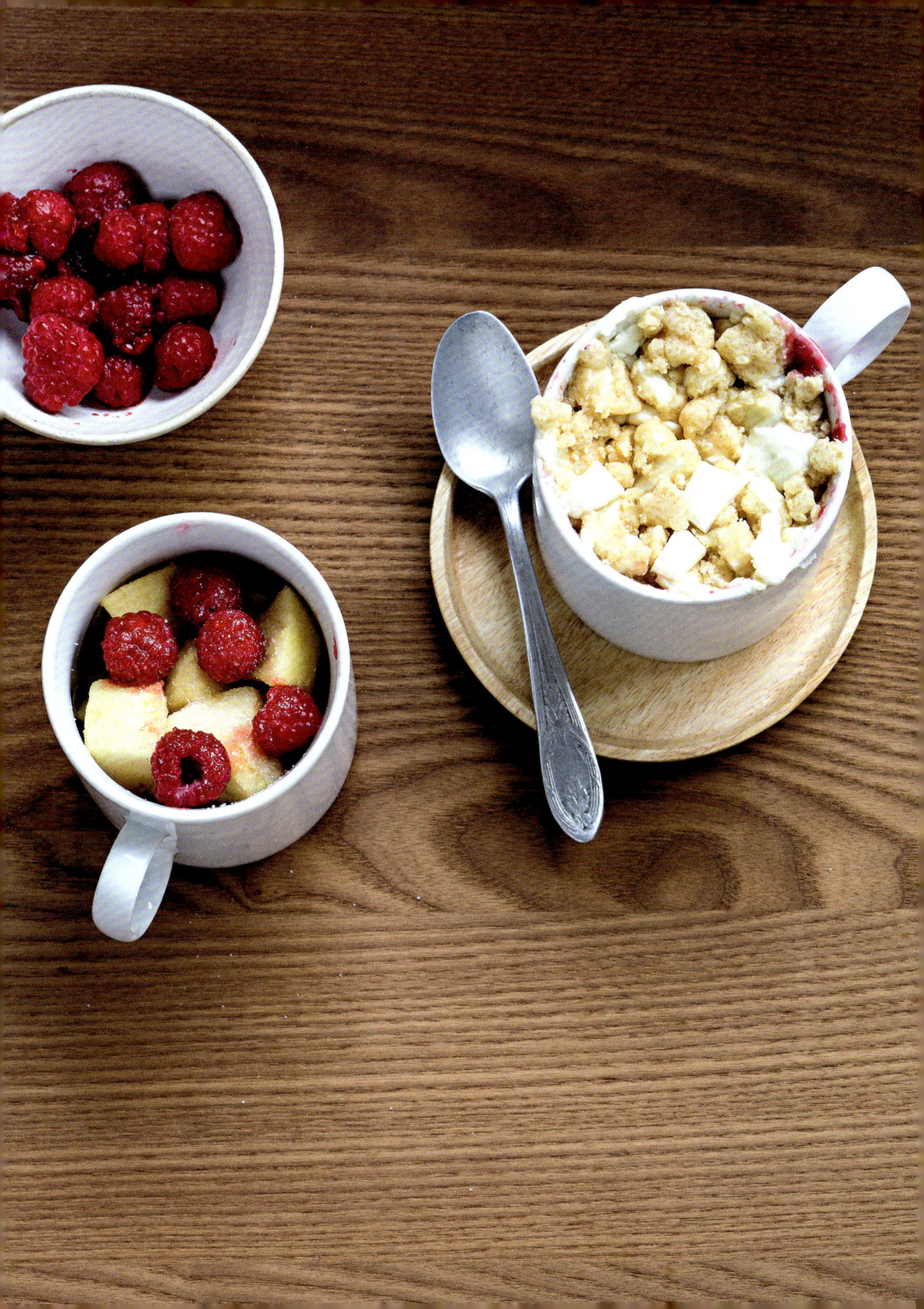

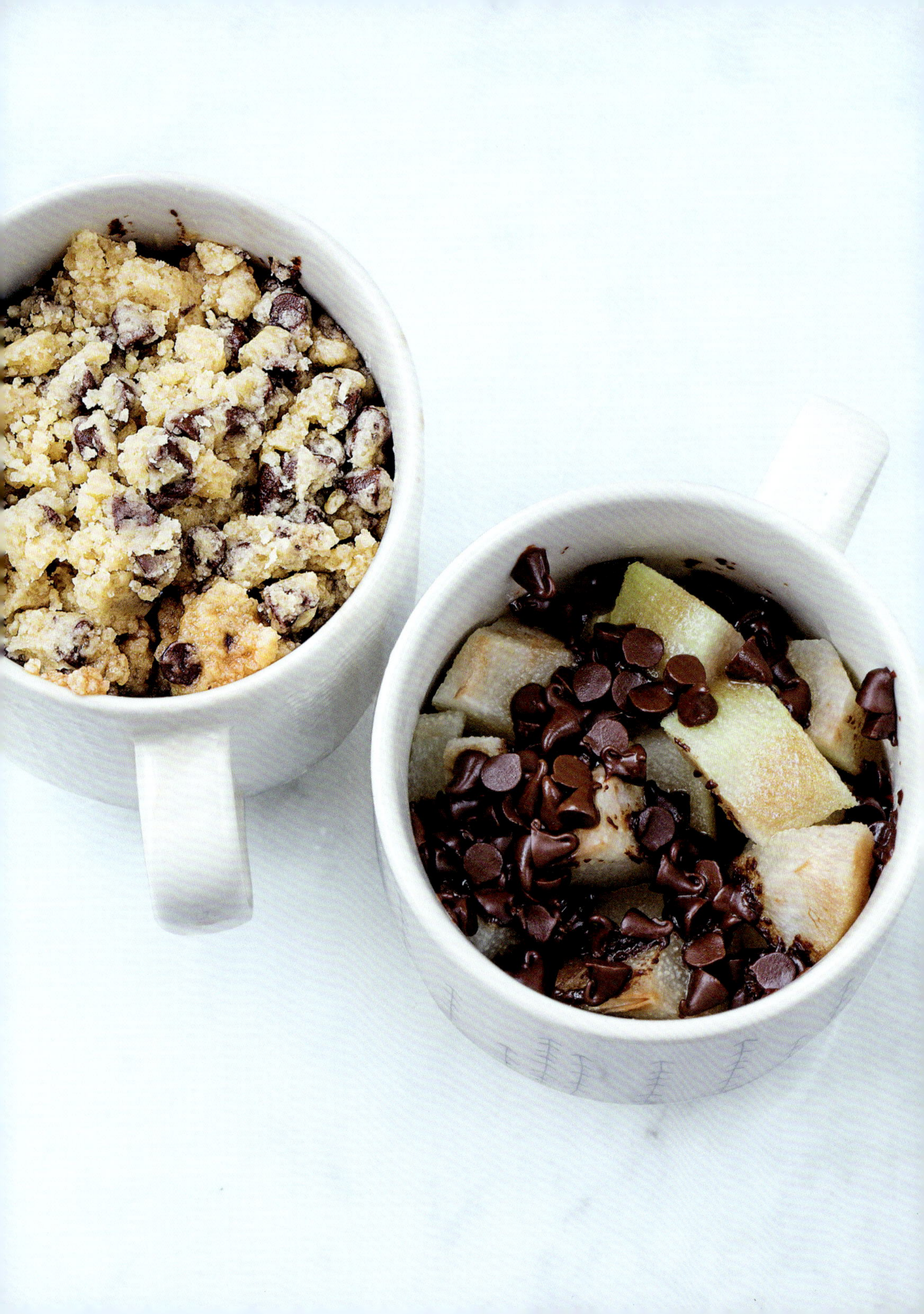

# Dark Chocolate & Pear Crumble

*Chocolate and pears are such a brilliant combination – the flavours just work together. And the darker the chocolate, the better it seems to be. Sure, you can buy a bag of chocolate chips for cooking, but if you happen to have a bar of 85% cocoa chocolate, chop that up and chuck it in, and taste the difference.*

**SERVES 1**

**TAKES 6 minutes**

2 pears, peeled, cored and diced
1 tablespoon caster (superfine) sugar
a knob of butter
1 tablespoon dark chocolate chips

**Crumble**
1 slice of butter 5mm (¼in) thick (15g/½oz)
1 tablespoon soft brown sugar
3 heaped tablespoons plain (all-purpose) flour
1 tablespoon dark chocolate chips
a pinch of salt

In a mug, mix the pear with the sugar and butter. Cover the mug with cling film (plastic wrap) and pierce it several times.

Cook in the microwave for 1 minute. Pour off any excess liquid. Add the chocolate chips and stir again.

In a bowl, mix the butter, soft brown sugar, flour, chocolate chips and salt with your fingertips to form a coarse breadcrumb-like consistency.

Crumble it into the mug and cook in the microwave for 1 minute. Let it cool a little before eating.

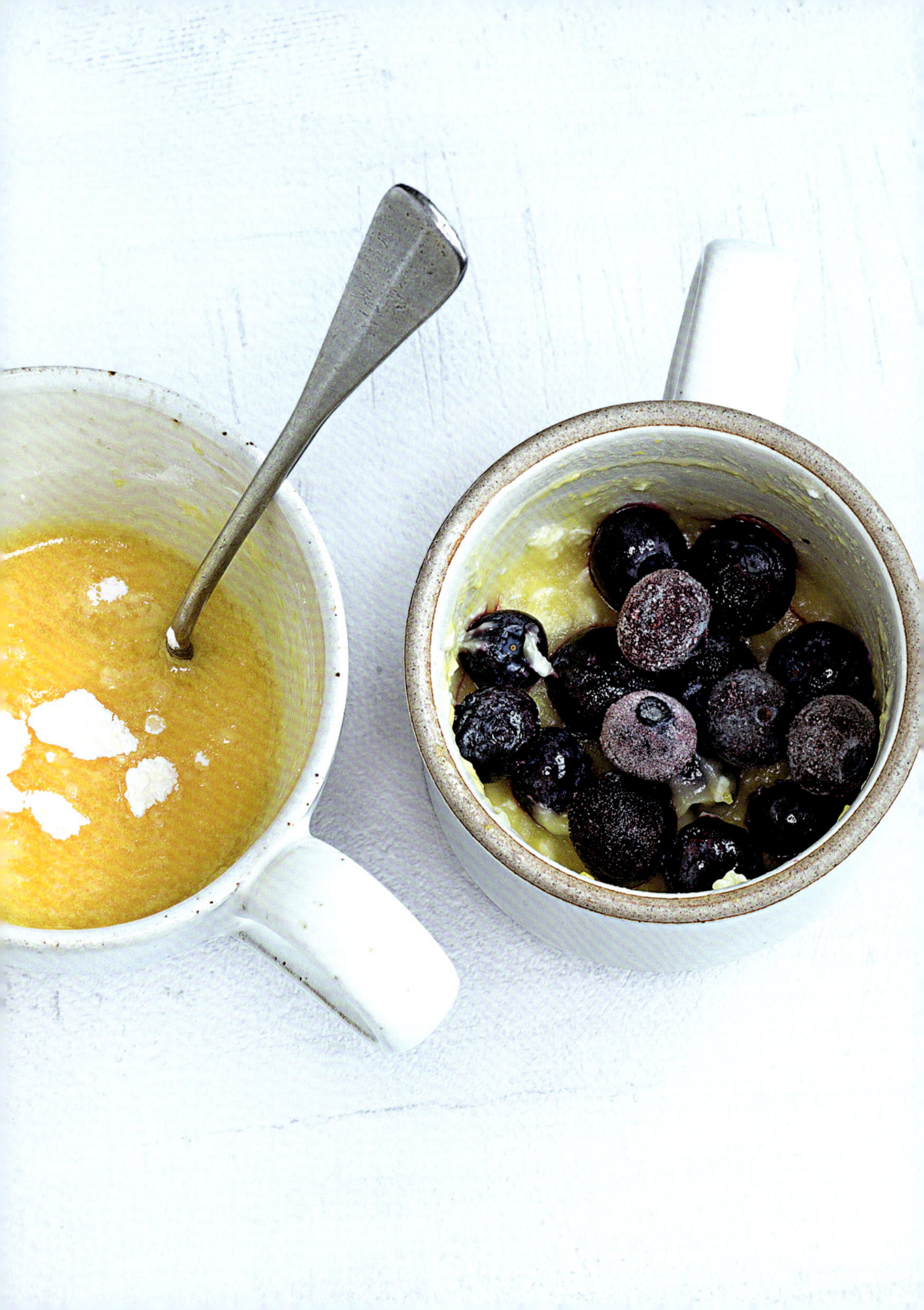

# Lemon Curd & Blueberry Crumble

*There are few things that provide such an immediate injection of flavour and joy to a dessert as lemon curd. It's sweet, it's tangy, it's the perfect pairing for blueberries, and if you don't happen to have a jar in the fridge, it's even possible to whip up your own in just 30 seconds in the microwave.*

**SERVES 1**

**TAKES 7 minutes**

50 g (2oz) lemon curd (shop-bought or homemade, see below)
1 tablespoon frozen blueberries

**Homemade Lemon Curd**
1 slice of butter 5mm (¼in) thick (15g/½oz)
1 small egg
juice of ½ lemon
2 tablespoons caster (superfine) sugar
1 teaspoon cornflour (cornstarch)

**Crumble**
1 slice of butter 5mm (¼in) thick (15g/½oz)
1 heaped tablespoon soft brown sugar
3 tablespoons plain (all-purpose) flour
zest of ½ lemon

If making the lemon curd from scratch, add the butter to a mug and melt in the microwave. Add the egg, lemon juice, sugar and cornflour and beat. Cover the mug with cling film (plastic wrap) and pierce it several times, then cook for 30 seconds.

If using shop-bought lemon curd, skip the first step and add the curd to the mug without cooking it. Add the blueberries and stir.

Cover and cook again for 30 seconds.

In a bowl, mix the butter, soft brown sugar, flour and lemon zest with your fingertips to form a coarse breadcrumb-like consistency.

Crumble it into the mug and cook in the microwave for 1 minute.

Let it cool a little before eating.

# Pineapple, Apple &
# Lotus Biscuit Crumble

*If you want a break from the ordinary, make this curious combination your next stop. The pineapple lends a touch of the tropical to a classic apple and cinnamon base, and the caramelized biscuits lend a depth of flavour to the crumble that you wouldn't believe possible from a microwave 'bake'.*

**SERVES 1**

**TAKES 6 minutes**

1 apple, peeled, cored and diced
1 tablespoon vanilla sugar
2 slices of pineapple in syrup, cut into chunks
1 teaspoon ground cinnamon
a knob of butter

**Crumble**
1 slice of butter 5mm (¼in) thick (15g/½oz)
1 tablespoon soft brown sugar
2 Lotus biscuits or other caramelized biscuits (cookies), crushed
1 heaped tablespoon plain (all-purpose) flour
a pinch of salt

In a mug, mix the apple, sugar, pineapple, cinnamon and butter together. Cover the mug with cling film (plastic wrap) and pierce it several times.

Cook in the microwave for 1 minute. Pour off any excess liquid and stir.

In a bowl, mix the butter, brown sugar, caramelized biscuits, flour and salt with your fingertips to form a coarse breadcrumb-like consistency.

Crumble it into the mug and cook in the microwave for 1 minute. Let it cool a little before eating.

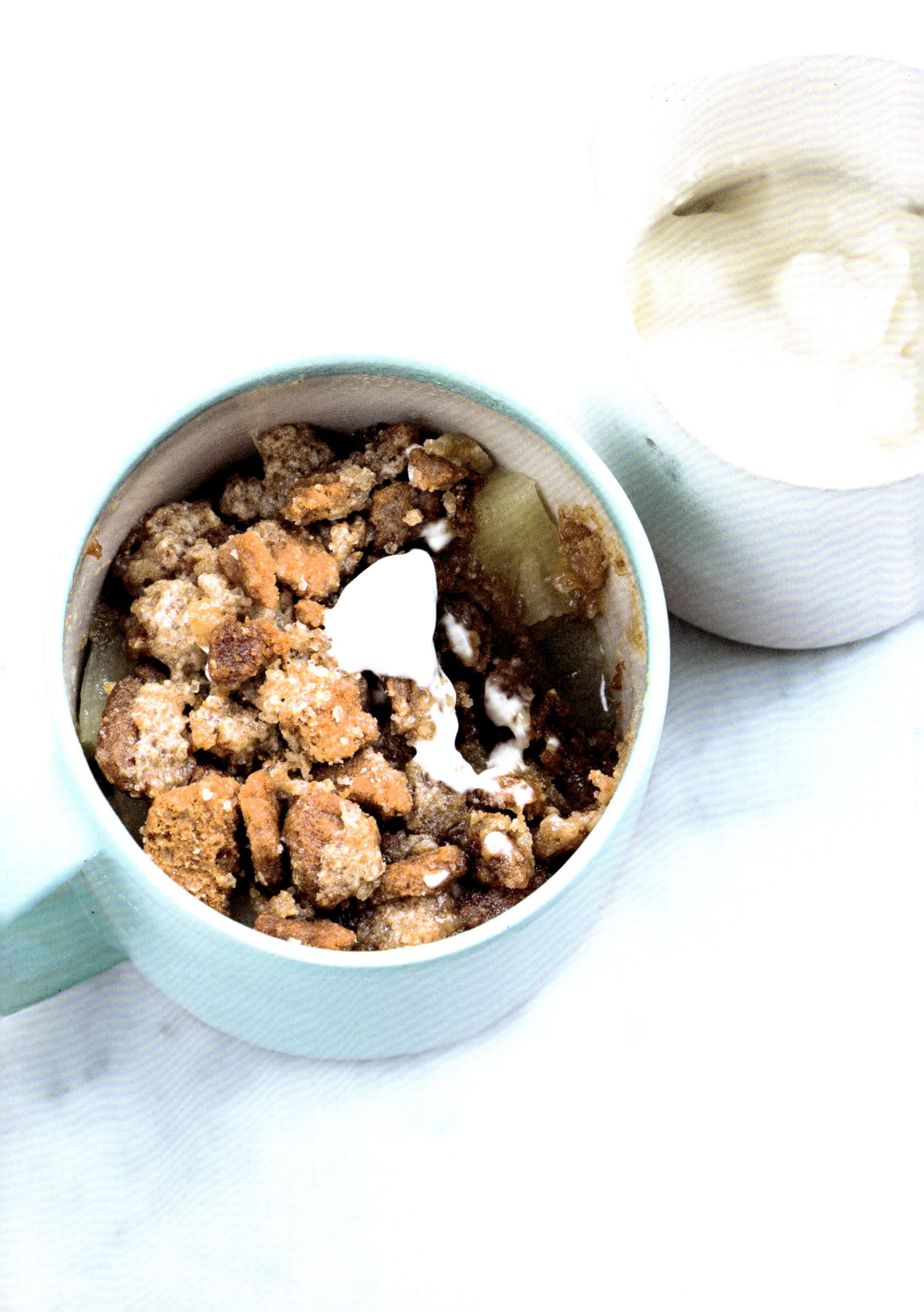

Melt-in-the-
# Middle
───────

# Milk Chocolate
# **Fondant**

*Lava cake, fondant pudding, molten-middle – whatever you call this beloved dessert, it is always met with the height of anticipation. How gooey will the middle be? Well, pretty reliably oozey if you're making it in the microwave – and a whole lot quicker!*

**SERVES 1**

**TAKES 5 minutes**

1 slice of butter 1cm (½in) thick (30g/1oz)
1 egg
4 tablespoons caster (superfine) sugar
1 teaspoon vanilla sugar
2 teaspoons single (light) cream
2½ tablespoons unsweetened cocoa powder
6 tablespoons plain (all-purpose) flour
½ teaspoon baking powder
2 or 3 squares of milk chocolate (10–15g/⅓–½oz)

Melt the butter in a bowl in the microwave for 20 seconds.

In a mug, beat in one by one the egg, sugar, vanilla sugar, cream, cocoa, flour, baking powder and melted butter.

Push the squares of milk chocolate into the middle of the mixture.

Cook in the microwave for 1 minute 20 seconds, or until risen but still gooey in the centre.

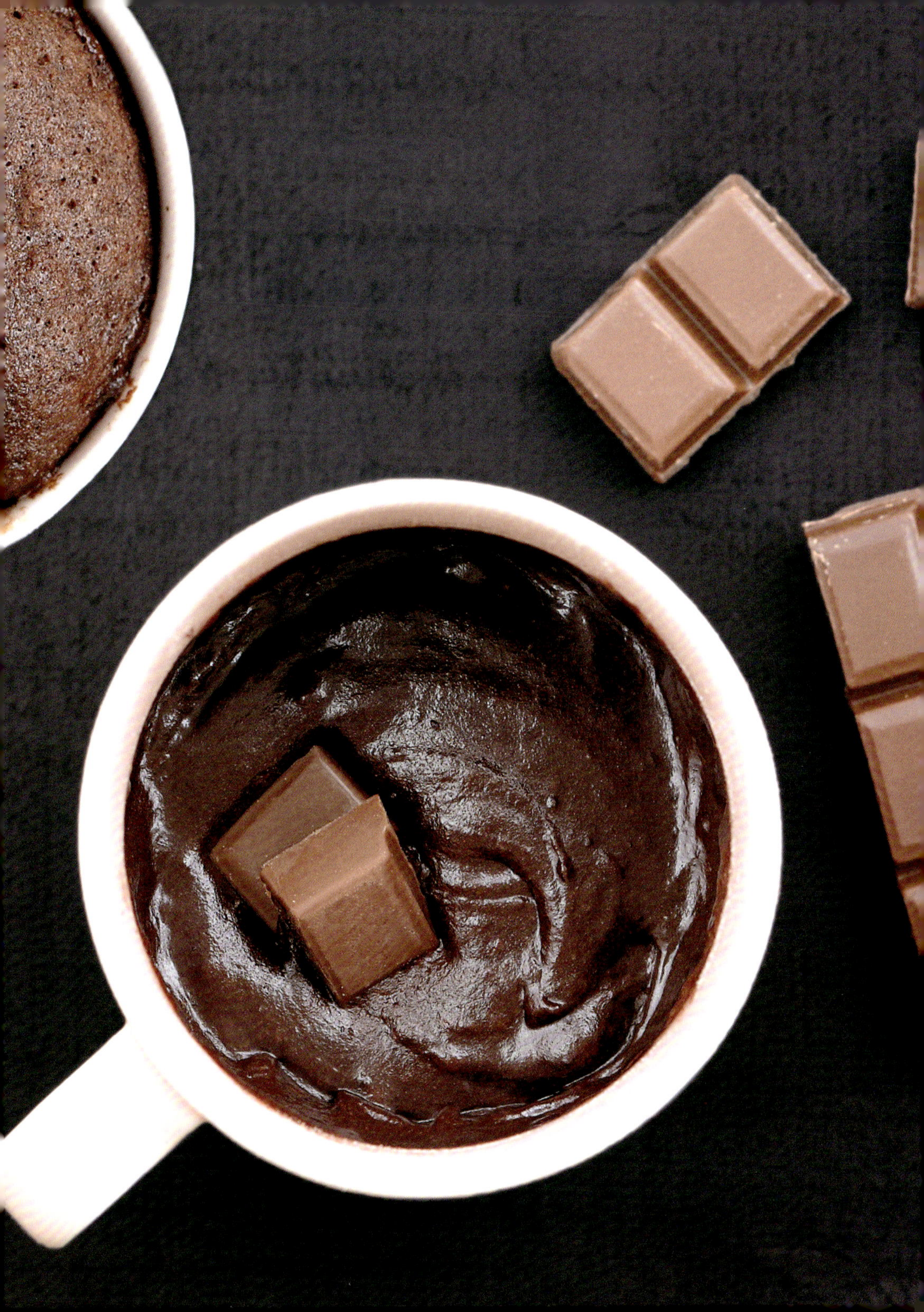

# White Chocolate
# Fondant

*Fondant puddings aren't often made with white chocolate, but there appears to be no real good reason for this. Rather than defaulting to the classic, give this paler and somewhat sweeter version a go – it will definitely satisfy a sweet tooth.*

**SERVES 1**

**TAKES 5 minutes**

1 slice of butter 1cm (½in) thick (30g/1oz)
6 squares of white chocolate (30g/1oz)
1 egg
2 tablespoons caster (superfine) sugar
4 tablespoons plain (all-purpose) flour
½ teaspoon baking powder

In a mug, melt the butter with four squares of the chocolate in the microwave for 40 seconds.

Beat the mixture until smooth, then allow it to cool slightly. One by one, whisk in the egg, sugar, flour and baking powder.

Push the remaining two squares of chocolate into the middle, then cook in the microwave for 1 minute 30 seconds, or until risen but still gooey in the centre.

Allow to cool for 1 minute before eating.

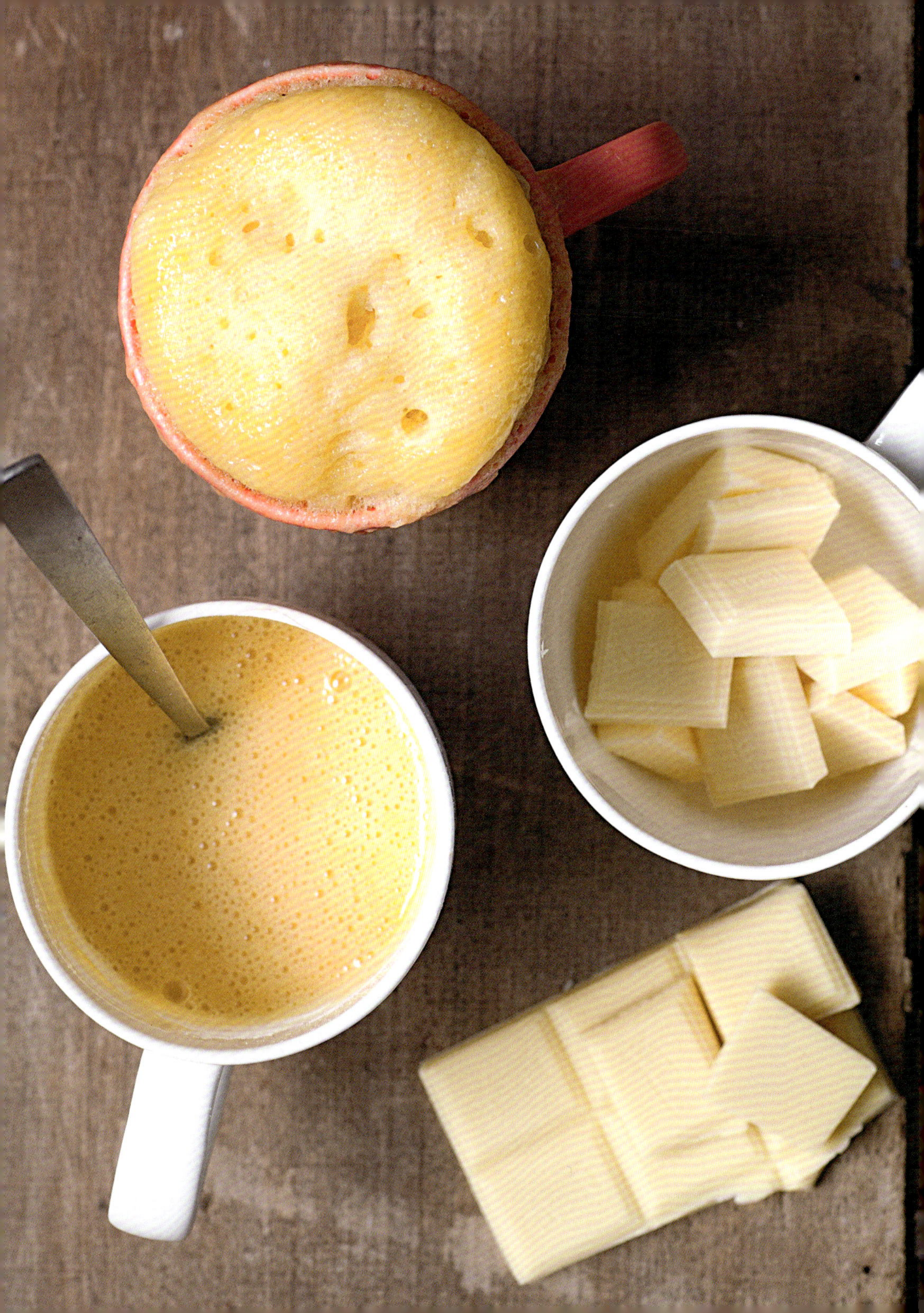

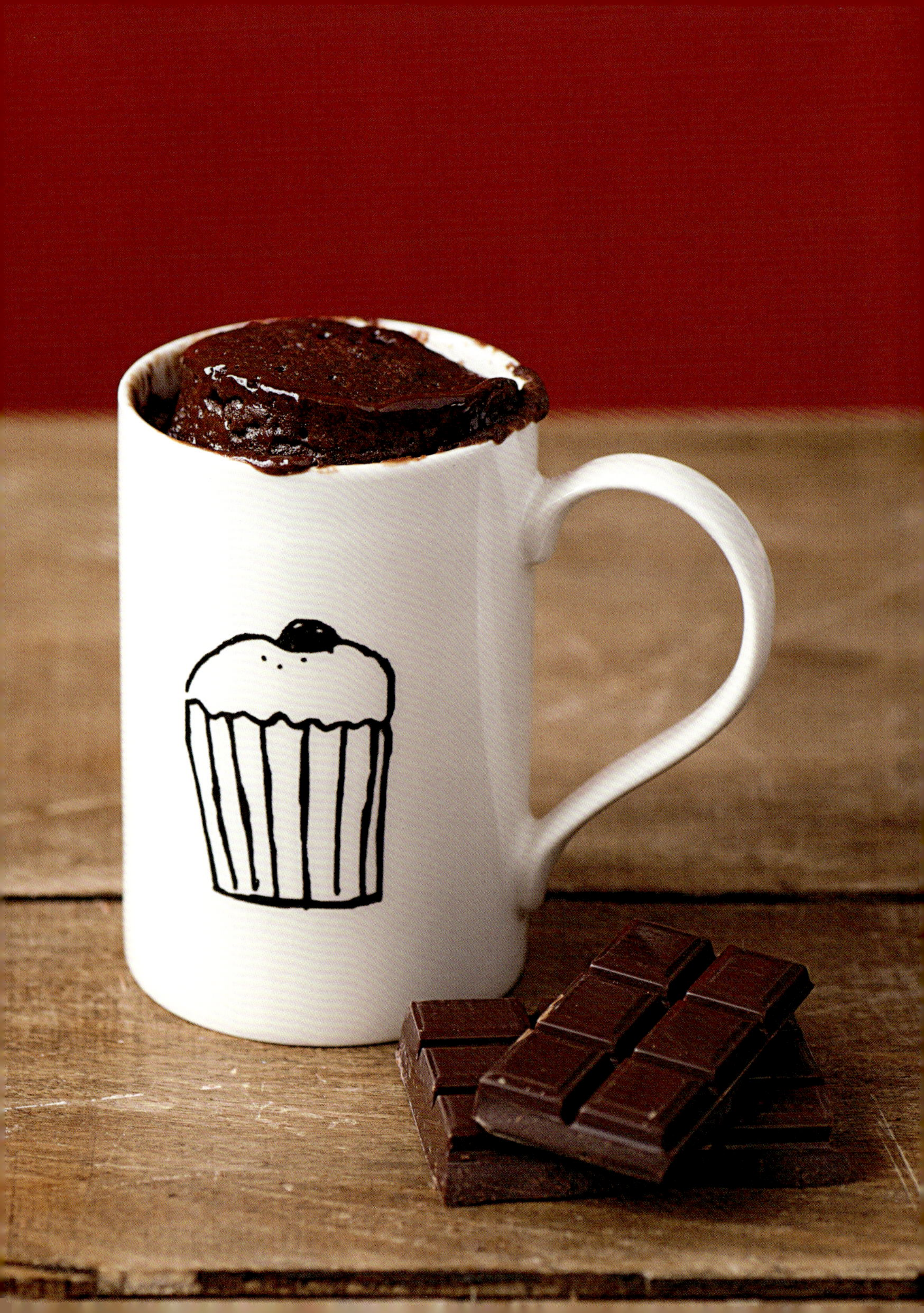

# Dark Chocolate
# **Fondant**

*A molten dark chocolate centre surrounded by light and fluffy chocolate sponge, this is pure indulgence. A single-serve mug provides the best vehicle for enjoying this – snatch it from the microwave and quickly hide yourself away to enjoy a quiet moment of pleasure.*

**SERVES 1**

**TAKES 5 minutes**

- 1 slice of butter 1cm (½in) thick (30g/1oz)
- 8 squares of dark chocolate (40g/1½oz) at least 55% cocoa solids
- 1 egg
- 2 tablespoons caster (superfine) sugar
- 4 tablespoons plain (all-purpose) flour
- ½ teaspoon baking powder

In a mug, melt the butter with six squares of the chocolate in the microwave for 30–40 seconds.

Beat the mixture until smooth, then allow it to cool slightly. One by one, whisk in the egg, sugar, flour and baking powder.

Push the remaining two squares of chocolate into the middle, then cook in the microwave for 1 minute 20 seconds, or until risen but still gooey in the centre.

Allow to cool for 1 minute before eating.

# Dark Chocolate & **Peanut Butter**

*There's really no reason a melting middle should be yet more chocolate. What joyous surprise as your spoon breaks instead into a well of liquid peanutty goodness! Smooth peanut butter is creamy and luxurious, or use a crunchy one for textural interest. You honestly can't go too far wrong.*

**SERVES 1**

**TAKES 5 minutes**

1 slice of butter 1cm (½in) thick (30g/1oz)
6 squares of dark chocolate (30g/1oz)
1½ teaspoons peanut butter
1 egg
1 tablespoon soft brown sugar
5 tablespoons plain (all-purpose) flour
½ teaspoon baking powder

**Middle & Decoration**
1 teaspoon peanut butter
1 teaspoon chocolate sprinkles

In a mug, melt the butter with the chocolate in the microwave for 30–40 seconds.

Beat the mixture until smooth, then allow it to cool slightly. One by one, whisk in the peanut butter, egg, sugar, flour and baking powder.

Cook in the microwave for 50 seconds. Push the teaspoonful of peanut butter into the middle and cook for a further 40 seconds, or until risen but still gooey in the centre.

Decorate with chocolate sprinkles. Allow to cool for 1 minute before eating.

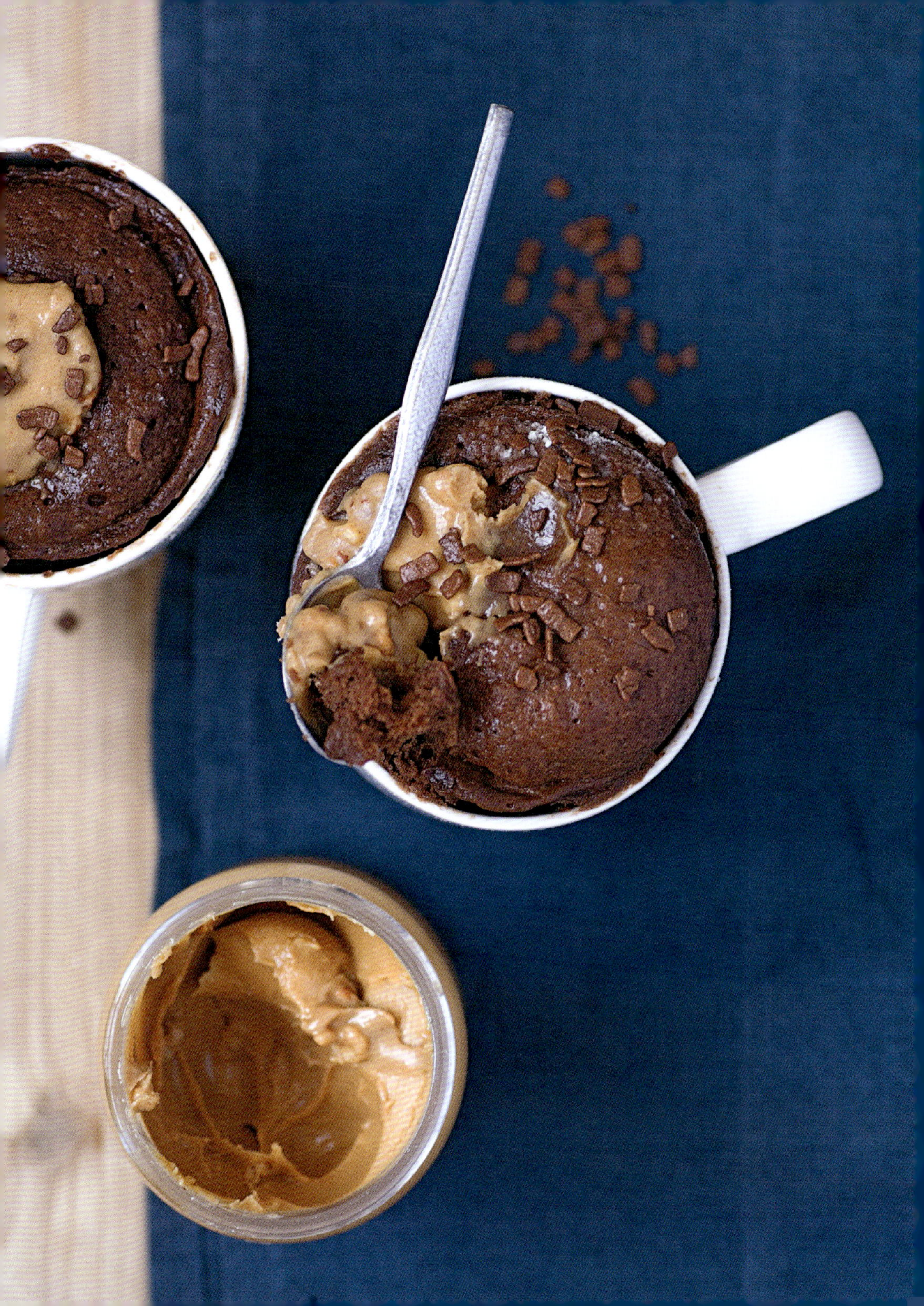

# Milk Chocolate &
# Salted Caramel

*This mug cake hits the target for ultimate pleasure – a rich, golden payload of sweet and salty caramel, delivered right into your mouth, and the mission can be accomplished in just 5 minutes!*

**SERVES 1**

**TAKES 5 minutes**

1 slice of butter 1cm (½in) thick (30g/1oz)
5 squares of milk chocolate (25g/1oz)
1 egg
2 tablespoons caster (superfine) sugar
4 tablespoons plain (all-purpose) flour
½ teaspoon baking powder

**Middle & Decoration**
1 large teaspoon salted caramel sauce
a pinch of chocolate sprinkles

In a mug, melt the butter with the chocolate in the microwave for 30–40 seconds.

Beat the mixture until smooth, then allow it to cool slightly. One by one, whisk in the egg, sugar, flour and baking powder. Cook in the microwave for 50 seconds. Spoon the caramel sauce into the middle and cook for a further 40 seconds, or until risen but still gooey in the centre.

Allow to cool for 1 minute. Decorate with chocolate sprinkles before eating.

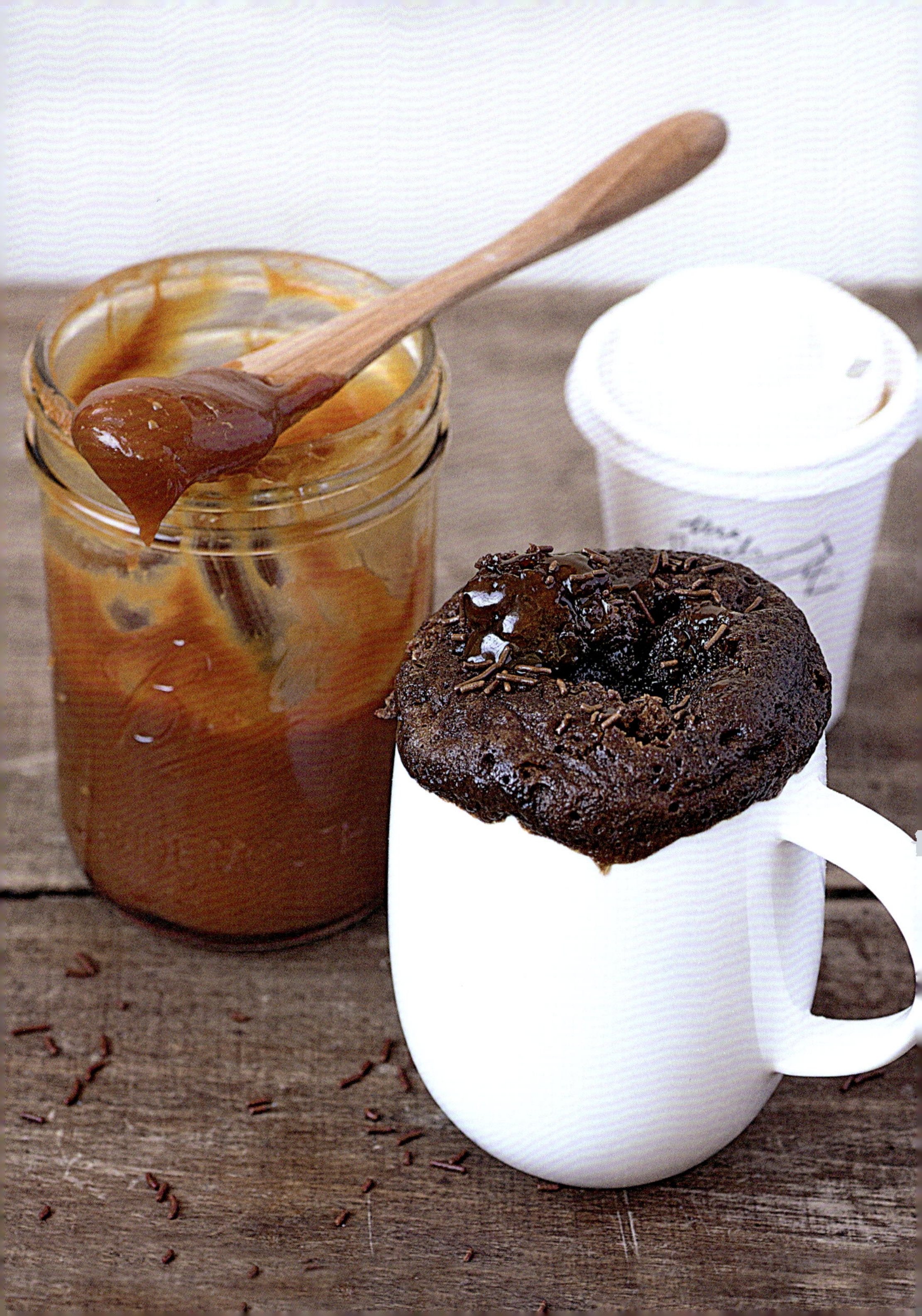

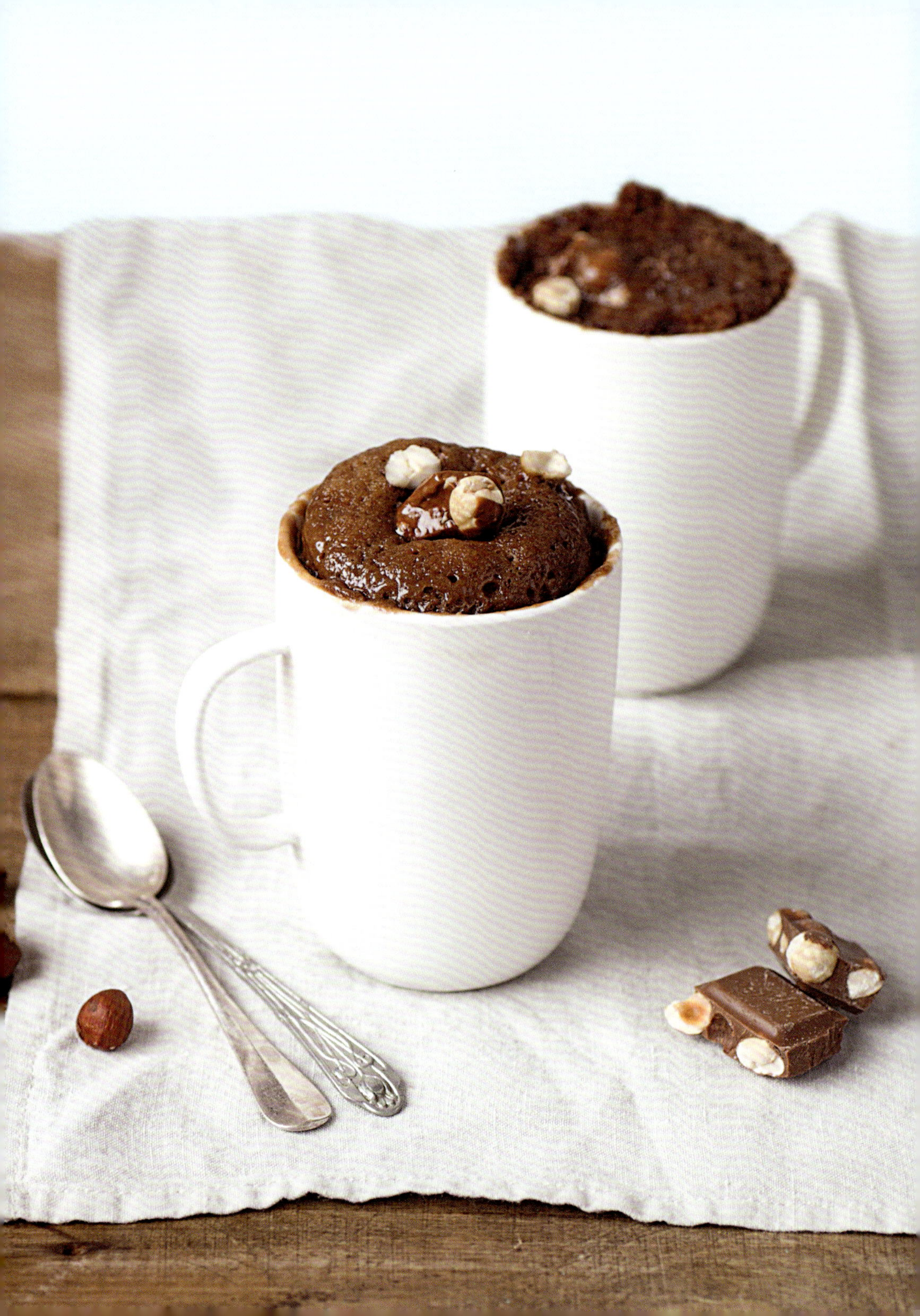

# Molten Chocolate &
# Hazelnut

*A riff on everyone's favourite nostalgic golden-foiled chocolate, breaking into the pleasure of a creamy chocolate hazelnut centre never gets tired. Even the ambassador would be impressed.*

**SERVES 1**

**TAKES 5 minutes**

1 slice of butter 1cm (½in) thick (30g/1oz)
7 squares of milk chocolate (35g/1¼oz)
1 egg
2 tablespoons caster (superfine) sugar
3 tablespoons plain (all-purpose) flour
2 tablespoons ground or chopped hazelnuts
½ teaspoon baking powder

**Middle & Decoration**
1 square of hazelnut chocolate (5g/¼oz)
a few crushed hazelnuts

In a mug, melt the butter with the chocolate in the microwave for 30–40 seconds.

Beat the mixture until smooth, then allow it to cool slightly. One by one, whisk in the egg, sugar, flour, ground hazelnuts and baking powder. Cook in the microwave for 50 seconds. Push the hazelnut chocolate square into the middle and cook for a further 40 seconds, or until risen but still gooey in the centre.

Allow to cool for 1 minute. Sprinkle with the crushed hazelnuts before eating.

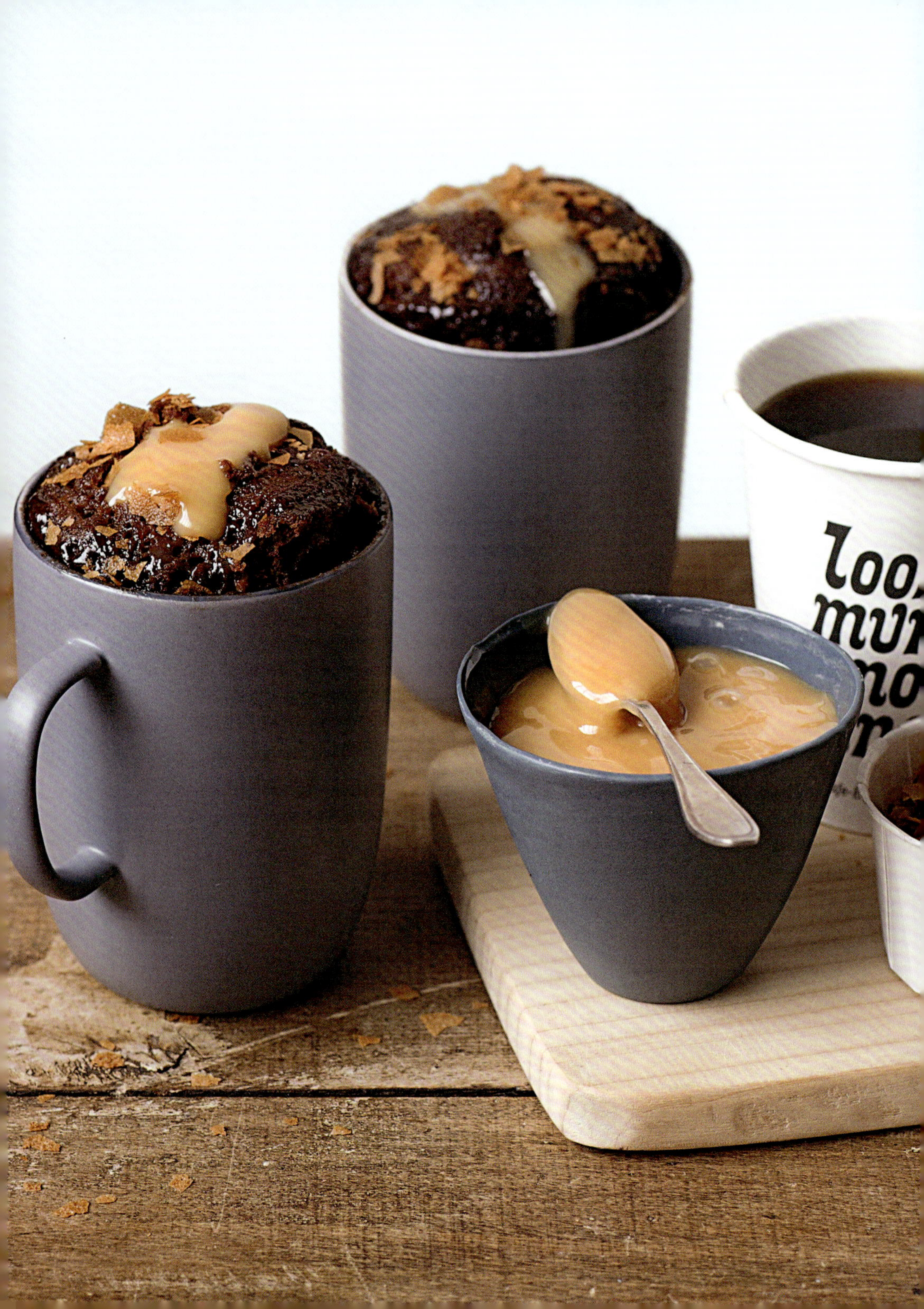

# Chocolate &
# Dulce de Leche

*You may have to look a little beyond your standard supermarket to get your hands on a jar of the classic Latin American spread dulce de leche, but it's well worth any effort. Use it to fill this decadent mug cake or, you know, just eat it out the jar with a spoon.*

**SERVES 1**

**TAKES 5 minutes**

1 slice of butter 1cm (½in) thick (30g/1oz)
6 squares of milk or dark chocolate (30g/1oz)
1 egg
2 tablespoons soft brown sugar
5 tablespoons plain (all-purpose) flour
½ teaspoon baking powder
2 wafer curls (rolled wafers), crumbled
2 tablespoons dulce de leche (caramelized milk)

In a mug, melt the butter with the chocolate in the microwave for 30–40 seconds.

Beat the mixture until smooth, then allow it to cool slightly. One by one, whisk in the egg, sugar, flour and baking powder. Sprinkle some crumbled wafer curls on top and reserve a little for decorating. Cook in the microwave for 50 seconds. Add the dulce de leche to the middle and cook for a further 40 seconds, or until risen but still gooey in the centre.

Allow to cool for 1 minute. Sprinkle the reserved wafer curls on top before eating.

# White Chocolate & Raspberry Jam

Pretty much all forms of raspberry jam will be delicious as the gooey middle of this sweet and simple mug cake, but it can definitely be elevated by using a fancy conserve with a high-fruit content in place of a standard seedless jelly.

**SERVES 1**

**TAKES 5 minutes**

1 slice of butter 1cm (½in) thick (30g/1oz)
8 squares of white chocolate (40g/1½oz)
1 egg
2 tablespoons caster (superfine) sugar
5 tablespoons plain (all-purpose) flour
½ teaspoon baking powder

**Middle & Decoration**
1 tablespoon raspberry jam (jelly)
½ teaspoon icing (confectioners') sugar

In a mug, melt the butter with the chocolate in the microwave for 30–40 seconds.

Beat the mixture until smooth, then allow it to cool slightly. One by one, whisk in the egg, sugar, flour and baking powder. Cook in the microwave for 40 seconds. Add the jam to the middle and cook for a further 50 seconds, or until risen.

Allow to cool for 1 minute and lightly dust with the icing sugar.

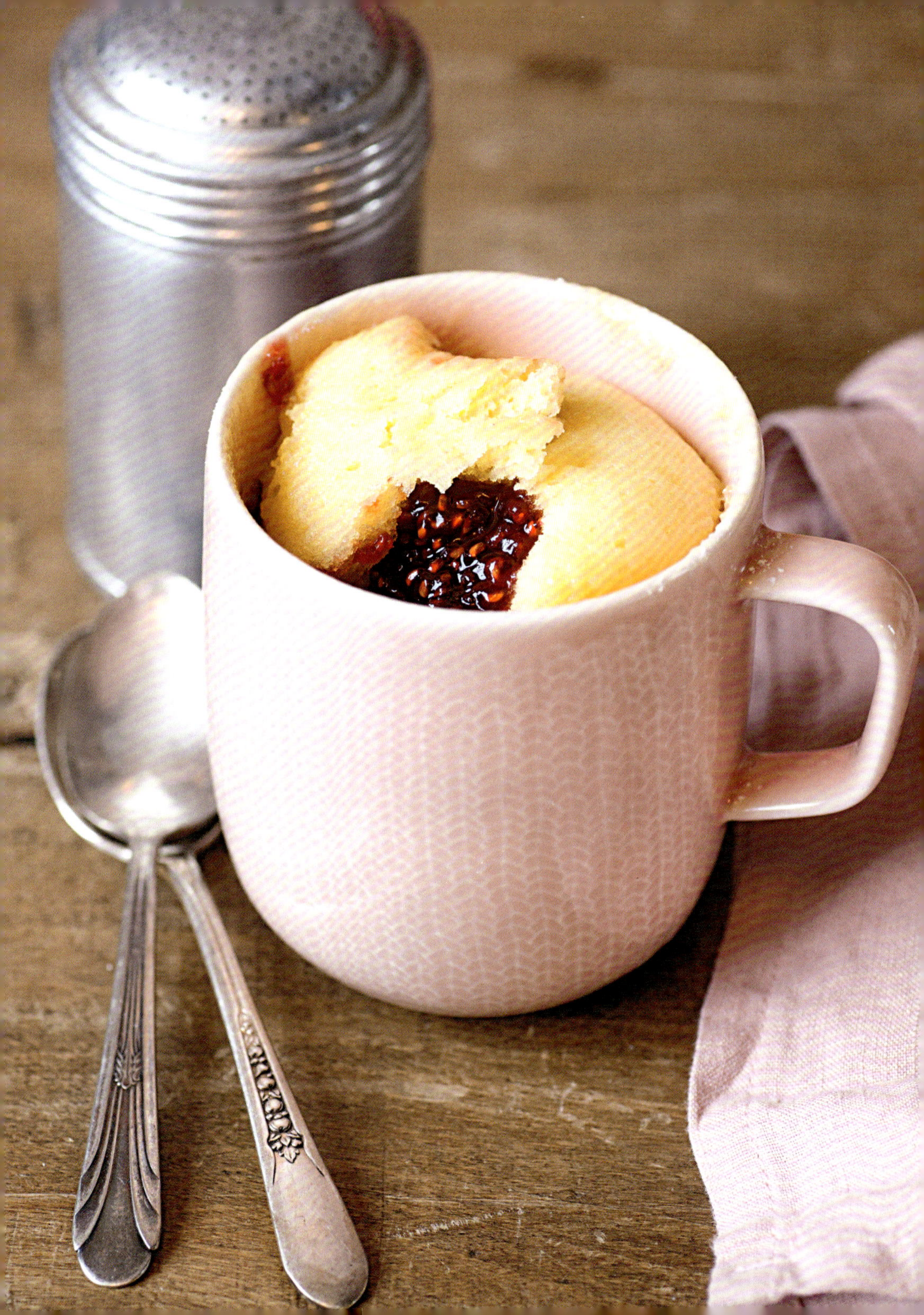

# Pistachio & White Chocolate

*In a world of beige and brown cakes, this lovely green mug cake stands out not just for its colour but also for its deliciousness. This is thanks to the pistachio paste – a creamy green nut butter which provides a perfect nutty canvas for the white chocolate centre and makes it pretty as a picture.*

**SERVES 1**

**TAKES 5 minutes**

1 slice of butter 5mm (¼in) thick (15g/½oz)
5 squares of white chocolate (25g/1oz)
1 egg
1 tablespoon caster (superfine) sugar
½ teaspoon pistachio paste
5 tablespoons plain (all-purpose) flour
½ teaspoon baking powder

### Middle & Decoration
1 square of white chocolate (5g/¼oz)
1 teaspoon melted white chocolate
a few crushed pistachios

In a mug, melt the butter with the chocolate in the microwave for 30–40 seconds.

Beat the mixture until smooth, then allow it to cool slightly. One by one, whisk in the egg, sugar, pistachio paste, flour and baking powder. Cook in the microwave for 50 seconds. Push the square of white chocolate into the middle and cook for a further 40 seconds until risen but still gooey in the centre.

Allow to cool for 1 minute. Dollop the melted white chocolate on top and sprinkle with the crushed pistachios before eating.

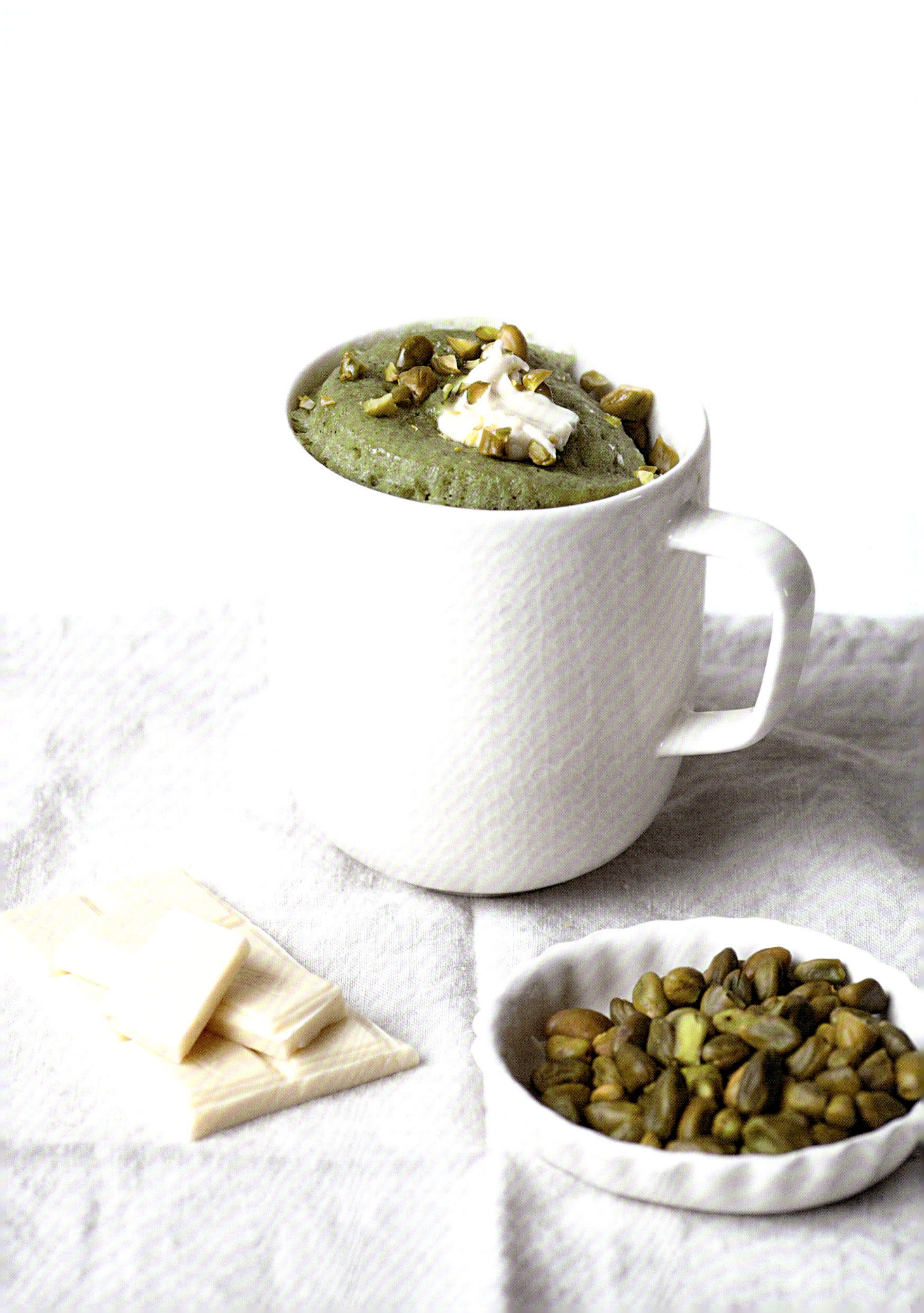

# Celebrations & Holidays

# Big
# Mug Cake

*Sharing is caring, so grab a second spoon and dig into the BIG treat together. And don't worry; it does make a much bigger cake than the others in the book, so no one will feel short-changed. The question is – do you have a mug that's up to the challenge? (Hint: you can just use a smallish microwave-safe bowl if not!)*

**SERVES 2 (or 1 very hungry person!)**

**TAKES 6 minutes**

1 slice of butter 2cm (¾in) thick (60g/2oz) or 60g (2oz) almond butter
12 squares of dark or milk chocolate (60g/2oz)
2 eggs
4 tablespoons soft brown sugar
1 tablespoon vanilla sugar or 1 teaspoon vanilla extract
1 drop of almond extract
8 tablespoons plain (all-purpose) flour
2 tablespoons ground almonds
1 teaspoon baking powder
a few flaked (slivered) almonds, to decorate

In a large 500ml (17fl oz) mug, melt the butter with the chocolate in the microwave for 50 seconds.

Beat the mixture until smooth, then allow it to cool slightly. One by one, whisk in the eggs, sugar, vanilla sugar, almond extract, flour, ground almonds and baking powder. Cook in the microwave for 2 minutes 30 seconds, or until risen and slightly springy to the touch.

Allow to cool for 1 minute. Decorate with flaked almonds and dig in.

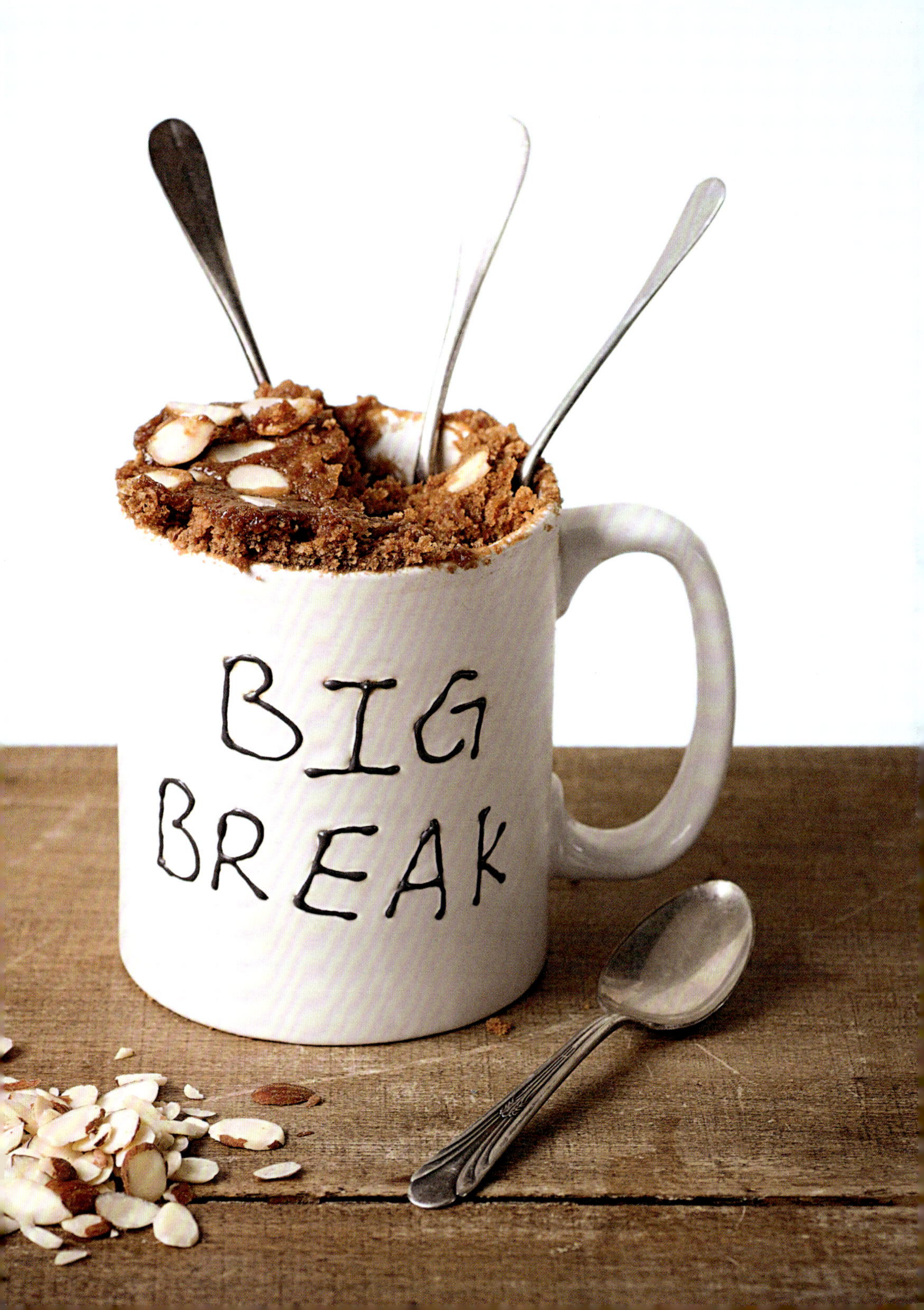
BIG
BREAK

# Birthday Sprinkles Cake

*Bring the party with this cute little personal birthday treat, freckled with colourful Funfetti sprinkles. With a swirl of buttercream and a teeny candle, filling your colleague's favourite mug with this tasty treat is sure to bring a smile to the face of anyone stuck in the office on their special day.*

**SERVES 1**

**TAKES 5 minutes**

2 tablespoons sunflower oil
3 tablespoons caster (superfine) sugar
1 egg
½ teaspoon vanilla extract
4 tablespoons self-raising (self-rising) flour
1 tablespoon sprinkles (such as Funfetti), plus extra to decorate
2 tablespoons ready-made buttercream icing, to decorate

In a mug, mix together the oil, sugar, egg and vanilla using a fork until smooth. Add the flour and mix until just smooth. Stir in the sprinkles.

Microwave for 1 minute 30 seconds, or until risen and springy to the touch. Set aside to cool for 10 minutes.

Once cool, either dollop or pipe on the buttercream icing. Scatter over a few more sprinkles and dig in.

*Tip: To make your own buttercream, beat 1 tablespoon softened salted butter with 4 tablespoons icing (confectioner's) sugar, a few drops of vanilla extract, ½ teaspoon milk of your choice, and a couple of drops of food colouring of your choice.*

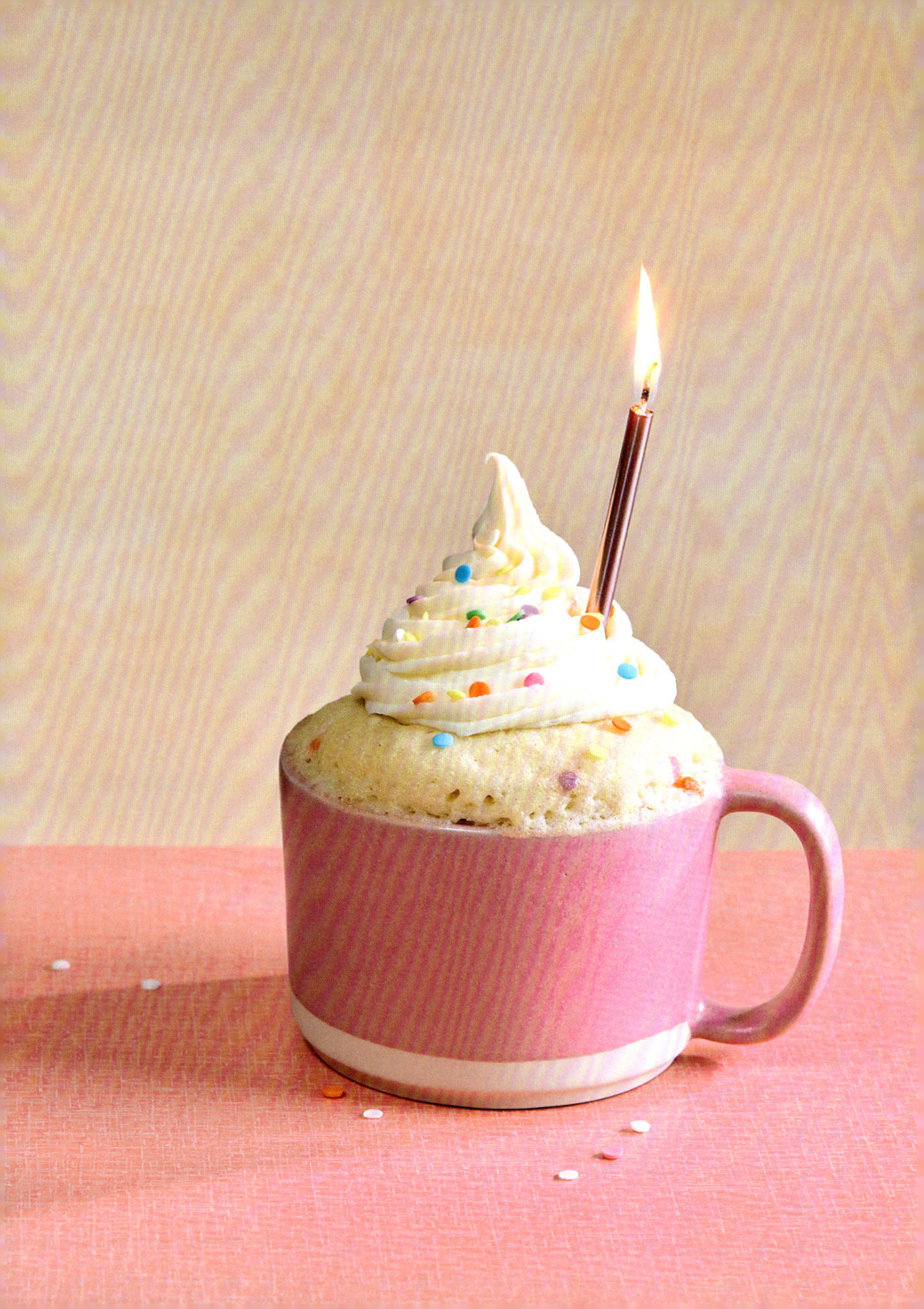

# Festive
# Gingerbread

*Sweetly spiced with the flavours of Christmas, and with the pleasing crunch of gingerbread pieces, this is a cosy hug in a mug. The festive decoration is optional here – this really is delicious with any extra adornment.*

**SERVES 1**

**TAKES 5 minutes**

2 tablespoons sunflower oil
3 tablespoons dark muscovado sugar
1 egg
1 tablespoon golden (light corn) syrup
1 teaspoon ground ginger
½ teaspoon mixed spice
4 tablespoons self-raising (self-rising) flour
2–3 mini gingerbread people or ½ large gingerbread person, broken into small pieces

**Decoration**
1 tablespoon icing (confectioner's) sugar
a few small sweets (such as Jelly Tots)

In a mug, mix together the oil, sugar, egg and syrup using a fork until smooth. Add the ginger, mixed spice and flour, and mix until just smooth. Gently stir the pieces of gingerbread into the top half of the batter.

Microwave for 1 minute 30 seconds, or until risen and springy to the touch. Set aside to cool for about 10 minutes.

To make the icing, mix the icing sugar with ½ teaspoon of water in a small bowl. Drizzle it over the cake, top with a few small sweets, then dig in and enjoy.

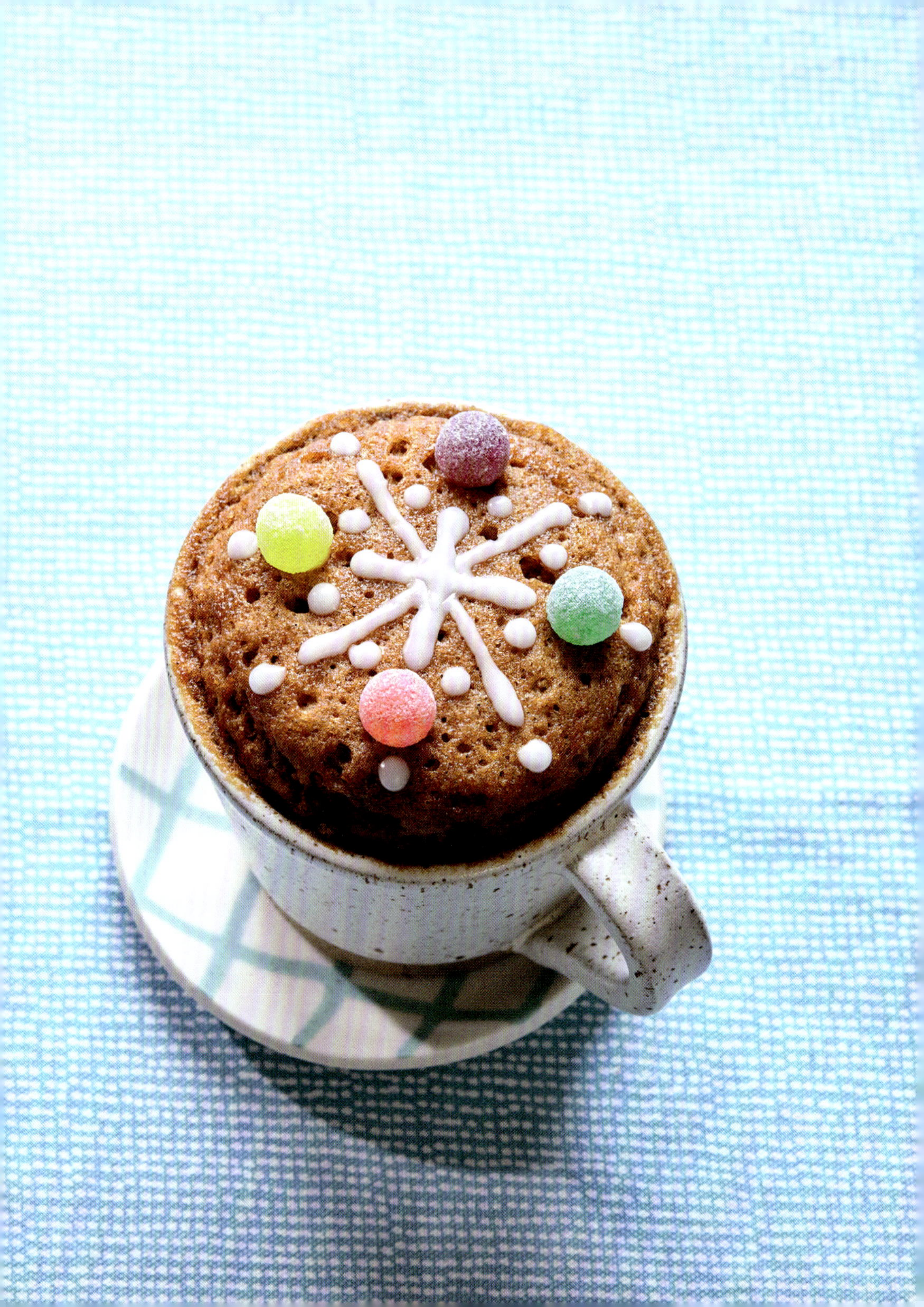

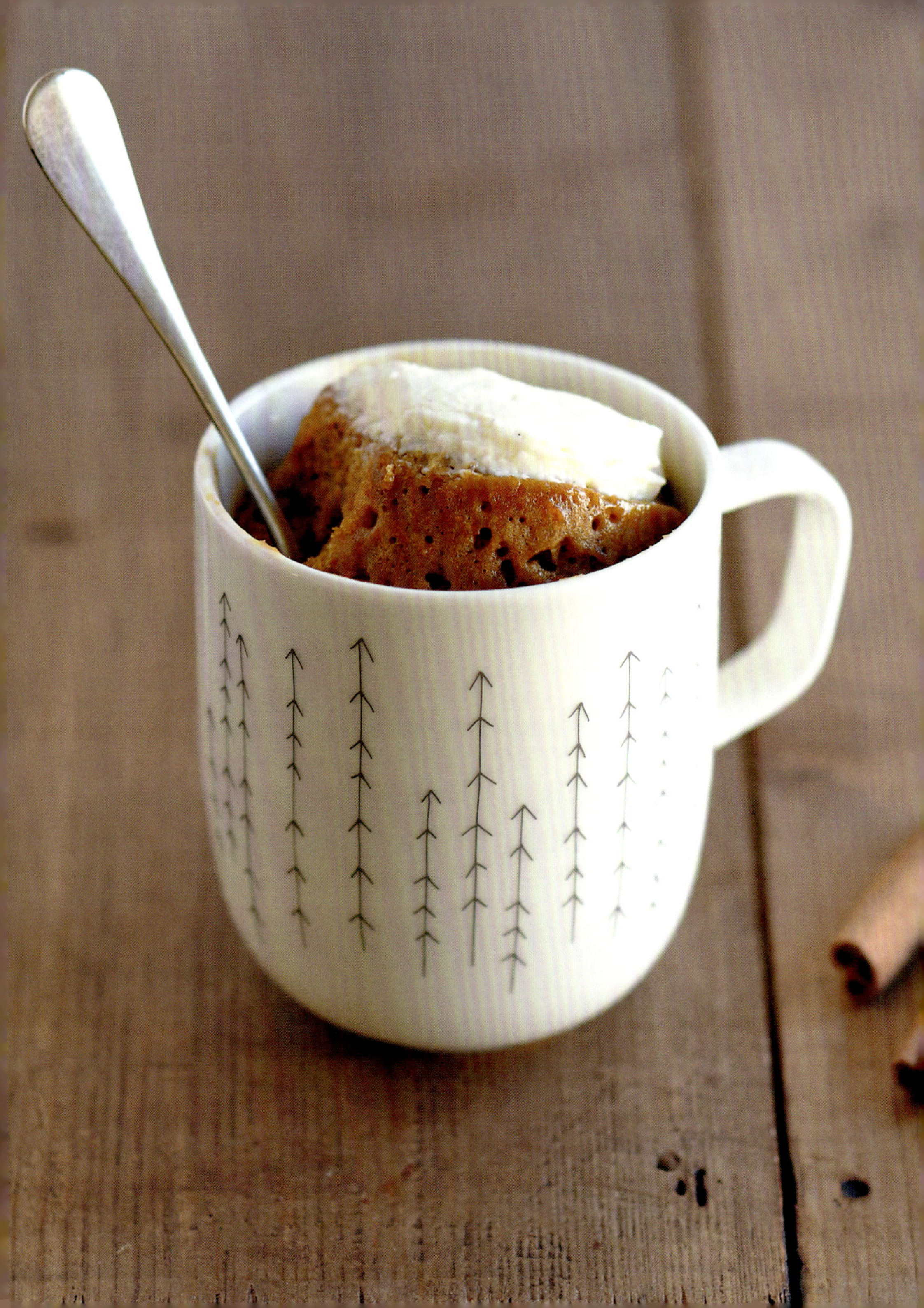

# Spiced Carrot Cake

*If you don't have the energy to bake a whole cake, squeeze all the goodness of a wholesome carrot cake into one single-serve mug, and top with its signature velvety cream cheese frosting.*

**SERVES 1**

**TAKES 5 minutes**

1 egg
4 tablespoons soft brown sugar
½ teaspoon vanilla sugar
2½ tablespoons sunflower oil
4 tablespoons grated organic carrots
6 tablespoons plain (all-purpose) flour
½ teaspoon baking powder
a pinch of cinnamon

### Cream Cheese Topping

3 tablespoons cream cheese
1 slice of butter 3mm (⅛in) thick (8g/⅓oz)
1 tablespoons icing (confectioners') sugar
½ teaspoon lemon zest

In a mug, beat in one by one the egg, brown sugar, vanilla sugar, sunflower oil, grated carrots, flour, baking powder and cinnamon.

Cook in the microwave for 1 minute 40 seconds, or until risen and springy to the touch.

To make the cream cheese topping, mix the cream cheese, soft butter, icing sugar and lemon zest in a bowl. Stir until nice and smooth, then top the mug cake with a thin layer of the icing.

# Hot Chocolate Cake with **Marshmallows**

*Cake-ify everyone's favourite bedtime beverage by filling your mug with a hot chocolate sponge, finished with melting marshmallows. It delivers all the simple pleasure of a mug of cocoa, and doesn't take much longer to prepare than its namesake drink.*

**SERVES 1**

**TAKES 6 minutes**

2 tablespoons sunflower oil
2 tablespoons caster (superfine) sugar
1 egg
1 teaspoon vanilla extract
3 tablespoons self-raising (self-rising) flour
1 tablespoon hot chocolate powder
1 heaped tablespoon mini or 3 regular marshmallows

In a mug, mix together the oil, sugar, egg and vanilla using a fork until smooth. Add the flour and hot chocolate powder, and mix until just smooth.

Microwave for 1 minute 30 seconds, or until risen and springy to the touch.

Scatter over the marshmallows, then microwave for a further 15 seconds. Allow a couple of minutes for the marshmallows to cool, then dig in and enjoy.

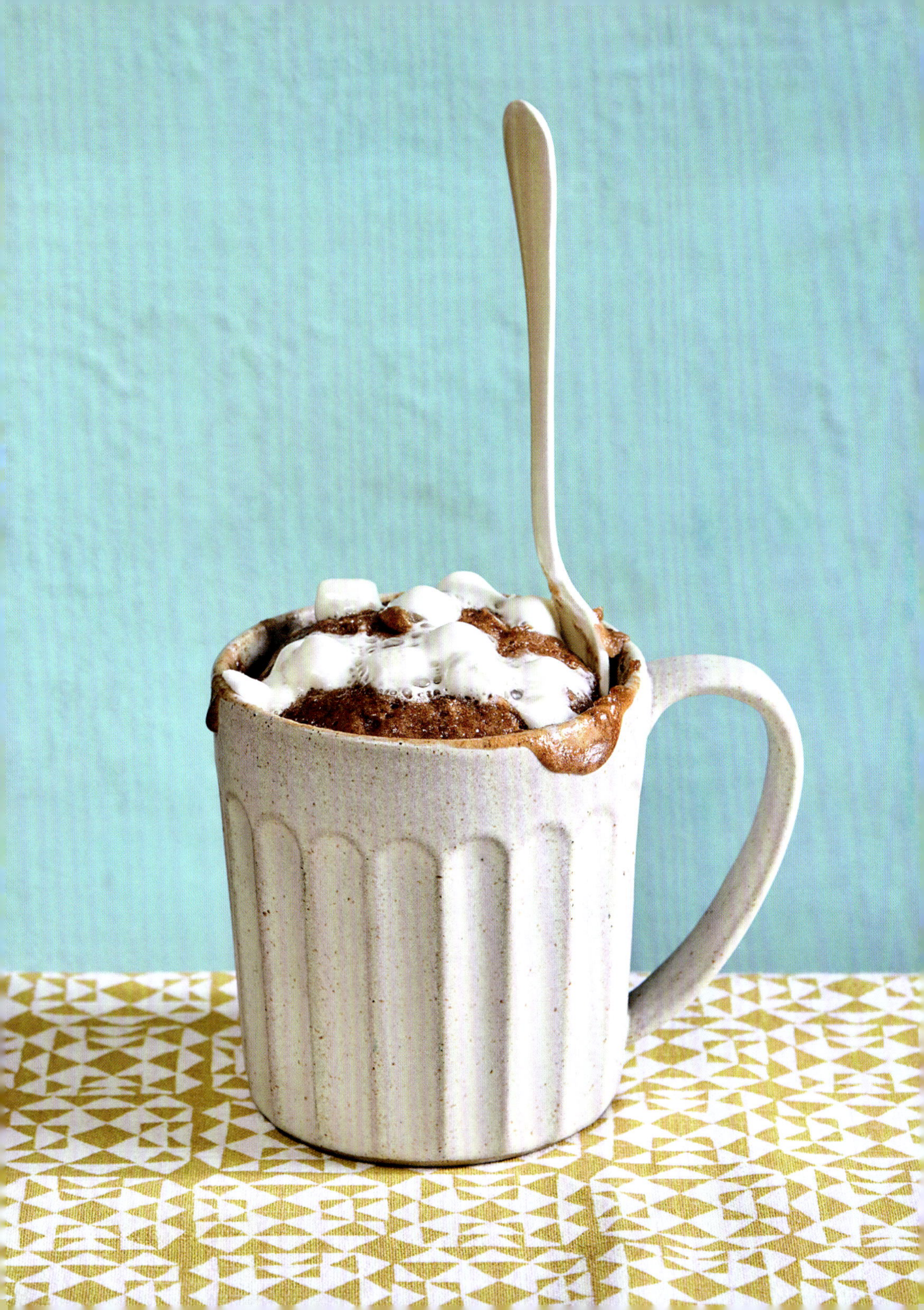

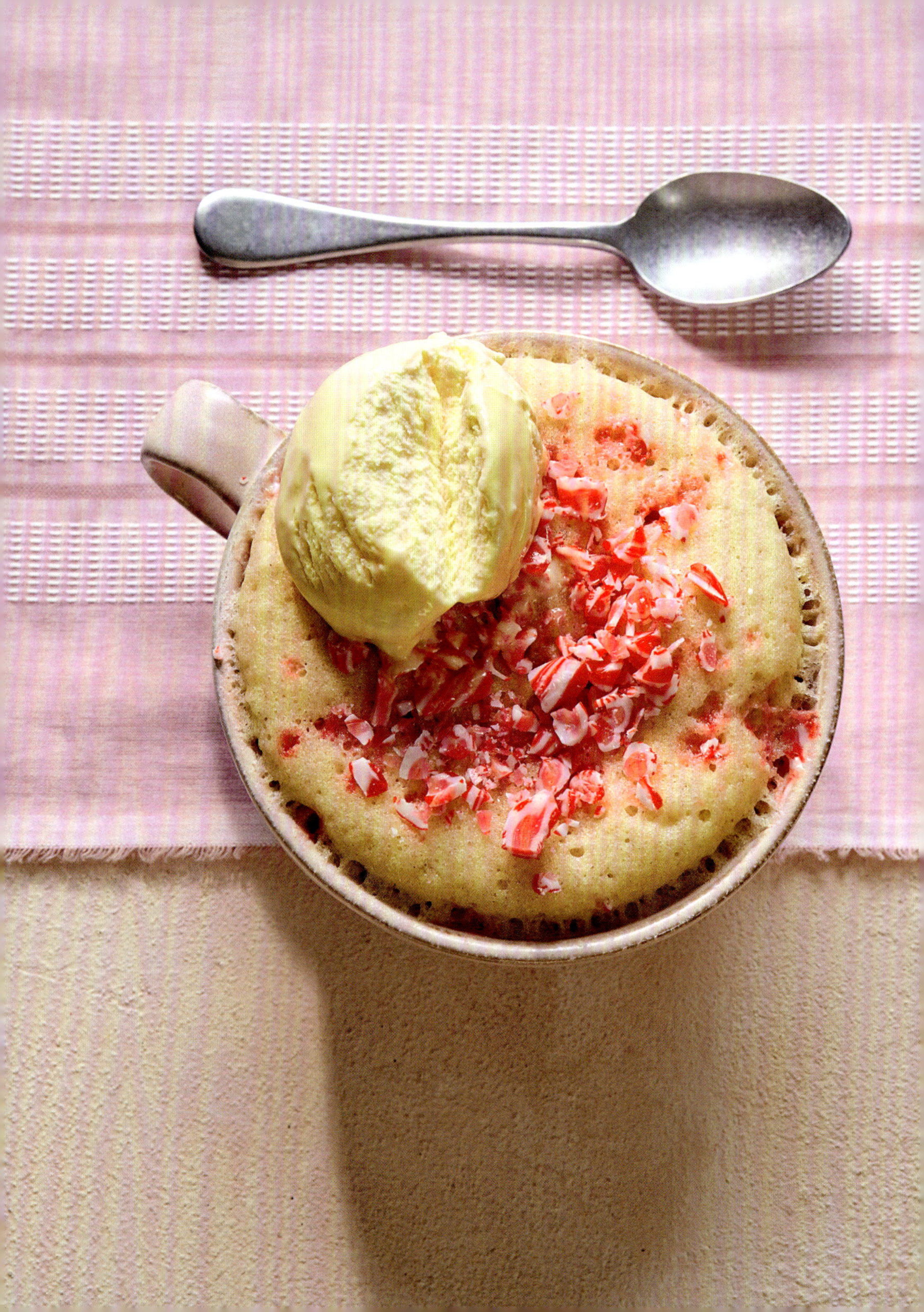

# White Chocolate Cake with a
# Candy Cane Crunch

*This is the perfect mug cake for beating those January blues. Once the Christmas tree comes down, repurpose those leftover candy canes by crushing them up and baking into this winter-warmer treat.*

**SERVES 1**

**TAKES 5 minutes**

1 candy cane
2 tablespoons sunflower oil
3 tablespoons caster (superfine) sugar
1 egg
½ teaspoon vanilla extract
4 tablespoons self-raising (self-rising) flour
1 tablespoon white chocolate chips or chunks
vanilla ice cream, to serve

Before you begin, smash up the candy cane in a small bowl using the bottom of a rolling pin, then set aside.

In a mug, mix together the oil, sugar, egg and vanilla using a fork until smooth. Add the flour and mix until just smooth. Gently fold most of the crushed candy cane and all the white chocolate chips into the top half of the batter.

Microwave for 1 minute 40 seconds, or until risen and springy to the touch. Sprinkle with the remaining crushed candy cane and enjoy with a scoop of vanilla ice cream.

# Easter
# Mini Egg Cake

*You really can't escape mini sugar-coated chocolate eggs in the run up to Easter – they are everywhere. If you want to get creative about how to consume your annual quota, try them in this super-quick and easy mug cake. They not only add a lovely chocolate hit, but make for a charming multi-coloured sponge, too.*

**SERVES 1**

**TAKES 5 minutes**

2 tablespoons sunflower oil
3 tablespoons golden caster (superfine) sugar
1 egg
½ teaspoon vanilla extract
4 tablespoons self-raising (self-rising) flour
4 candy-covered chocolate mini eggs, roughly chopped into quarters, plus 3 to decorate

In a mug, mix together the oil, sugar, egg and vanilla using a fork until smooth. Add the flour and mix until just smooth. Gently fold the chocolate egg pieces into the top half of the batter.

Microwave for 1 minute 30 seconds, or until risen and springy to the touch.

Finish by sprinkling over more chopped mini eggs and enjoy.

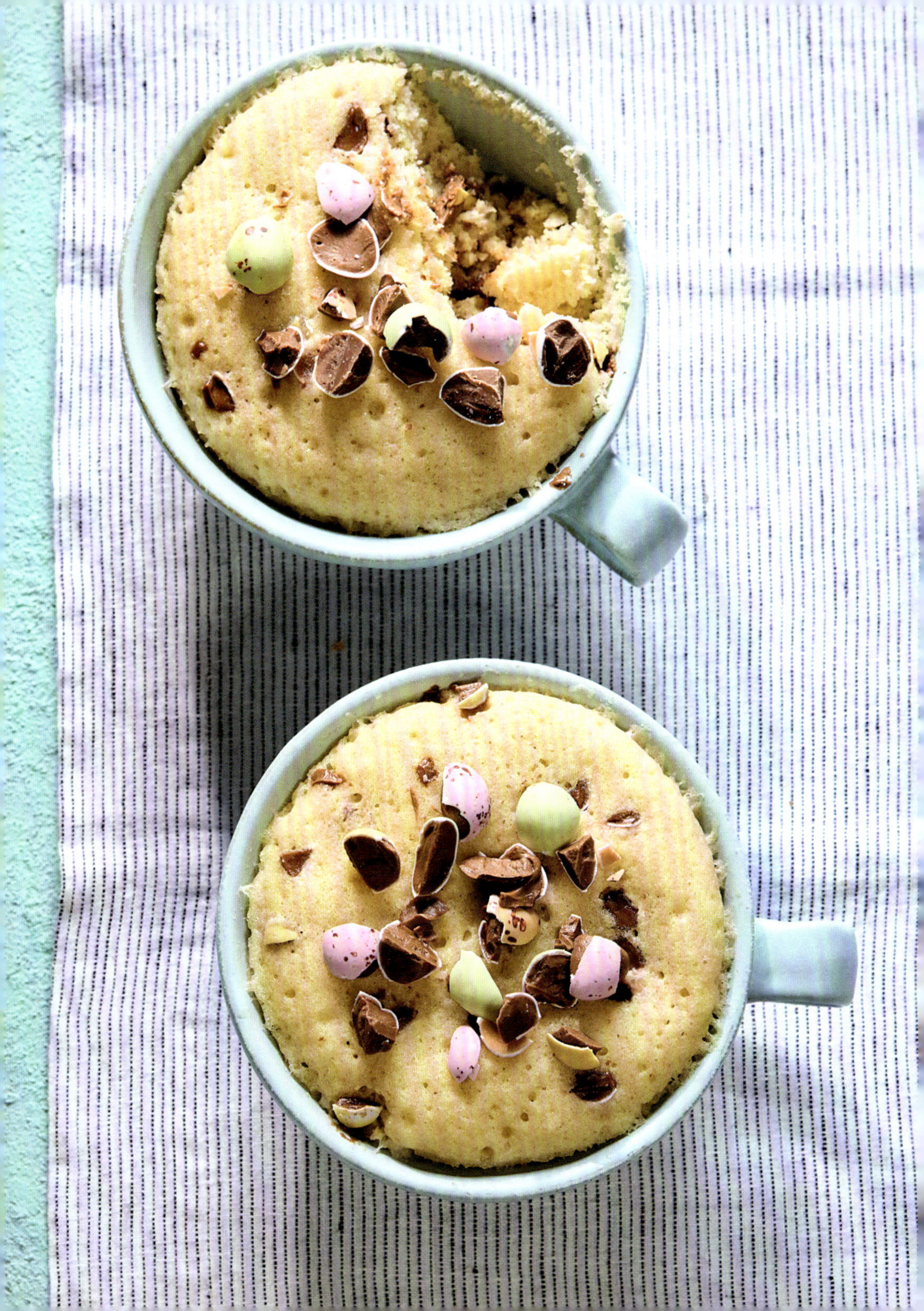

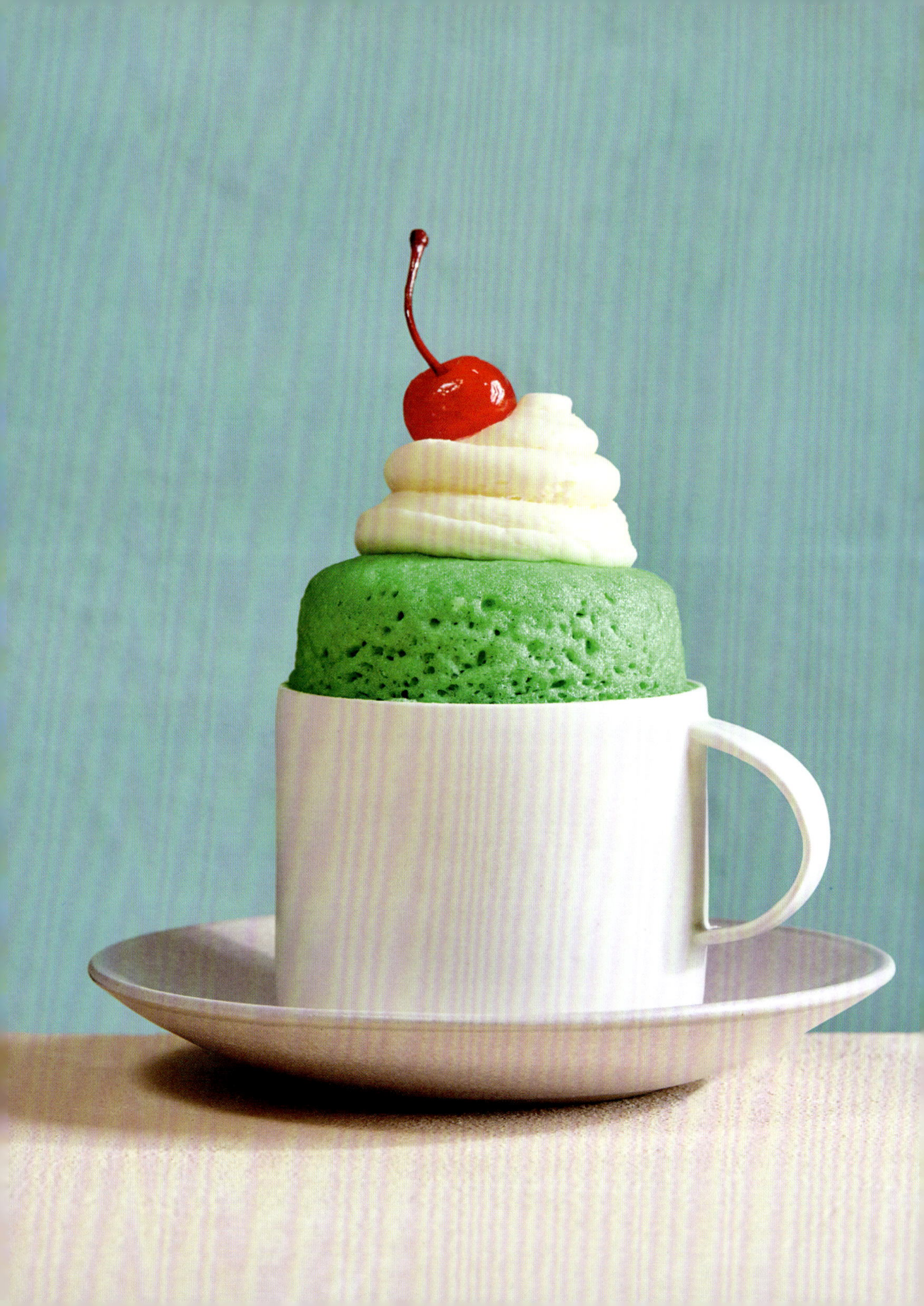

# Peppermint
# Shamrock Cake

*Celebrate St Paddy's Day with this fun minty mug cake that's greener than a leprechaun's trousers. It may not come with a pot of gold, but it does come with a cherry on top!*

**SERVES 1**

**TAKES 4 minutes**

2 tablespoons sunflower oil
3 tablespoons caster (superfine) sugar
1 egg
½ teaspoon vanilla extract
¼ teaspoon peppermint extract
a few drops of green food colouring
4 tablespoons self-raising (self-rising) flour

**Decoration**
3 tablespoons ready-made buttercream icing
a maraschino cherry

In a mug, mix together the oil, sugar, egg, vanilla and peppermint extracts and the green food colouring using a fork until smooth. Add the flour and mix until just smooth.

Microwave for 1 minute 30 seconds, or until risen and springy to the touch. Leave to cool for about 10 minutes, then dollop or pipe on the buttercream icing. Top with the cherry, then dig in and enjoy.

Tip: To make your own buttercream, beat 1 tablespoon softened salted butter with 4 tablespoons icing (confectioner's) sugar, a few drops of vanilla extract, ½ teaspoon milk of your choice, and a couple of drops of food colouring of your choice.

# Irish Cream
# Cheesecake

*A golden and buttery biscuit base sits underneath a thick layer of Irish-cream cheese topping in this decadent mug (cheese)cake. Don't forget to factor in the chilling time – this one requires a little more patience. It's not as immediately gratifying as most of the other recipes, but boy is it worth the wait.*

**SERVES 1**

**TAKES 6 minutes**

- 1 teaspoon butter, melted, plus extra for greasing
- 1 digestive biscuit (graham cracker), crushed
- 2 tablespoons icing (confectioner's) sugar
- 2 tablespoons sour cream
- 2 tablespoons cream cheese
- 1 egg
- 2 tablespoons Irish cream liqueur (such as Baileys)
- unsweetened cocoa powder, to decorate

Grease the inside of a mug with a little butter.

In the greased mug, mix together the crushed biscuit and melted butter, then press down to make a base.

In a small bowl, mix the icing sugar with the sour cream, cream cheese, egg and Irish cream liqueur using a hand whisk. Pour the mixture into your mug.

Microwave for 50 seconds. Leave to rest for 5 seconds, then microwave for a further 20 seconds. Leave to rest for 5 seconds, then microwave for another 20 seconds. Chill the cheesecake in the refrigerator for at least 45 minutes. Dust with cocoa and dig in.

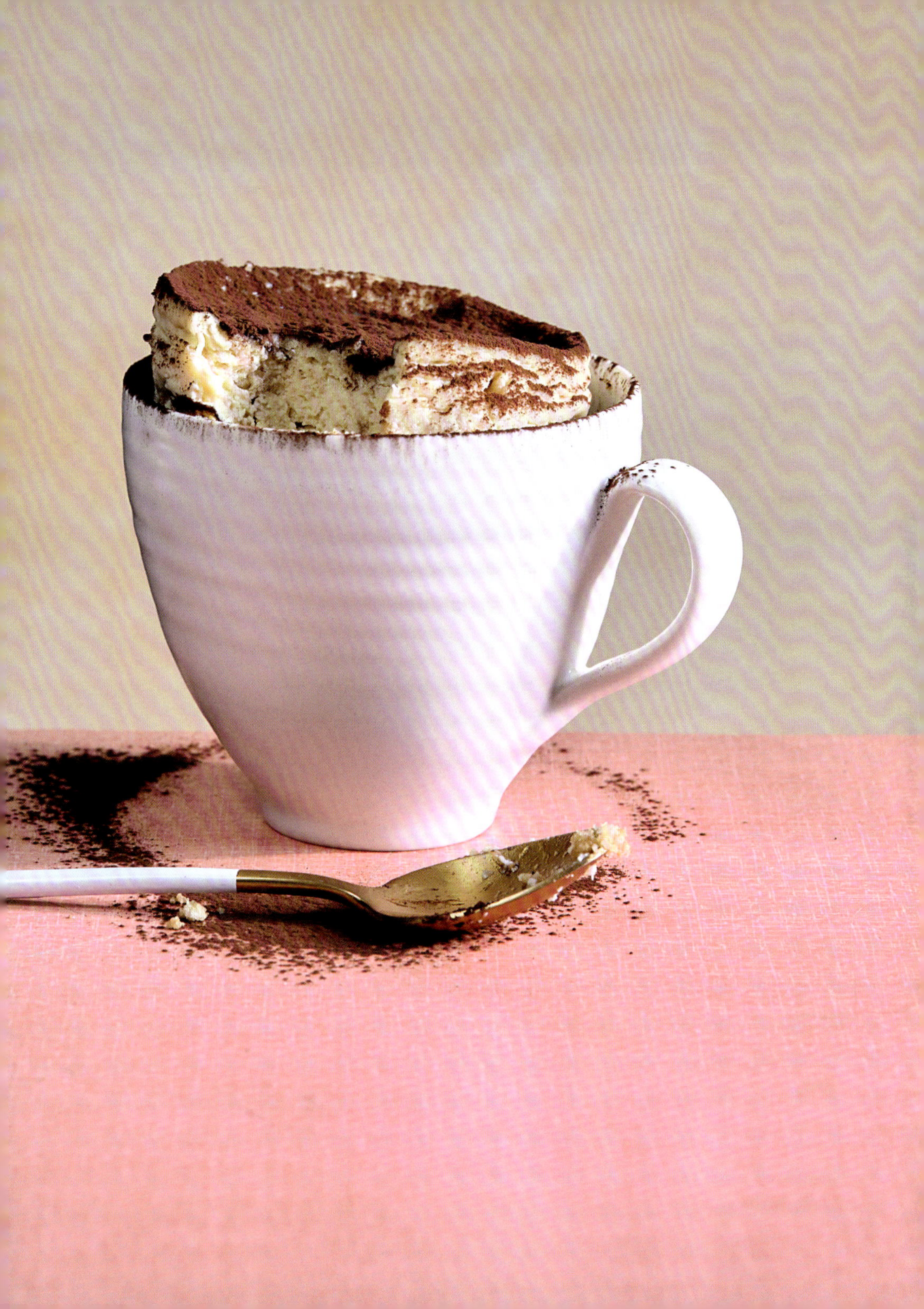

## Classic
# Red Velvet Cake

*The queen of cakes, some would say, the red velvet cake is known for its great balance of delicate cocoa flavour with a slightly tangy undertone – provided here by buttermilk. It's not overly sweet, but this mug version results in a truly light and lofty sponge which is the perfect crimson base for the luxurious cream cheese frosting.*

**SERVES 1**

**TAKES 5 minutes, plus cooling**

- 3 tablespoons soft brown sugar
- 3 tablespoons plain (all-purpose) flour
- 1 teaspoon unsweetened cocoa powder
- ¼ teaspoon bicarbonate of soda (baking soda)
- ¼ teaspoon baking powder
- 1 egg
- ½ teaspoon vanilla extract
- 1 tablespoon buttermilk
- 2 tablespoons sunflower oil
- ½ teaspoon red food colouring gel
- 3 tbsp ready-made cream cheese style icing

In a mug, mix together the brown sugar, flour, cocoa, bicarbonate of soda and baking powder using a fork. Add the egg, vanilla, buttermilk, oil and food colouring and mix until just smooth.

Microwave for 1 minute 30 seconds, or until risen and springy to the touch. Set aside to cool for about 10 minutes.

After about 10 minutes, either dollop or pipe on the cream cheese icing and dig in.

*Tip: You could also top this with the cream cheese topping on page 157, just omit the lemon zest.*

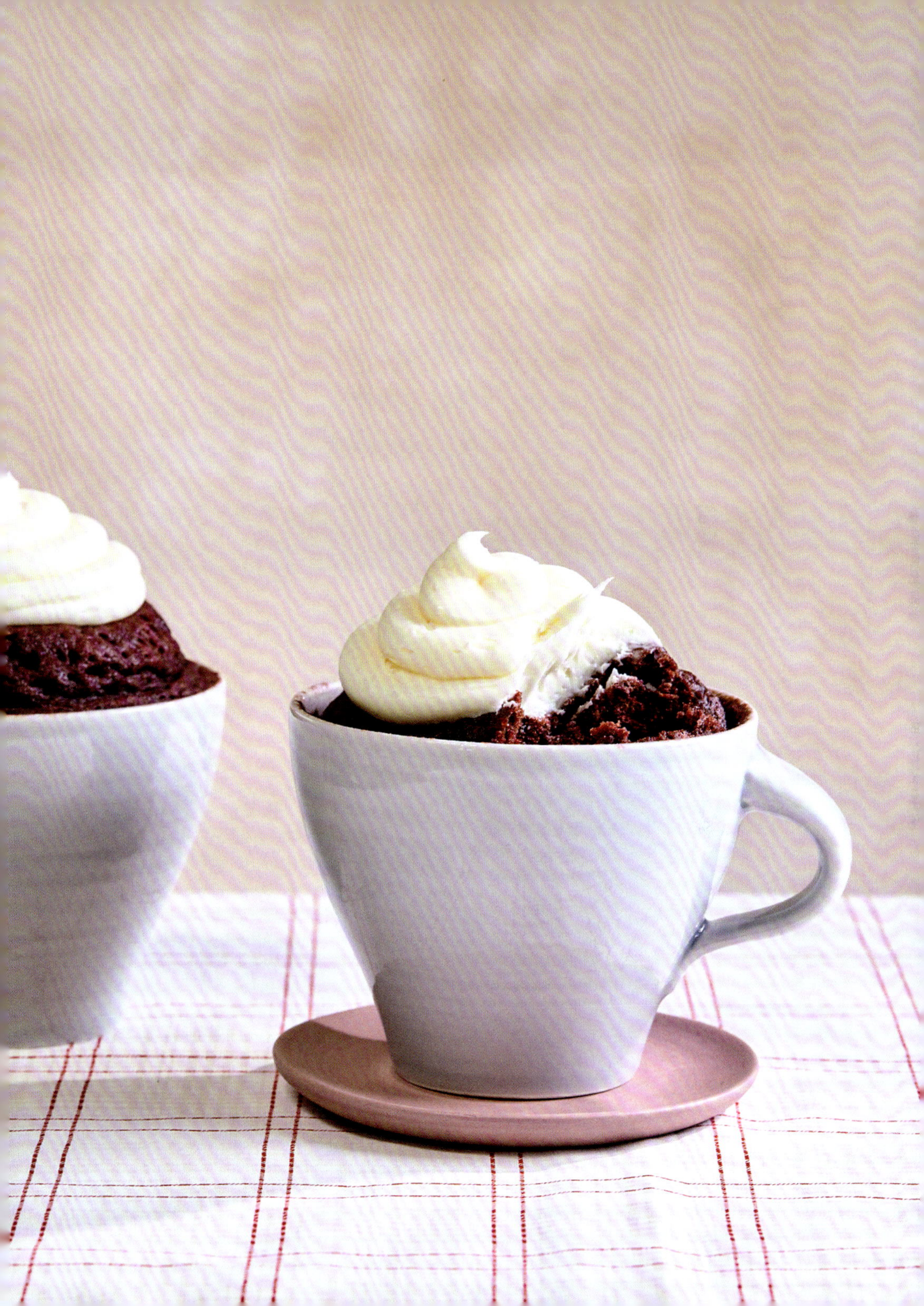

# Index

## A

after-dinner mint-choc mug cake 65
almonds
    almond mug cake with frangipane & custard 70
    big mug cake 150
    chocolate & amaretto cake 46
    classic apple crumble 108
    hazelnut, almond & pistachio cake 73
    mug cookie with lemon & poppy seeds 17
    orange zest & almond cake 39
    raspberry & almond Bakewell 85
    white chocolate, almond & pear cake 20
amaretto
    almond mug cake with frangipane & custard 70
    chocolate & amaretto cake 46
apples
    apple & blackberry crumble 117
    apple & caramel crumble 113
    apple & pecan crumble 114
    apple, chocolate & nut crumble 118
    apple, white chocolate & raspberry crumble 120
    banana, apple & peanut crumble 111
    classic apple crumble 108
    pineapple, apple & Lotus biscuit crumble 126
    red berry, apple & shortbread mug crumble 27

apricot jam: hazelnut, almond & pistachio cake 73

## B

Baileys: Irish cream cheesecake 166
Bakewell, raspberry & almond 85
bananas
    banana, apple & peanut crumble 111
    chocolate mug cake with banana & coconut 29
berries: red berry, apple & shortbread mug crumble 27
big mug cake 150
birthday sprinkles cake 152
Biscoff spread: dark chocolate cake with a Biscoff middle 96
Black Forest cake, dark chocolate 33
blackberries: apple & blackberry crumble 117
blueberries
    blueberry-ricotta swirl cake 24
    lemon curd & blueberry crumble 125
butter caramels: salted butter caramel cake 93
buttermilk: classic red velvet cake 168

## C

candy cane crunch, white chocolate cake with 161
caramel
    apple & caramel crumble 113
    caramel & chocolate truffle cake 90

chocolate & dulce de leche 143
chocolate, caramel & coffee cake 95
dark chocolate cake with a Biscoff middle 96
marble mug cake with coffee & chocolate 103
milk chocolate & salted caramel 138
mocha mug cake with coffee cream 98
pick-me-up espresso martini 104
salted butter caramel cake 93
whipped cream cappuccino cake 100
carrot cake, spiced 157
cheesecake, Irish cream 166
cherries: dark chocolate Black Forest cake 33
cherries, glacé
    right-side-up pineapple cake 34
    toasted coconut & cherry cake 82
chocolate
    after-dinner mint-choc mug cake 65
    apple, chocolate & nut crumble 118
    apple, white chocolate & raspberry crumble 120
    big mug cake 150
    caramel & chocolate truffle cake 90
    chocolate & amaretto cake 46
    chocolate & dulce de leche 143
    chocolate & hazelnut marble cake 45

chocolate & hazelnut praline cake 78
chocolate, caramel & coffee cake 95
chocolate mug cake with banana & coconut 29
chocolate mug cake with double-choc chips 62
chocolate mug cake with orange & cinnamon 59
classic cocoa cake 42
classic mug cake with milk chocolate 48
classic red velvet cake 168
coconut mug cake with chocolate sauce 68
dark chocolate & cream cheese swirl 60
dark chocolate & peanut butter 136
dark chocolate & pear crumble 123
dark chocolate Black Forest cake 33
dark chocolate cake with a Biscoff middle 96
dark chocolate fondant 135
Easter Mini Egg cake 162
hot chocolate cake with marshmallows 158
marble mug cake with coffee & chocolate 103
marshmallow & chocolate rocky road 86
milk chocolate & Oreo cake 52
milk chocolate & salted caramel 138
milk chocolate fondant 130
mocha mug cake with coffee cream 98
molten chocolate & hazelnut 141
mug cookie with chocolate chips 57

mug cookie with M&M's 54
pick-me-up espresso martini 104
pistachio & white chocolate 146
triple chocolate & vanilla cake 51
whipped cream cappuccino cake 100
white chocolate, almond & pear cake 20
white chocolate & cranberry mug cookie 19
white chocolate & raspberry jam 144
white chocolate & raspberry matcha mug cake 30
white chocolate cake with candy cane crunch 161
white chocolate fondant 132
chocolate and hazelnut spread: molten centre Nutella cake 77
cinnamon, chocolate mug cake with orange & 59
coconut, desiccated (dried shredded)
  chocolate mug cake with banana & coconut 29
  coconut mug cake with chocolate sauce 68
  rum & pineapple tropical cake 23
  toasted coconut & cherry cake 82
coffee
  chocolate, caramel & coffee cake 95
  marble mug cake with coffee & chocolate 103
  mocha mug cake with coffee cream 98
  pick-me-up espresso martini 104

whipped cream cappuccino cake 100
coffee-flavoured liqueur: pick-me-up espresso martini 104
cranberries: white chocolate & cranberry mug cookie 19
cream
  almond mug cake with frangipane & custard 70
  apple, chocolate & nut crumble 118
  chocolate & hazelnut marble cake 45
  coconut mug cake with chocolate sauce 68
  hazelnut, almond & pistachio cake 73
  marble mug cake with coffee & chocolate 103
  milk chocolate & Oreo cake 52
  mocha mug cake with coffee cream 98
  rum & pineapple tropical cake 23
  strawberry & meringue Eton Mess cake 37
  triple chocolate & vanilla cake 51
  whipped cream cappuccino cake 100
  white chocolate, almond & pear cake 20
  zesty lemon cake 14
cream cheese
  dark chocolate & cream cheese swirl 60
  Irish cream cheesecake 166
  spiced carrot cake 157
crumbles 106–27
  apple & blackberry crumble 117
  apple & caramel crumble 113
  apple & pecan crumble 114
  apple, chocolate & nut crumble 118

**171**
Index

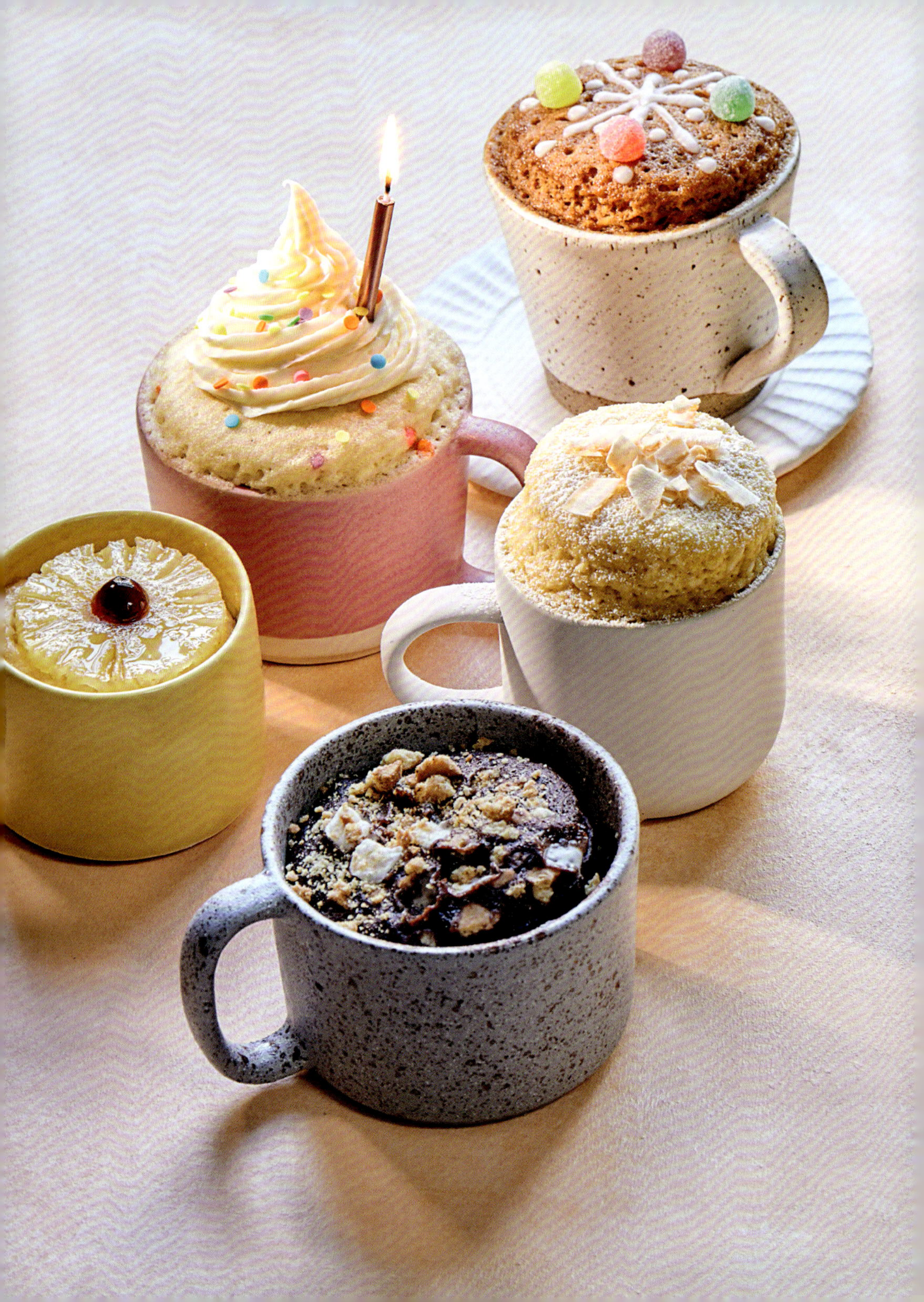

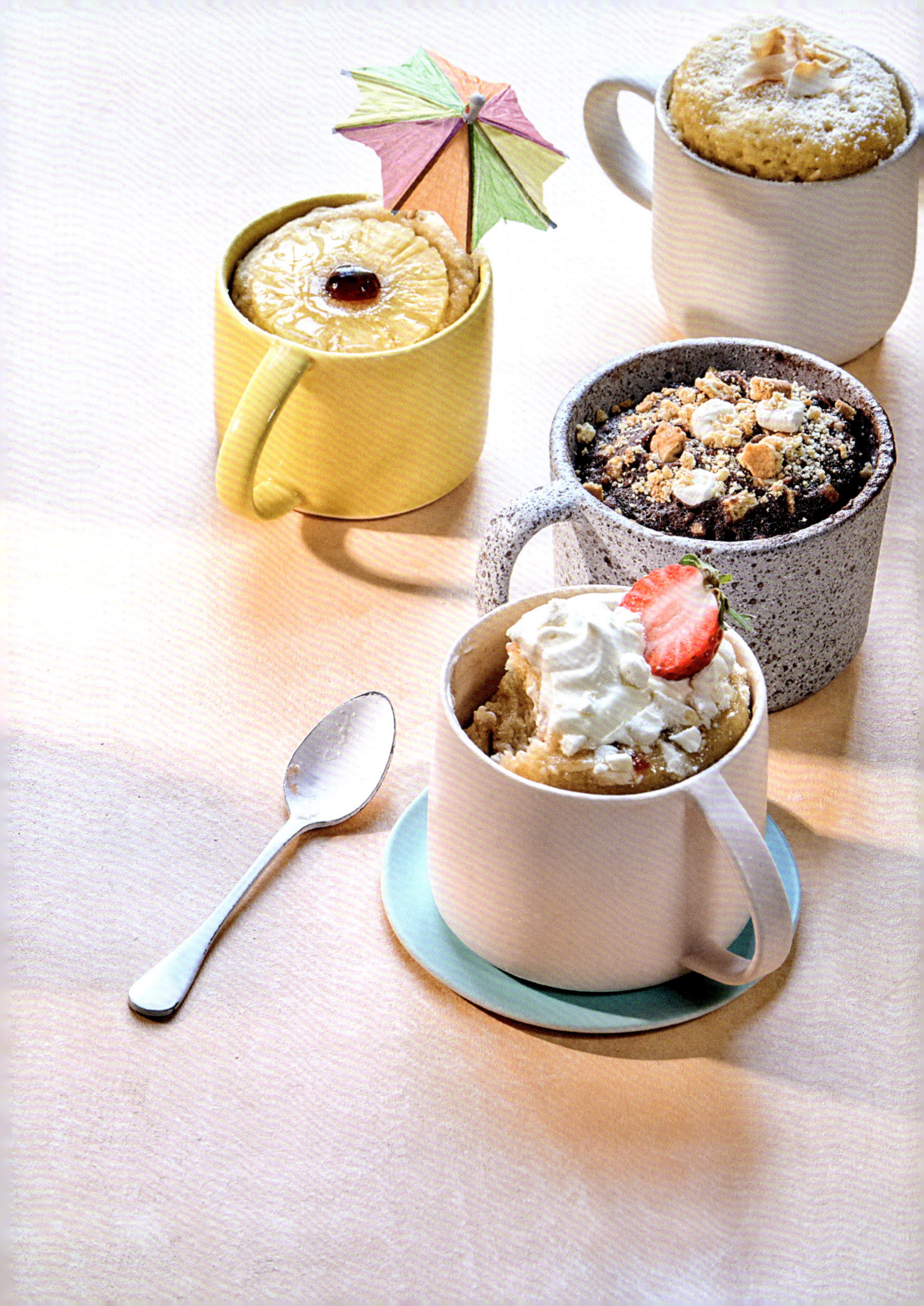

apple, white chocolate & raspberry crumble 120
banana, apple & peanut crumble 111
classic apple crumble 108
dark chocolate & pear crumble 123
lemon curd & blueberry crumble 125
pineapple, apple & Lotus biscuit crumble 126
red berry, apple & shortbread mug crumble 27
custard, almond mug cake with frangipane & 70

# D
digestive biscuits (graham crackers)
  Irish cream cheesecake 166
  marshmallow & chocolate rocky road 86
dulce de leche
  apple & caramel crumble 113
  chocolate & dulce de leche 143

# E
Easter mini egg cake 162
Eton Mess cake, strawberry & meringue 37

# F
festive gingerbread 154
fondants
  dark chocolate fondant 135
  milk chocolate fondant 130
  white chocolate fondant 132
frangipane: almond mug cake with frangipane & custard 70

# G
gingerbread, festive 154

# H
hazelnuts
  apple, chocolate & nut crumble 118
  chocolate & hazelnut marble cake 45
  chocolate & hazelnut praline cake 78
  hazelnut, almond & pistachio cake 73
  molten chocolate & hazelnut 141
hot chocolate cake with marshmallows 158

# I
Irish cream cheesecake 166

# L
lemon curd & blueberry crumble 125
lemons
  blueberry-ricotta swirl cake 24
  mug cookie with lemon & poppy seeds 17
  zesty lemon cake 14
Lotus biscuits
  dark chocolate cake with a Biscoff middle 96
  pineapple, apple & Lotus biscuit crumble 126

# M
M&M's, mug cookie with 54
marble cakes
  chocolate & hazelnut marble cake 45
  marble mug cake with coffee & chocolate 103
marshmallows
  hot chocolate cake with marshmallows 158
  marshmallow & chocolate rocky road 86
martini, pick-me-up espresso 104
matcha green tea: white chocolate & raspberry matcha mug cake 30
meringues: strawberry & meringue Eton Mess cake 37
Mini Egg cake, Easter 162
mint chocolate: after-dinner mint-choc mug cake 65
mocha mug cake with coffee cream 98
molten centre Nutella cake 77
molten chocolate & hazelnut 141
mug cookies
  mug cookie with chocolate chips 57
  mug cookie with lemon & poppy seeds 17
  mug cookie with M&M's 54
  white chocolate & cranberry mug cookie 19

# N
Nutella: molten centre Nutella cake 77
nuts
  apple, chocolate & nut crumble 118
  nutty mug cakes 66–87
  *see also individual types of nuts*

# O
oats: classic apple crumble 108
orange marmalade: chocolate mug cake with orange & cinnamon 59
orange zest & almond cake 39

Oreo biscuits (cookies): milk chocolate & Oreo cake 52

## P

PB&J cake, sweet & salty 81
peanut butter
   banana, apple & peanut crumble 111
   dark chocolate & peanut butter 136
   peanut butter & sesame mug cookie 74
   sweet & salty PB&J cake 81
pears
   dark chocolate & pear crumble 123
   white chocolate, almond & pear cake 20
pecan nuts
   apple & pecan crumble 114
   apple, chocolate & nut crumble 118
   marshmallow & chocolate rocky road 86
peppermint shamrock cake 165
pick-me-up espresso martini 104
pineapple
   pineapple, apple & Lotus biscuit crumble 126
   right-side-up pineapple cake 34
   rum & pineapple tropical cake 23
pistachios
   hazelnut, almond & pistachio cake 73
   pistachio & white chocolate 146
poppy seeds, mug cookie with lemon & 17
praline chocolate: chocolate & hazelnut praline cake 78

## R

raisins
   almond mug cake with frangipane & custard 70
   mug cookie with chocolate chips 57
raspberries
   apple, white chocolate & raspberry crumble 120
   white chocolate & raspberry matcha mug cake 30
raspberry jam
   raspberry & almond Bakewell 85
   sweet & salty PB&J cake 81
   white chocolate & raspberry jam 144
red berry, apple & shortbread mug crumble 27
red velvet cake, classic 168
ricotta cheese: blueberry-ricotta swirl cake 24
right-side-up pineapple cake 34
rocky road, marshmallow & chocolate 86
rum & pineapple tropical cake 23

## S

salted butter caramel cake 93
salted caramel
   caramel & chocolate truffle cake 90
   milk chocolate & salted caramel 138
sesame seeds: peanut butter & sesame mug cookie 74
shamrock cake, peppermint 165
shortbread biscuits: red berry, apple & shortbread mug crumble 27
spiced carrot cake 157
strawberry jam
   strawberry & meringue Eton Mess cake 37
   sweet & salty PB&J cake 81
swirl cake, blueberry-ricotta 24

## T

triple chocolate & vanilla cake 51
tropical cake, rum & pineapple 23
truffle cake, caramel & chocolate 90

## V

vanilla: triple chocolate & vanilla cake 51
vodka: pick-me-up espresso martini 104

## W

wafer curls: chocolate & dulce de leche 143
walnuts: apple, chocolate & nut crumble 118
white chocolate
   apple, white chocolate & raspberry crumble 120
   chocolate mug cake with double-choc chips 62
   pistachio & white chocolate 146
   triple chocolate & vanilla cake 51
   white chocolate, almond & pear cake 20
   white chocolate & cranberry mug cookie 19
   white chocolate & raspberry jam 144
   white chocolate & raspberry matcha mug cake 30
   white chocolate cake with candy cane crunch 161
   white chocolate fondant 132

## Z

zesty lemon cake 14

# Picture
# Credits

Photography on pages 7, 8, 10, 35, 36, 38, 47, 63, 64, 80, 83, 84, 87, 91, 99, 105, 153, 155, 159, 160, 163, 164, 167, 169 and 172–173 © Clare Winfield

Photography on pages 15, 16, 18, 21, 22, 25, 44, 55, 56, 69, 71, 72, 75, 92, 102, 109, 131 and 156 © Richard Boutin

Photography on pages 26, 110, 112, 115, 116, 119, 121, 122, 124 and 127 © David Japy

Photography on pages 28, 31, 32, 43, 49, 50, 53, 58, 61, 76, 79, 94, 97, 101, 133, 134, 137, 139, 140, 142, 145, 147 and 151 © Sandra Mahut